John Nolen & Mariemont

Creating the North American Landscape

Gregory Conniff
Edward K. Muller
David Schuyler
Consulting Editors

George F. Thompson
Series Founder and Director

Published in cooperation with the Center
for American Places, Santa Fe, New Mexico,
and Harrisonburg, Virginia

Millard F. Rogers, Jr.

JOHN NOLEN &

MARIEMONT

✦ ✦ ✦ ✦ ✦ ✦ ✦ ✦ ✦ ✦ ✦ ✦ ✦ ✦ ✦ ✦

Building a New Town in Ohio

The Johns Hopkins University Press ✦ *Baltimore and London*

© 2001 The Johns Hopkins University Press
All rights reserved. Published 2001
Printed in the United States of America on acid-free paper

2 4 6 8 9 7 5 3 1

The Johns Hopkins University Press
2715 North Charles Street
Baltimore, Maryland 21218-4363
www.press.jhu.edu

Library of Congress Cataloging-in-Publication Data
Rogers, Millard F.
John Nolen and Mariemont : building a new town in Ohio /
Millard F. Rogers, Jr.
p.   cm. — (Creating the North American landscape)
Includes bibiographical references and index.
ISBN 0-8018-6619-7
1. Nolen, John, 1869–1937.   2. Mariemont (Ohio)—History.
3. City planning—Ohio—Mariemont—History.   I. Title.   II. Series.
NA9085.N64 R64 2001
711'.4'0977177—dc21   00-011511

A catalog record for this book is available from the British Library.

Title page illustration: John Nolen (1869–1937), town planner of Marie-mont, Ohio. Commissioned in 1920 to design a new town founded by Mary Emery, Nolen called Mariemont a "national exemplar" of town planning.

Page 249 is an extension of the copyright page.

To Nina and Seth

CONTENTS

PREFACE
AND ACKNOWLEDGMENTS

This book chronicles the birth and early history of Mariemont, a masterpiece of town planning by America's preeminent urban designer, John Nolen. In the first quarter of the twentieth century, Nolen joined a wealthy financial backer and a visionary impresario, forming an impressive triumvirate. In my estimation, this merger produced the finest work of Nolen's career.

The founding mother of this village in southwestern Ohio, a few miles east of Cincinnati, was Mary Muhlenberg Emery (1844–1927). She inherited great wealth upon the death of her husband, Thomas J. Emery (1830–1906), and for the next twenty-one years she followed a course of compassionate giving. Emery's fortune consisted partly of massive real estate holdings and housing development in Cincinnati and elsewhere in the United States, so his family's business related comfortably to the idea of creating a well-designed suburban community that would serve as a model for the nation. It was not surprising, therefore, that Mary Emery contributed the funds to create the new town, Mariemont.

Although Mariemont was not promoted as a philanthropy, Nolen's new town depended totally on Mary Emery's financial largesse from its beginnings until years after her death. Mariemont's genesis and early development, impossible without Mary Emery's generosity, were intertwined with the life of her secretary, manager, and surrogate son, Charles J. Livingood (1866–1952). He served Mrs. Emery as business agent and personal representative to the many institutions she supported. Furthermore, he played an influential role as trusted advisor in her philanthropic endeavors. It fell to Livingood in 1910 to develop the concept of Mariemont and to mastermind its implementation. He answered to Mrs. Emery, but it was he who summoned the talents of John Nolen and made most of the important decisions affecting Nolen's planning efforts and the town's development.

Between 1920 and 1925, the period when John Nolen was employed to design Mariemont, a rare patron-planner relationship developed. The main storytellers of this relationship and of Mariemont's beginnings are Nolen and Livingood. In their voluminous correspondence they recorded how this internationally renowned planned community was initiated. Their exchange of ideas, suggestions, queries, and orders created a rare, perhaps unique, record in the history of American town planning. This prompted my research on the evolutionary process, the decisions made, and the planning by Nolen, Mary Emery, and Livingood. To record Nolen's many achievements in designing towns and suburbs and discuss these apart from their pertinence to Mariemont is not the purpose of this study. Nolen's extensive oeuvre requires separate books. The extended history of Mariemont after 1925 is not within the purview of my book. By that year, all of Nolen's work and most of the construction ever undertaken by the Mariemont Company according to Nolen's original plan were completed.

My interest in Mariemont began during my tenure as director of the Cincinnati Art Museum, 1974–94, when I was in daily contact with Mary Emery's legacy as a great patron of that institution. Little did I realize in 1974, when my family and I arrived in Cincinnati and settled in Mariemont, that this gem of suburban living was one of her philanthropies. Thus, I had another relationship with this lady's legacy that soon aroused my curiosity. Research began in earnest upon my retirement in 1994. Archives, historical societies, newspapers, libraries, court records, and published references were searched for information on Mariemont, Nolen, and Livingood. Articles about soon-to-be-built Mariemont had flowed into various publications shortly after Nolen's plans were announced in 1922. I researched and recorded these articles, later ones, and numerous unpublished materials. My bibliography attempts to list all important references to Mariemont, particularly those written by Nolen.

Without question, the greatest collection of original documents pertaining to Mariemont is housed with the papers of John Nolen in the Carl A. Kroch Library, Cornell University. As Nolen saved every scrap of paper, it seems, that came to his office (as well as copies of letters and memoranda that left it), the Cornell holdings provide a complete picture of the town planner's involvement with this monumental enterprise. Letters, blueprints, photographs, and other papers at Cornell (134 cubic feet of materials) illustrate the chronology of the Nolen-Livingood partnership in designing Mariemont. These papers suggest, too, Nolen's modus operandi as he evolved Mariemont's plan for Livingood, who was acting on behalf of Mrs. Emery. In the written exchange between Nolen and Livingood, the town planning process is recounted in rich detail. The influences of the English Garden City movement, Cincinnati's altruistic urge for better housing for workers, and earlier planned communities in the United States are displayed throughout the Nolen papers at Cornell University.

Unfortunately, the bulk of Livingood's personal papers and his correspondence with architects whom he selected for the Mariemont project have disappeared (exempting those materials in the Nolen Collection at Cornell University). Copies of Livingood's diaries and a few letters and other documents remaining in descendants' hands were generously given to me by Livingood's grandson, Virginius Hall Jr. Interviews with Elizabeth Livingood McGuire, youngest daughter of Charles J. Livingood, added immeasurably to my understanding of her father's role with Mariemont and Mary Emery. Also important in my research were the files, photographs, blueprints, and other records housed at the Mariemont Preservation Foundation. This Ohio foundation owns the largest collection of plans and photographs pertaining to Mariemont and its architects.

The John Nolen Research Fund, administered by Cornell University, awarded two grants to me for research and travel in 1995 and 1996. These grants, for which I am deeply grateful, permitted the study of Nolen materials pertaining to Mariemont and now housed in the Carl A. Kroch Library. There I inspected nearly one thousand documents, letters, and memoranda by Nolen and more than three hundred blueprints and drawings by him and his associates. Of particular interest were two unusual parts of the Nolen collection: a photograph album of fifty-nine images of the Mariemont site before any construction changed its topography and a dozen glass slides illustrating portions of lectures on Mariemont delivered by Nolen.

Many individuals and institutions assisted my research, and I acknowledge with gratitude the Boston Public Library: Kim Tenney; Cincinnati Art Museum: Terrie Benjamin, Mona Chapin, William Clark, Ran Mullins, Cathy Shaffer; *Cincinnati Enquirer:* Owen Findsen; Cincinnati Historical Society: Laura Chace, Anne Shepherd; Cincinnati Public Library; Cornell University, Carl A. Kroch Library: Herbert Finch, Lorna Knight; The Thomas J. Emery Memorial: Henry Hobson Jr.; Thomas Hogan III; Walter Langsam Jr.; Mariemont Preservation Foundation: Fred Rutherford, Janet Setchell; New-York Historical Society: May Stone; Barbara Nolen Strong; Taft, Stettinius & Hollister, Cincinnati: James R. Bridgeland Jr.; University of Cincinnati, Archives, Zane L. Miller, Jean Wellington, DAAP Library; University of North Carolina: John Nolen Planning Collection; University of Pennsylvania Architectural Archives: Julia M. Converse. To my wife, Nina, who shares my interest in Mariemont and who patiently endured and encouraged my research and writing, I express my heartfelt thanks.

I hope that this story of Mariemont's beginnings has lessons for many in the complex interplay among John Nolen, Mary Emery, and Charles Livingood, who fashioned together what became known as the national exemplar of town planning in America. Town planners, developers, architects, philanthropists, foundations, and government officials may learn from Nolen's experiences with Mariemont. Urban dwellers and those who seek suburban life may take heart in reading about Mariemont's birth throes, hoping to implement in their environments some portion of a town planner's vision and impressive accomplishments.

John Nolen & Mariemont

I ✦ NEW TOWN, NEW CONCEPT

A present-day traveler's first encounter with the village of Mariemont, just ten miles east of Cincinnati along the spine of U.S. Route 50, might suggest a quaint town in the Cotswolds region of England. Half timber and stucco abound on dwellings and commercial buildings; an aged graveyard abuts a gray stone church with a lichen-covered roof; red brick and crisp white wooden trim help define the Georgian style of schools and offices bordering the highway. Diverting into residential streets to the right and left, the traveler sees rows of tightly grouped, two-story townhouses distinguished by their simple, classical details. In summer, trees and green spaces dominate in every direction. The age of the village seems indeterminate. Its orderly appearance amid the visually chaotic communities surrounding it, where little aesthetic control is evidenced, offers a tranquil oasis of harmony between nature and architecture. But its appearance provokes questions: How can a Norman-style church sprout up in the Midwest? Were the shops and residential sections originally so well spaced and related to each other? Is automobile traffic calmed by the town square and adjoining beech woods? Why is this village so unlike other suburban communities? How did Mariemont happen?

A visitor to Mariemont's site in the early 1920s, traveling on the same U.S. Route 50, a two-lane highway, saw only orchards, corn fields, and patches of vegetables growing on acreage dotted with a few farmhouses. One narrow road intersected the highway near an architectural landmark, the Ferris house, built shortly after 1800. The scenery was rural and agricultural. But on April 23, 1923, an elderly lady dressed in the stylish fashion of earlier decades stood on the lawn with a crowd of onlookers and pressed a silver spade into the ground to begin the village of Mariemont. The lady was Mary Muhlenberg Emery, widow of

The Mariemont Memorial Church was begun in 1923 and designed by New York City architect Louis E. Jallade in the Norman Revival style. Its medieval roof stones once covered a tithe barn in the Cotswolds, near Tetbury, England.

the wealthy real estate developer and landowner Thomas J. Emery. Many knew her as Cincinnati's most generous philanthropist, the Lady Bountiful (as the press labeled her), so her role as founder of a new residential community was not surprising. The public, however, knew little about her personal life and that of the Emery family, long acknowledged as one of America's richest dynasties.

The Emery clan descended from English-born Thomas Emery (1798–1857), who settled in Cincinnati in 1832 and became a land agent and moneychanger. His success came quickly in the bustling river city of twenty-eight thousand residents, largely owing to his factory, which processed lard oil as a by-product of the local meat-packing industry. Emery's three sons led the enterprise after their father's death, forming a business known as "Thomas Emery's Sons," which would prosper throughout the nineteenth century and far into the twentieth. Production of lard oil and candles led the sons into real estate and housing, which formed the foundation for the family's wealth. The company was directed by Thomas J. Emery (1830–1906) and John J. Emery (1835–1908), with some astute assistance from their younger brother, J. Howard Emery (1838–86). Their landholdings were concentrated in Cincinnati but eventually stretched from San Francisco to Denver, Chicago, and New York. A sophisticated New Yorker was introduced into the close-knit Emery family as the Civil War raged in the South.

In 1862, eighteen-year-old Mary Muhlenberg Hopkins arrived in Cincinnati from Brooklyn. Born in New York City on December 19, 1844, the oldest child of Richard Hubbell Hopkins (1798–1863) and his wife, Mary Barr Denny (1807–93),[1] Mary's upbringing in the home of a middle-class merchant gave her the means for an exceptional education before the family moved west to Cincinnati. This American city was the most cultured one apart from the eastern seaboard she left behind, and there she married Thomas J. Emery in 1866.[2] The community could not foresee the significance this alliance would have forty years later.

Dominating the town square, the Mariemont Inn was designed by Cincinnati architects Zettel & Rapp in the Tudor Revival style. Retail shops, a restaurant, and a savings bank occupy the ground floor of the inn, which was under construction in 1925.

Designed by Philadelphia architect Robert R. McGoodwin and begun in 1924, the single-family houses of painted brick on Albert Place echo residences built in Letchworth, England, the original garden city and an important influence on Mariemont.

The decade of the 1880s opened propitiously for the Emery brothers and for Mary. She had two sons, Sheldon and Albert, and the family's real estate holdings expanded with large apartment buildings along the new streetcar lines branching out from downtown. By 1881, Mary and Thomas Emery had built a splendid stone mansion overlooking the Ohio River, just as their children were reaching adolescence. Tragedy dampened the Emerys' happiness, however, when their youngest son, Albert, died in an accident in 1884, and six years later Sheldon succumbed to pneumonia. Sheldon had attended Harvard University but never graduated. A classmate and friend wrote comfortingly to the grieving Mary Emery that his "heart at this moment goes out to you as to my own Mother."[3] The letter writer, Charles Jacob Livingood, began shortly thereafter a new career that brought him to Cincinnati and employment with the Emery businesses. Eventually, after the death of Thomas J. Emery in 1906, Livingood was at Mrs. Emery's side as advisor, manager of her husband's estate, surrogate son, and friend.

Livingood's education and background helped him in his future role, but his friendship with Sheldon Emery was his introduction to a successful relationship with Mary Emery. His father was a prosperous lawyer and real estate developer in Reading, Pennsylvania. After public and private schooling, Livingood entered Harvard in 1884 in the class of 1888, as did Sheldon Emery.[4] After Sheldon's death, Livingood started at the bottom of the employment ladder with the Emerys, and from 1890 to 1906 he supervised rental apartments while attaching himself more and more to his employers, particularly Mary. During this period, the Emerys demonstrated little philanthropic interest compared with Mary's later beneficent nature as a wealthy widow. During her husband's lifetime, the Episcopal church received most of the Emerys' charitable giving.

By 1900, Thomas Emery's Sons was the largest property owner in Cincinnati. The candle and lard oil business reached customers from the east to the west coast of the United States and even into Europe, where more candles were sold by the Emery Candle Company in Germany than in Ohio.[5] Cincinnati was home to many other dynamic industries, including carriage making, soap and meat by-products, breweries, printing inks, furniture, and yeast. Steamboat traffic crowded the river front, and railroads made the city an important hub.

Mary Muhlenberg Emery (1844–1927), philanthropist, arts patron, and founder of Mariemont, the new town outside of Cincinnati, Ohio. Photographed about 1910, the year when the first land purchases for Mariemont were made.

As the family prospered and to escape Cincinnati's humid and hot summers, Thomas Emery purchased in 1901 an estate in Middletown, Rhode Island, a few miles outside of Newport, and named it *Mariemont*. The title combines two French words, *Marie* to honor his wife and *mont* to signify the hill at the center of the estate. This summer residence, eventually surrounded by extensive gardens designed by the noted Frederick Law Olmsted Studio, would give its name in twenty years to a remarkable planned community near Cincinnati. For

After the death of her husband, Thomas J. Emery, in 1906, Mary Emery's principal advisor was Charles J. Livingood (1866–1952). He appointed John Nolen, directed the creation of Mariemont, and selected the new town's architects.

both the estate and the new town, an Anglicized pronunciation (*marry-mont*) was preferred by the Emerys.

In 1905, as Thomas Emery's health declined, he sought the dry desert and hot baths of Algeria. While preparing to sail for home from Cairo, he died suddenly on January 15, 1906.[6] Except for a few minor bequests, his widow, Mary Muhlenberg Emery, was his sole heir. No inventory of the estate's assets and worth was submitted to the probate courts, but estimates in the press valued

Thomas Emery's fortune at 25–35 million dollars.[7] With the death of her husband, Mary entered her loneliest years and a new era of philanthropy. She envisioned her future course of philanthropy as a duty and a pleasure, aided by Livingood, who preempted the role of manager and advisor now that her husband was gone.

Mrs. Emery, retiring by nature but well known in Cincinnati as the wife of a leading businessman, began twenty-one years of generous giving in 1907, one year after her husband's death. This new direction in her life identified her as Cincinnati's leading patron of causes and programs. Christ Church in Cincinnati was an early beneficiary, receiving a spacious new parish center. She built a home for working girls in Paris with her anonymous gift of $250,000. A highly regarded technical school in Cincinnati, the Ohio Mechanics Institute, was offered $500,000 for a new building. Newport was blessed with a palacelike Army-Navy YMCA, constructed with her gift of $250,000. She enlarged her Olmsted-designed gardens at Mariemont, Rhode Island, and made her first acquisitions of paintings, taking steps to form the art collection of old master pictures she would bequeath at her death to the Cincinnati Art Museum. Paintings by Titian, Hals, Mantegna, Gainsborough, Murillo, and Van Dyck joined others, eventually forming what Mary Emery titled the Edgecliffe Collection, in honor of the family home overlooking the Ohio River in Cincinnati. By her sixty-sixth year, in 1910, she had demonstrated her broad interest in humanitarian activities. As the young century in America embraced the flow of immigrants and industrial barons flourished, Mary Emery embarked on her most costly, long-lasting benefaction: a planned community, Mariemont.[8]

Shortly after her husband's death, Mary apparently contemplated several projects that she felt would improve housing in Cincinnati. She considered building a large apartment building in the downtown area or a series of small homes in the suburbs, all intended to relieve crowded, unsanitary tenement living. These ideas were discarded. With Livingood's urging, Mary Emery agreed that the English garden city was the appropriate model for a planned community that she would finance.[9]

Several reform movements in nineteenth-century America attempted to address housing problems of the poor and of low-income workers. New York, Boston, Chicago, Saint Louis, Baltimore, and Minneapolis, among other large cities, expanded with population explosions just before and after 1900. Outcries for housing improvements were fanned by volunteer and philanthropic groups.[10] Some benevolent factory owners built company towns, such as Pullman, Illinois, designed by Solon S. Beman in 1880 and financed by George M. Pullman for his railroad car workers. Some sterling examples of planned housing arose in the aftermath of World War I, with communities designed for workers at places like Yorkship Village in Camden, New Jersey, begun in 1918 by Electus D. Litchfield. A notable "streetcar suburb," created in 1912 and influential in Mariemont's planning, was Forest Hills Gardens, Queens, New York. This masterful concept was developed by the Russell Sage Foundation to offer industrial workers good housing in locations near their employment.

Housing conditions in Cincinnati, as elsewhere, were ripe for improvement. After the Civil War, Cincinnati was considered one of the three most densely populated cities in the United States.[11] The nineteenth century brought a flood of blacks from the South and immigrants from Europe (especially from Germany), who crowded into the downtown basin of the city, filling the tenements and substandard shelters. The city was squeezed into a half-circle bordered on the south by the Ohio River and on other sides by hills. The worst housing occupied streets between the downtown businesses and the river. After World War I, substandard housing extended beyond a twelve-block radius of downtown to the north and west. Living in ramshackle houses and apartments in these areas, the poor had few neighborhood amenities and little hope that their wages would permit them to move to better parts of the city and better housing.

Philanthropic efforts in Cincinnati by the Model Homes Company, organized by Jacob Schmidlapp in 1914, and the city's Better Housing League, founded in 1916, were led by housing reformers who worked assiduously to ease the city's housing problems for the underprivileged. By 1920, when the federal census recorded a population of 401,247 for Cincinnati (an increase of 10.4% over the previous decade), the city had no plan to deal with its growth, land use, and housing problems. Cincinnatian Alfred Bettman formed the United City Planning Committee in 1915 with private funds, but a formal plan was not accomplished until 1925. Although Mary Emery was aware of the league's existence and supported its goals for social betterment, the efforts of this program and others came too late to generate the Mariemont concept in Mary Emery's mind. She knew their leaders not only through her late husband's real estate and housing interests but also as social equals.

Before Schmidlapp founded his company, he had built nearly one hundred houses for poor residents, locating them outside the tenement-ridden basin area. The first venture of his company was Washington Terrace, a project for blacks, recognized as "the first attempt by Cincinnati reformers to build housing for wage earners on a 'community plan.'"[12] Schmidlapp's enterprise included community enhancements, such as an assembly hall, a store, and recreation areas, which Mariemont would embrace in the 1920s on a much larger scale.

The Better Housing League, under Bleecker Marquette's leadership during a remarkable period between 1918 and 1954, fostered a plan opposing tenement construction, urged zoning ordinances and the enactment of a reasonable building code, and sought "appropriate community housing for the metropolis," which emphasized houses for wage earners rather than the poor.[13] The Better Housing League was supportive of the Mariemont concept, largely because the new town evolved from a well-executed plan and intended its housing for those able to pay modest rents.

As early as 1909 but probably in 1910, Mrs. Emery assigned Livingood the responsibility of developing the community of Mariemont.[14] It became Livingood's duty to execute his principal's direction. The magnitude of her financial backing would not be known until a decade later.

With Mary Emery's authorization, Livingood studied and visited European and American planned communities for three years, beginning in 1910, seeking the prototypes and character that would be consolidated into the new venture.[15] His travel assignment was not his sole occupation during this period, of course, for he had numerous responsibilities with Mr. Emery's estate and Mary's growing philanthropies. But Livingood's frequent trips to Europe and America's East Coast as a veteran employee of Thomas Emery's Sons introduced him to housing experiments that would frame his concept for a planned community. He attended international planning and housing congresses and met Octavia Hill and Sir Raymond Unwin, pioneers of the housing movement in England. He studied the early Krupp building colonies at Essen, Hellerau, Nuremburg, and Leipzig in Germany, as well as Norwegian examples and some in Sweden, France, and Italy. Finally, he claimed to have inspected housing developments in Ankara, Turkey, and Johannesburg, South Africa.[16] In Livingood's brief autobiography he noted the English prototypes that later proved to be influential: Letchworth, Port Sunlight, Hampstead Garden Suburb, Bournville, Harborne Tenants, Croydon, and Ealing.[17]

Livingood listed Letchworth in England as the first community he studied in preparation for his efforts with the new suburb of Cincinnati. It is appropriate that Livingood turned to this model, for its initiator was Sir Ebenezer Howard (1850–1928), renowned for his accomplishments as visionary, writer, and planner. Howard's book, *To-morrow: A Peaceful Path to Real Reform,* first published in 1898, was issued in revised form in 1902 as *Garden Cities of To-morrow.* It remains a provocative and philosophical text on town planning, expressing Howard's strategies for achieving harmony in urban life. The book applied his ideas in practical terms at Letchworth, called the first garden city, thirty-five miles north of London. Much of the fabric of Letchworth does not apply to Mary Emery's community, Mariemont, such as Letchworth's principle of land ownership held in trust, limited profit to its owners, the greenbelt that rings the city, expected population numbers, and the large acreage required. However, Howard's garden city had many elements assimilated later by Mariemont, including his concern that "unity of design and purpose" should clearly be a key element.[18]

The garden city's influence and model, at least in the particular elements that could be adapted to American needs, "prevailed over most of the world."[19] In the United States, the Resettlement Association and other federal initiatives modeled as many as sixteen new towns and suburbs after Ebenezer Howard's concept.[20] Mariemont's planner, John Nolen, venerated the garden city ideal, even including a plan of Letchworth as his initial illustration in *New Towns for Old,* his most important published statement on his planning goals and philosophy. The Farm City Corporation of America and the greenbelt towns (Greenbelt, Md.; Greenhills, Ohio; and Greendale, Wis.) descended from the garden city as "the closest derivations of the Garden City theories."[21]

Howard's garden city efforts in the twentieth century blossomed first with Letchworth in 1903. The concept was subject to various interpretations, with the term *garden city* applied indiscriminately to many unplanned urban and suburban communities. Quite a few towns even used that term in their names. By 1919, the Garden Cities and Town Planning Association had adopted a definition, in consultation with Ebenezer Howard, that was accepted by architects and planners. This definition required the garden city to have a surrounding rural belt with land held in public ownership or in trust, and the garden city had to be "of a size that makes possible a full measure of social life."[22] Some planned communities, including Mariemont, did not follow Howard's garden city concepts explicitly, so the term cannot be strictly applied to Mary Emery's project.

Aside from the administrative, financial, and philosophical differences between Letchworth and Mariemont, the English model had many positive elements that appealed to Livingood, such as its appearance, its infrastructure, and its plan. Letchworth's architects, Barry Parker (1867–1947) and Raymond Unwin (1863–1940), were talented but conservative. Letchworth houses had steeply pitched roofs and abundant windows and were available as both attached and freestanding dwellings. Green spaces and allotment gardens were placed throughout the neighborhoods. Gently curving streets led to boulevards and esplanades linking residential with shopping regions and separating an industrial section.

The second community listed and investigated by Livingood was Port Sunlight, a company town between Liverpool and Chester, begun in 1888, a decade earlier than Letchworth. Taking its name from a popular soap manufactured by the Lever empire, Port Sunlight was the beloved housing scheme of William Hesketh Lever (1851–1925), later Lord Leverhulme. Its layout married land assigned to the Lever Brothers factory with land for their workers and their families. Schools, a church, an inn and pub, plus other amenities were provided by Lever alongside the rows of impeccably designed and crafted attached houses. Port Sunlight was much smaller than Letchworth (only about 220 acres to Letchworth's 3,826 acres), and Lever's project employed a roster of architects chosen, for the most part, by Lever himself (whereas Letchworth relied primarily on Parker and Unwin). Port Sunlight is but one of several industrial communities built for workers in England during the nineteenth century where the founder provided the land, its financing, the architects, and the philosophical roots. A paternalistic enterprise, Port Sunlight has a decidedly old English look in half-timbered, Cheshire vernacular style admired by Lever and his principal architects, William and Segar Owen. The town's appearance and plans equaled Letchworth's, Livingood felt, and references to the two English towns as prototypes or models for Mariemont were credited frequently in print.

The third planned community on Livingood's list was Hampstead Garden Suburb, a magnificent undertaking begun in 1906. It combined the talents and energies of its founder, Henrietta Barnett, its planners, Parker and Unwin, and its best-known architect, Edwin Lutyens (1869–1944). Close to London, it relied on that great city for most employment and was only a tube ride away on the Underground. Hampstead Heath and the openness of the rolling fields recommended the site to its founder, who hoped to maintain the rural look of the setting, especially around its edges. Originally the site covered 243 acres, with its houses expected to attract both middle-class and affluent buyers. Hampstead's architectural styles interlaced Georgian Revival with German medievalism, red brick for some buildings and rounded arches in others. America's City Beautiful movement and the design achievements of the World's Columbian Exposition, held in Chicago in 1893, influenced its planners somewhat, especially in the grand scale of the central square and Lutyens's impressive churches, but Hampstead provided telling lessons for Livingood. He saw and remembered, no doubt, the "intervals of verdure, the intimate and modest scale throughout, and the effect of privacy."[23]

Unfortunately, Livingood's recorded observations made concurrently with his visits to towns in Europe and America, between 1910 and 1913, are unknown. We lack his spontaneous comments from those years when he collected ideas, influences, and visual images. There are brief mentions, however, in his diary entries noting later visits. In June 1930, he drove out to Letchworth and Welwyn Garden City from London, writing his impression of "seeing the Garden Cities of Welwyn and Letchworth which have nothing on Mariemont." At Hampstead Garden Suburb, near London, he hoped to talk to Dame Henrietta Barnett, that town's founder. He missed seeing her, but he roamed through the town. He disliked the cinder sidewalks and the rutted streets, he wrote, but the brick houses and tile roofs impressed him.[24]

A diary entry in 1933, apparently his final one commenting on planned communities, recalled his visit to Hellerau, a Krupp community, twenty-one years earlier. Livingood first saw this development in 1912, when it had barely been completed. He was disappointed in its appearance in 1933, noting the washed-away streets, broken fences, and unpainted houses.[25] Livingood's 1933 visit to planned communities in England elicited equally bleak observations on their future prospects, beginning with his trip by rail to Welwyn Garden City and Letchworth.

> Of course we went, and neither [of the two communities of Welwyn and Letch-worth] indicates a complete success (W. built by Louis de Soissons, still work-ing on smaller projects as it has grown only through County Council grants and most of its industries languishing) while Letchworth, slowly expanding, much better houses and gardens, seems to be at a standstill. Its industries too are dead in the main, and no new ones. The shops, however, in Town Center seem all to be occupied—but then such is the case generally in the towns we have seen thus far. I notice that planting strips, grass between sidewalk and kerb or house have been cemented over. Some building going on in both places.[26]

In addition to European planned towns that Livingood could study in prepa-ration for the community near Cincinnati, he is thought to have visited some American models, such as Salem Rebuilding Trust in Salem, Massachusetts; Bellerica Garden Suburb in Massachusetts; the American Viscose Company's community for its workers in Marcus Hook, Delaware; Forest Hills, New York; Goodyear Heights, near Whitinsville, Massachusetts; Indian View, near Worcester, Massachusetts; Yorkship Village, at Camden, New Jersey; and a vil-lage at Perryville, Maryland.[27] Of these, Forest Hills provided the best exam-ple to be emulated, at least in part, as the earliest American example that es-poused the garden city philosophy. But the constituency of Forest Hills Gardens differed from Mariemont's intent, at least initially, to serve wage earners and renters in its Dale Park district. The Queens, New York, development was not a social experiment to benefit blue-collar workers, and a more affluent middle class found it especially attractive soon after its opening.

Forest Hills Gardens, developed by the Russell Sage Foundation, had the blessing and funding of Olivia Slocum Sage, who, like Mary Emery, inherited her husband's fortune and set about doing good works in her spouse's memory. There were several other parallels between Forest Hills Gardens and Mariemont in their administrative structures, their original financing, their reliance on traditional architecture, and their future. Sage acquired 142 acres in 1909, and construction was carried out in 1910–12. Direct control of the operation was the responsibility of the Sage Foundation Homes Company, a creature of the parent Sage Foundation. Frederick Law Olmsted's firm was the planner, and Grosvenor Atterbury, the distinguished architect who later worked at Mariemont, designed the houses with the intention of appealing to low-income residents. The planned community was within easy reach of New York City, a plus for residents, but land was expensive and Atterbury's style was costly. The cozy appearance, gently winding streets, and blend of single and attached housing would be revisited in Mariemont. Forest Hills Gardens depended on the work of Parker and Unwin and on the example of Hampstead Garden Suburb as "a sequentially organised community based on a continuous line of movement from the railroad station to Forest Park, a metaphoric journey from town to open country."[28]

After Livingood had studied planned communities in Europe and the United States between 1910 and 1913, selecting the site for Mary Emery's new town became his preoccupation. Livingood did not need to look beyond the farm fields that dotted the outskirts of the Queen City. Interurban traction lines moved into thriving neighborhoods and through acres of corn and hay to outlying communities such as Milford, Terrace Park, and Newtown to the east of Cincinnati. Only ten miles from the center of Cincinnati, Livingood found a beautiful site overlooking the Little Miami River, a patchwork of farms with a few modest buildings. The land was served by railway lines and a main road. Wooster Pike, a federal highway (U.S. 50), ran through it. Interestingly, the chosen location contained the important Madisonville archeological site under control of Harvard University, Livingood's alma mater.

The earliest dwellers on the land now within the borders of Mariemont, Ohio, were prehistoric Indians. They lived and died on a densely wooded plateau that jutted out one hundred feet above the Little Miami River, abutting a ravine known today as Whiskey Creek. Since the late nineteenth century, this Indian village and cemetery, called the Madisonville Site, has taken its name from a nearby neighborhood in Hamilton County. Madisonville was the home of the site's discoverer and first excavator, Dr. Charles Louis Metz (1847–1926). A physician by occupation but an active archeologist by avocation, Dr. Metz in

1878 explored earthworks and mounds on property then belonging to the Stites and Ferris families.[29]

Metz was attracted to the plateau by the abundance of arrowpoints, flint chips, and carved shells found on the surface, as well as human remains in shallow burials uncovered by the rains. Local farmers knew the area as Ferris Woods, but Metz and his fellow amateur archeologists labeled it Pottery Field. During the autumn and winter of 1878–79, Metz hired laborers to prospect there by digging holes and trenches in carefully marked plots. In March 1879, Metz was awed by the extent of the burial ground, hut circles, trash pits, and fireplaces beginning to be uncovered. Extensive, well-planned excavations then began and continued until 1881, unearthing hundreds of skeletons, earthenware pottery, and cache-pits.[30] Professor F. W. Putnam of Harvard University's Peabody Museum recognized the site's significance, and he arranged with Metz and the Madisonville Literary and Scientific Society to pay a portion of the costs of exploring the site. Work was sporadic under Harvard's sponsorship until 1891, when Metz and others undertook additional excavations for several years. In 1897, the property's owner and a descendant of the pioneer family that had settled and farmed the area, Miss Phoebe Ferris, deeded twenty-five acres of land that included the Madisonville Site to Harvard University.[31]

Excavations by the Peabody Museum continued at the site until 1911, recording more than twelve hundred burials and thousands of artifacts, including glass and copper beads, tobacco pipes, stone tablets, woven basket fragments, spoons, combs, awls and needles, bone tools, grinding stones, and axheads.[32] The original occupants of the Madisonville Site were part of the Fort Ancient culture. From about A.D. 1000 to 1400, they occupied the bluff above the Little Miami River. Subsequent occupancy of the region by the Shawnee Tribe lasted until about 1600. There was some contact between Europeans and the Shawnee residents, as evidenced by the many beads and iron fragments that resulted from trading, but the area was abandoned by these first Americans long before white settlers arrived in this portion of Ohio.

Passage of the Northwest Ordinance by the U.S. Congress on July 13, 1787, organized the governing structure of a vast region that eventually became the states of Ohio, Michigan, Indiana, Illinois, and Wisconsin. This act enabled colonization and land acquisition by settlers hungry for farm and forest lands.

One eager real estate entrepreneur was John Cleves Symmes, who received the original eighteenth-century land grant for a large tract in southwestern Ohio. Symmes, chief justice of New Jersey, induced a group of friends to join him as shareholders to purchase about 312,000 acres in the virgin wilderness that fronted on the Ohio River and was bounded by the Little Miami and Great Miami Rivers. This was known as the Miami Purchase. On December 7, 1787, Symmes conveyed one section of this land, about 640 acres (comprising the present village boundaries of Mariemont), to Major Benjamin Stites. Members of the Stites, Ferris, Peck, Knapp, and Lockwood families soon settled in the region, with Eliphalet Ferris and his brother Joseph erecting brick dwellings on the rich farmland. Eliphalet's house, begun about 1802, became the center point in Mariemont's eventual layout, the triangulation station from which all survey coordinates and measurements for the future village were determined.

Livingood ended his studies of European and American planned communities just before World War I consumed millions of lives in four years of destruction. As the United States entered World War I in 1917, Mary Emery and Livingood witnessed the first acquisitions of land that would become her planned community. Livingood, acting as the founder's personal representative, had chosen the site by 1915. He studied available, inexpensive land in Cincinnati's suburbs, places such as Pleasant Ridge, Kennedy Heights, Sharonville, and Price Hill. These areas beckoned because they were relatively free of dust and smoke from coal-burning furnaces, but the distances from downtown Cincinnati would make the new community too isolated from the population center and employment. In this respect Livingood shied away from the Letchworth model, which was thirty-five miles from London, too far for easy commuting, he felt. Port Sunlight, near Liverpool, Harborne Tenants, in Birmingham, and the Krupp Colonies, in Essen, were all within or adjacent to large cities. The American models that provided some insights but were quite dissimilar as developments were Goodyear Heights in Whitinsville, Massachusetts; Indian View, near Worcester, Massachusetts; and the so-called war towns of Perryville, Maryland, and Yorkship Village, in Camden, New Jersey.[33]

The original site for Mariemont covered a little over 253 acres, a spread of farmland, ravines, and woods in Columbia Township, an unincorporated region dotted with simple frame houses and bisected by two main roads. It was

General View

In July 1922, John Nolen assembled a scrapbook of photographs taken in June 1922 at the undeveloped Mariemont site by his associate, Philip W. Foster. This general view across gently rolling hills shows a pastoral and wooded landscape dotted with a few farmhouses.

not divided into building lots, and it was sparsely settled. On the banks of the river below the fields and orchards was a railroad right of way with freight and passenger service. This location met Livingood's criteria admirably. The land area was bordered on its north by built-up blocks of houses, just beyond a streetcar line that served communities east of the city. To the west was the small neighborhood of Fairfax, originally part of the Ferris family lands. Beyond the eastern boundary were more farms and woodlands. It was Livingood's original intention to extend the northern boundary of the site beyond the streetcar line, but when he discovered that his purchase negotiations involved more than two hundred owners, he decided against this extension.

Close by Livingood's chosen site were several well-established suburbs of Cincinnati: the middle-class neighborhoods of Madisonville, Linwood, and Oakley. Another nearby suburb, Hyde Park, had a wider range in its economic classes and housed many of Cincinnati's wealthiest families in spacious mansions on streets not far from the bungalows of the less affluent.[34] During Mariemont's construction period, beginning in 1923, the rural region abutting the new town on the northeast began to attract many of Cincinnati's richest citizens. This area, called Indian Hill, offered building lots of one, three, and five acres, and quite a few large estates emerged in the 1920s. As examples, Julius Fleischmann's Winding Creek Farm covered sixteen hundred acres, and Mary Emery's nephew, John J. Emery, built his home at Peterloon, an estate of twelve hundred acres.[35]

Although land purchases began in 1915, the land apparently was not surveyed for the proposed village project until three years later. For this task, Livingood hired a civil engineer and surveyor from Cincinnati, Thomas B. Punshon, to prepare a survey of the acres he had selected. This survey was completed in August 1918.[36] The tattered, original blueprint of Punshon's survey now in the

Photographs from John Nolen's scrapbook, July 1922, show farm fields and woods where streets, houses, a school, a church, and other buildings would be constructed. Existing houses and road names were noted in his captions.

Site for TOWN CENTER from Wooster Pike

Site for VILLAGE GREEN (woods at right)

Although no new buildings were yet built in Mariemont in July 1922, signs were already in place to indicate future locations of sites, such as the town center (bottom).

Nolen Papers at Cornell University embraces the core area of present-day Mariemont. The survey's western boundary is the Harvard tract; the northern boundary is Murray Avenue, with a small section set aside beyond that limit for the part called Resthaven. To the east the border is Indianview Avenue, already assigned to house lots by an earlier developer and eventually to become part of Mariemont. The southern boundary is the Little Miami River. The white lines of the blueprint include two main roads, Wooster Pike, arcing east and west through the farm fields and orchards, and Plainville Pike (now Plainville Road), coursing from the north to a dead end at an unnamed road to the rail yards just below the bluffs of the Little Miami River. The blueprint is covered with red- and yellow-pencil drawings and notes in Livingood's hand, indicating his suggested placement of buildings, streets, and neighborhoods.

That his concept for Mariemont and the detailed placement of elements within it were already quite developed sometime after 1918 but before his first encounter with town planner John Nolen in 1920 is evidenced on the Punshon survey blueprint. Livingood's notations in colored pencil record specific locations for the "Village Church," "solid rows of cheap houses," and a "Hotel," among many other proposals.[37] Livingood walked over the acres of fields and woods before and after purchases were made. As he became familiar with the terrain, he conceptualized the complete community even before he commissioned the town's designer.

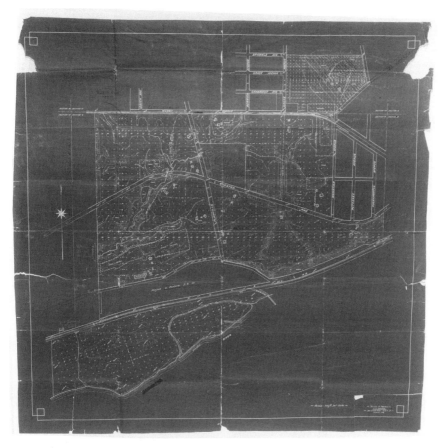

Thomas B. Punshon, a Cincinnati surveyor, was commissioned by Charles J. Livingood in August 1918 to make the first survey of the land purchased by Mary Emery for Mariemont. Livingood used this document at his first meeting at the office of John Nolen, annotating the blueprint with colored pencils to suggest locations for future buildings.

Livingood's selected acreage was owned by about thirty parties.[38] Because he wanted to avoid publicity for the unannounced project and to fend off speculators and unreasonable holdout owners, he created a screen that would shield Mary Emery and the Emery interests as land purchases were made. A realtor in Chicago, William Ellis, was employed to act as purchaser, with a Cincinnatian, William A. Hall, as Ellis's local agent. Hall did not know for whom he was acting, other than for Ellis, nor did he know how the land would be used. A bank in Philadelphia issued the checks to buy the property. Unknown except to Livingood and a few trusted colleagues, the money was Mary Emery's.

Livingood visited each parcel of land before it was purchased, and more than once his early morning or nocturnal prowlings were interrupted by an irate farmer and his shotgun.[39] The local agent arranging purchases, William Hall, dropped in on a landowner after Livingood completed his inspection, and negotiations invariably ended with an agreement to sell to Hall, who said he represented a Chicago buyer.

The clandestine purchases began in 1915, ceased during 1916 and 1917, when World War I occupied people's minds and hearts, and resumed in 1918. The final acquisition was not made until 1922.[40] During this period of land purchases, rumors about the intended use of the property flew about Cincinnati. Someone suggested that the Pennsylvania Railroad was acquiring the property for a huge repair shop. Another consigned the property to the Baltimore & Ohio Railroad. One of the more romantically inclined thought that, because of the great open spaces, the river view, and the rugged beauty of what is now Dogwood Park, a motion picture studio was to be built there.[41] Other guesses proposed that a cemetery was planned for the site. Another thought that Henry Ford was buying land to connect his factories with coal distribution centers in Cincinnati.

By 1922 the last parcel for the Mariemont project had been purchased. Sensing that the time was at hand for a public announcement of the spectacular plan of Mary Emery, Livingood met with the general manager of the city's leading newspaper, the *Cincinnati Enquirer,* to offer him the story. The manager promised confidentiality and release of the story only when Livingood and town planner John Nolen outlined their concept at a meeting of Cincinnati's prestigious Commercial Club on April 22, 1922.

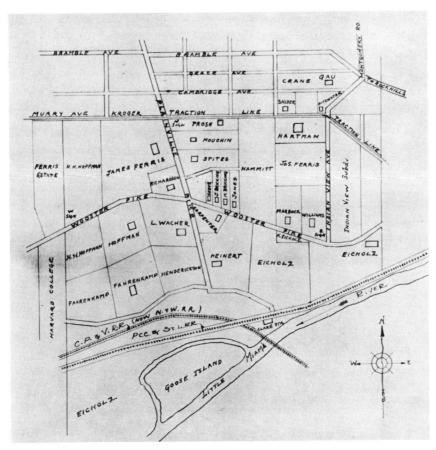

John Nolen's first record of owners from whom Mary Emery purchased land for Mariemont was drawn on notepaper and photographed for his scrapbook, July 1922.

But two years before the final land purchase, in September 1920, a visitor on a secret mission called at the Cambridge, Massachusetts, office of town planner John Nolen. Although the exact date of the visit is unknown, Nolen's secretary recorded the meeting and emphasized its peculiar secrecy. In the detailed, eight-page report she compiled in 1938, one year after Nolen's death, Nolen's affiliation with the Mariemont project from first to last involvement is outlined. Secretary Parsons's account of this first meeting is fascinating.

In September, 1920, the office had a mysterious visitor. It happened that Mr. Nolen was away, and so he was received by Mr. Foster [Philip W. Foster] then

Mr. Nolen's associate. The gentleman produced a map with all names carefully erased, and stated his errand in substance as follows: To discuss a scheme for the development of some property as a small community to house people employed in near-by factories. The major portion of the site had been acquired, but various parcels of land were still outstanding, and for that reason he wished to keep the scheme, its location, and his own identity secret.

The community was not to be known as a "model" village, as he disliked the word model. But all developments were to be along the highest lines, and his desire was to produce a result that would be followed as an example throughout the country. The village or town was to be for all classes of people, and would have some special features, one being a development on a cooperative basis for pensioned employees.

Our visitor, having had some training as an engineer, had worked up an interesting scheme in crayon. He was anxious to find some one to take on the planning who would have new and advanced ideas and high ideals, and not be governed by "cut and dried" customs. He was definitely afraid of getting some one too old or too busy to really give the scheme the necessary thought and attention. His selection of Mr. Nolen was the outcome of years of frequenting city planning conferences, judging the outstanding planners by their addresses and accomplished work.

At the close of the interview, which apparently had been satisfactory to him, he stated, in strict confidence, his name—Charles J. Livingood.[42]

In a memorandum written for Nolen's information by Nolen's partner and associate in his firm, Philip Foster, and probably the source for Parsons's detailed account of the visit, it is recorded that "Mr. Livingood had with him a blue print of the survey with a very interesting scheme worked up in crayon." Foster's report concluded with the quoted price for Nolen's services, fifty dollars per day and expenses, with his fee assessed for time used in traveling. No price was quoted for general planning work.[43] This first encounter between the nation's preeminent town planner and the man directly responsible for executing Mary Emery's vision began a partnership that flourished for five years, providing the soul and substance of Mariemont.

Nolen's "mysterious visitor" was silent for over a month, but in November he invited the town planner to visit him in Cincinnati. Again, Livingood played the dramatic actor.

Your Mr. Foster told me, when I came last month [*sic*] to your office and in confidence disclosed my project, on what terms and conditions he thought you would be willing personally when in the neighborhood to view the property I am securing for a town. I write to ask whether you will be presently, that is, before the weather gets to be too severe for tramping about, near Cincinnati? I am using this paper simply to reassure you as to my responsibility, and must still request that you do not disclose your errand, for you are very well known to many of my acquaintances. If you will therefor before arrival telegraph me I will meet you at the train and bring you to my home where I think it would be best for you to stay until we shall have surveyed the property and discussed my plans. I shall be wearing a bit of red ribbon in my overcoat lapel.[44]

According to Secretary Parsons's account, Foster had already ascertained, even before Livingood's letter arrived, that the survey of the proposed town focused on the Cincinnati region. Thus, the letter from Livingood was not a surprise, though the continuing mystery of the project intrigued Nolen.

Nolen was never at a loss for encouraging, appropriate words to write to clients, and he responded eagerly to Livingood's invitation. Livingood perpetuated the secrecy of the visit in a telegram he signed "Chas. J. Livingston" [*sic*]. In scheduling his first person-to-person meeting with Livingood, Nolen fueled interest in his past accomplishments, sending with a letter "the most recent example of our work, a report on city planning for Flint; also some other publications in which you may be sufficiently interested to glance over."[45] Livingood's knowledge of Nolen and his accomplishments, however, was not dependent on publications sent to him by the planner. Nolen was well known and well published when Livingood embarked on the Mariemont project. Acting on behalf of his patron and sponsor, Mary Emery, Livingood knew that Nolen had no equal as the leader of town planning in America.

When Livingood reached Nolen in 1920, the town planner was fifty-one years of age. Born in 1869 in Philadelphia, he had graduated from Girard College at age fifteen and worked for the Girard Estate for six years, 1884–90. After graduating from the University of Pennsylvania in 1893 with his bachelor's degree, Nolen had served as secretary of the American Society for the Extension of University Teaching. A trip to Europe in 1901–2 undoubtedly gave Nolen his first look at the cities and parks that partially influenced his later town planning. In 1905 he received a master's degree in landscape architecture, then a relatively new discipline, from Harvard University. After graduation, Nolen established his office in Harvard Square, Cambridge, his home base for the remainder of his long career. He and his staff soon developed a large practice in town planning as well as landscape architecture.

Nolen was the premier town planner in the United States at the time of Livingood's visit. His competitors were other top-level town planners, including Harland Bartholomew, Edward H. Bennett, Robert Whittier, and Charles H. Cheney. In the heyday of the 1920s, there were at least twenty-three consulting firms available to private patrons, civic institutions, or government commissions.[46] During these same years, about one hundred plans for municipalities were produced. Most of these focused on small cities and towns, as did Nolen's master plan for Mariemont.

Nolen's principal associate in 1920 when Livingood appeared at his office door was Philip W. Foster, a name carried in conjunction with Nolen's on all plans and documents pertaining to their practice together after 1914. Foster had been hired by Nolen in 1912, and he served as chief designer between 1914 and 1920. Blessed with administrative skills, Foster had become an associate in the firm by 1920 and directed the day-to-day activities of the staff.[47] Other employees in Nolen's office at different times were Earle Draper, Russell Black, Irving Root, and Justin Hartzog. These men all made their marks as town planners later in their careers.

Many town planning and landscape design accomplishments were already behind Nolen when Livingood made his first contact, and these were substantial enough and sufficiently pertinent to the proposed new community of Mariemont to satisfy Livingood. John Nolen was a prolific writer and lecturer as well as a practicing planner, promoting careful studies and solutions for new cities and towns, replanning of existing communities, and good design for landscape settings, particularly for parks. By 1920, Nolen's completed projects included the new suburb of Myers Park (1911) near Charlotte, North Carolina; improvements for Cohasset, Massachusetts (1916); Union Park Gardens, near Wilmington, Delaware, a town for the Liberty Land Company (1918) that would accommodate shipbuilders; and one of his better-known planned communities, Kingsport, Tennessee (1919). In addition to the Flint, Michigan, project Nolen mentioned in his first letter to Livingood, Nolen's other involvement contemporary with Mariemont included plans for Bristol, Connecticut; Asheville, North Carolina; and various enterprises in Florida.

A seemingly tireless traveler who usually spent two weeks each month away from his office to visit clients and their sites, Nolen's heaviest workload occurred between 1920 and 1929. For the first five years of this period, he was engaged to design Mariemont. Between 1905 and 1935, when he worked on more than four hundred projects, Nolen was the busiest planner in the United States.[48] The choice of Nolen, based on his recognized reputation and experience, also may have been colored somewhat by Nolen's earlier plan (1910) for Reading, Pennsylvania, Livingood's birthplace, and by Nolen's alumni affiliation with Harvard, Livingood's alma mater. For whatever reasons, it was a wise selection.[49]

2 · NOLEN'S
TOWN PLAN UNFOLDS

John Nolen's views on town planning were shaped by his predecessors in the field, the opportunities offered in America, his affinity for the landscape environment, and his expert organizational skills. As the best-known practitioner of town planning in the United States, his record by 1920 expressed his art clearly. He could articulate his abilities to his patrons quite effectively, both in writing and in conversations. He was an avid lecturer, utilizing his large collection of more than four thousand slides. In spite of a busy practice, Nolen was a prolific writer for technical journals and conferences. His initial career field, landscape architecture, had led him to specialize in town planning, where he felt the impress of Frederick Law Olmsted, America's leading landscape architect in the late nineteenth century. When commissioned by Livingood, Nolen probably was unaware that the Olmsted Brothers had designed Mary Emery's gardens at her Rhode Island estate. Nolen referred to Olmsted as "the leader of the movement" for city planning, a man who had a "commonsense application of the city planning ideal."[1]

Nolen admired the British Housing and Town Planning Act of 1909, which provided a suggested procedure to follow for Canada and the United States. In his own country, he felt the stimulation of the National Conferences on City Planning, first organized in 1909. By 1911, his own work reflected the English Garden City movement and the teachings of Ebenezer Howard. His indebtedness to Howard and particularly to the Letchworth experiment of 1903 was acknowledged often.[2]

Close to his home base, Nolen found predictions of Roger W. Babson, a statistician and economist from Wellesley, Massachusetts, especially useful in his work. Babson's observations are quoted extensively in Nolen's *New Towns for Old,* prophetically delineating the problems to come in America's cities and towns.[3] The large-scale exodus from cities to suburbs old and new, the growing dominance of the automobile in everyone's life, and the oppressiveness of many urban surroundings were accurate and foresightful readings by Babson. But Babson's observation most pertinent to Nolen's planned communities by the time of World War I was his prediction that suburban development would come not along rail lines snaking out from city to city, as had occurred in the nineteenth century, but with roads that would permit the migration of great numbers of city dwellers to points about fifteen or twenty miles distant from city centers. There, with roads and the automobile's abilities, the new suburbs would blossom, Babson forecasted. Nolen's pleadings for the planned development of new and model suburban communities and for the replanning of existing cities, while recognizing the achievements of the English Garden City prototypes, coincided with Babson's findings.

Nolen's thesis for town planning was elucidated many times in his writings and lectures; in quite a few instances, he edited and reused portions of one lecture in another. He was a consistent preacher of his sermon, promoting his cause again and again. Within his corpus of hundreds of articles, pamphlets, and lecture manuscripts are three full-length books, *Replanning Small Cities* (1912), *New Ideals in the Planning of Cities, Towns, and Villages* (1919), and *New Towns for Old* (1927). In the later work, Nolen's concepts and practices, his ideals and recommendations were solid, having been tested across the nation. While *New Towns for Old* is not a summary or history of town planning, it carefully explains his views, formed over many years of successful practice. It serves as the most meaningful single document for an appreciation and understanding of the man and his work.

Although Nolen engaged in numerous planning projects for established cities, improving the constricting grid layouts and widening streets, his true genius was best expressed in new towns, like Mariemont, developed on open or sparsely settled land. He lamented the wasteful use of land and the prevalence of unplanned cities while urging attention to suburban growth and the creation of new towns.[4] Nolen's necessary guidelines were stated simply in *New Towns for Old* and in other writings, providing a litany he followed assiduously. His ingredients for all new towns he planned, including Mariemont, were simply worded and concise.

1. The new town or city should have the right location, the right site geographically.

2. The local plan for a town should be based upon topographical conditions, and be worked out in right relation to railroads, main highways, water frontages or other controlling natural features.

3. The character of the new town should be rightly conceived with reference to its purpose and the use of the land.

4. The probable size of a town must have some consideration; otherwise the fundamental planning, the parts not easily changed, cannot be satisfactorily determined.[5]

With his notebook in hand and his philosophy in mind, John Nolen stepped from the train in Cincinnati on November 29, 1920, to meet his secretive commissioner, Charles J. Livingood, identified by a lapel ribbon. He then embarked on what Nolen would regard later as his favorite project. Mary Emery remained reclusive on this visit, and Nolen did not meet her. Nolen's secretary recorded this first face-to-face encounter with Livingood. The town planner was to design a "complete, self-contained satellite town on the outskirts of Cincinnati— an attempt not only to help the local situation, but to do it in such a manner that it could be duplicated wherever initiative, capital and sound planning could be combined."[6]

Nolen and Livingood spent hours walking over the acres already acquired by Livingood, with Nolen jotting comments in pencil on seven pages of a small notepad. His heading for his handwritten notes is the earliest known use of the new town's name, Mariemont. Nolen's notes, clearly a collaboration between the two men, first outlined the nature of the plans to be produced. He suggested a scale of two hundred feet to the inch for "street layout, location & design of institutional group, plaza, market, Factory section, station, parks, etc. & services—type of dwellings with simple lotting." Nolen's plans in "blackline prints" would be supplemented by watercolor renderings. No construction plans were required. Nolen's financial terms, specific requirements for needed surveys, and questions to be resolved concluded his notes. The final page recorded Nolen's rough layout of existing roads on the property. Nolen's proposal launched a sequence of events to be orchestrated in the following years.[7]

Nolen's brief notes listed the need for "a personal conference with you," meaning Livingood, "for discussion, criticism, and approvals" of plans and project details. It was clear from that time until the conclusion of Nolen's employment that Livingood was in charge and would be the final authority. Mrs. Emery's name sometimes was invoked to strengthen Livingood's role. A more complete survey than Punshon's was requested by Nolen at this meeting, as 337 acres were speculated within the project's boundaries of "Bottom lands and Uplands." The town planner's proposed fee during the first year's consultation was $2,400 plus drafting costs and travel expenses, to be paid quarterly, monthly, or bimonthly.[8]

With completion of Nolen's first viewing of the Mariemont acres (the land as yet unnamed officially), Livingood scratched out a letter by hand in early December to the newly employed designer. Again, Nolen's secret mission was noticed.

> I hope you have forgiven me for my hasty exit—leaving you up in the air about catching your train. That Dr. Gau [one of the residents on land owned by Mrs. Emery] did, as did others, tell the collector of rents about the big limousine seen on the property but the news has gone back to all that you were a collegemate of mine looking over the property at the suggestion of the Chicago owners. Have started the surveyor on task of securing information desired. In meantime here is a clean sheet 200′ blue print for you.[9]

Nolen responded that he was "safely back from my visit, full of enthusiasm for the project." Thanking his host for his hospitality, he said he was sending two books and a list of others for Livingood's reference.[10] This exchange of letters between Nolen and Livingood began an extensive correspondence focusing on the Mariemont project that continued for five years. Almost without exception, the letters were typewritten, and each writer addressed the other formally: "Dear Mr. Livingood" and "My dear Mr. Nolen," never "Dear Charles" or "Dear John." Theirs was a serious business arrangement from first to last.

Nolen set to work before Christmas in 1920 to draft an outline of "the general scope of the first year's work for 'Mariemont.'" By the first week of the new year, his listed responsibilities for his patron had been mailed. This document, lengthy but well constructed, set the course for all that Nolen pursued as he designed the new town. It elucidates the modus operandi of a town planner's initial work for a project of this magnitude.

> The first step . . . would be to establish a general plan for the whole project, and supply such details and cross sections as would make the ideas proposed for your consideration as clear as possible. The general plan would be drawn, probably, at the scale of 200 feet to the inch corresponding with the topographical survey. It would show the street and road layout, the public reservations such as parks and playgrounds, special sites for public or semi-public buildings, lot lines, and other essential features of the development. This general scheme should be supplemented by plans for the special sections in which community life would center, these to be drawn at a larger scale, probably 60 feet to the inch, following your larger scale survey. All these plans would be printed in black lines on white paper and rendered in color, in order to bring out more clearly and attractively the design and the principal ideas upon which the design would rest.
>
> Our work for 1921 would include: (1) consultation with you from the very beginning, and careful study of the whole of the property and the surrounding territory and the local conditions affecting it; (2) a preliminary study for the development; (3) personal conferences to go over the general scheme and its details, leading to approval, and (4) a general plan of the entire development, with larger detail drawings, as suggested, of the special features. The general plan would be accompanied by a typewritten descriptive report giving the main points of the scheme up-to-date, with photographs, statistics as to the number of lots, length of roads and other essential information relating to the property and the first stages of its development. It would also include a clear indication of the provision to be made for community life and the policy to be followed in the orderly and economic consideration of what would be in some respect an independent town or suburb. We would endeavor to make these plans as complete, definite, and attractive as possible, but of course they would be design, not construction plans. In addition to the plans as outlined above, we should expect to act as consultants during the year 1921, and in every way to give your project close attention and whole-hearted service.[11]

Nolen's letter, once accepted by Livingood, served as his contract, the only one he ever had for the immense undertaking he was about to begin. He ended his explicit outline by suggesting that one year, 1921, probably would not be enough to see Mariemont properly launched. Although Livingood wanted to commit only to one year's employment of Nolen, the town planner could foresee a longer occupation. By January 8, Nolen's initial layout or plan for the new town was progressing, news that must have excited Livingood.[12] By mid-January, Nolen had suggested that his associate, Philip Foster, visit the site in February and bring with him the first layout. From the beginning contact, Foster was a close collaborator with Nolen in Mariemont's development and in dealings with Livingood. And because he was closely integrated into the planning and construction stages, Foster was invaluable as an understudy for Nolen, especially when Nolen's busy schedule saddled him with demanding travel to the various cities and towns he was commissioned to plan.

Before Foster made his first visit to the Mariemont site, Livingood acknowledged Nolen's letter of January 4 and its terms but indicated clearly that Nolen was contracted for only one year and that his proposed plan might be accepted or rejected.[13] Livingood's cautiousness persisted throughout the years of Nolen's involvement, sometimes protecting his financial commitment, sometimes curtailing Nolen's recommendations and replacing them with his own. Livingood recognized his shortcomings as a town planner, for he wrote Nolen that "I am not a professional planner, merely a practical business man with some ideals, and therefor should not set my view up against yours." However, he expected his views to be observed. Nolen's acquiescence usually followed. In a few brief sentences, Livingood summarized his expectations.

> I want you to GIVE THE BEST that is in you on this project, such study of the problem that you will be proud to have been the means of solving it . . . namely, the planning of a comprehensive whole which shall represent the latest "thought and practice" on the subject of A MODEL COMMUNITY, model in the lay-out, model as to methods of street construction etc. etc. While our hope is to provide homes for the working classes we wish also to *set a standard.*

Nolen readily agreed with Livingood's assertion that termination of his services might occur "at any time that you and your principal so desire," and he bubbled over with excitement for the future. He recited his confidence in developing a new standard for a town, adding that "Mariemont might be the first to be put into effect." He told Livingood that he had studied a Farm City project and had met with the director of the Russell Sage Foundation to discuss town planning.[14]

As planned, Foster's visit to Cincinnati occurred on February 8–9 and was the only on-site inspection made by either Nolen or Foster in 1921. Livingood was delighted with the plan presented to him, with its beautifully rendered design.[15] He then wrote to Nolen to outline six points to be changed, modified, or redrawn. The "bottom lands" should not be available for factory sites because of frequent flooding, unless dikes were to be built. He preferred the bluffs for factories or light manufacturing, citing the advertising value. Livingood thought the plan to place a road across the Harvard College tract was "idle" due to "broken ground and local conditions," and he wanted the "institutional section designed more in accordance with my plan, for so many reasons that I cannot go into them here." The "Community House" was to be placed near the stadium, "where I had it," Livingood stated. The hotel, he concluded in his letter, "right on the square, near the garage," was what he wanted. It was to be "a sort of respectable roadhouse . . . more used than would be a quite resort-like place off there in the woods."

Although Livingood's comments were tactfully expressed as suggestions rather than absolute dictates, his placement of the hotel and the community house (eventually they became the Mariemont Inn and the community center) were sited as he preferred. The highway never crossed through the Harvard College tract and its prehistoric Indian mounds and burials. The factory plots, fortunately, never were placed on the attractive bluffs or in the bottom lands, for Nolen eventually won land for the industrial section to the west of town in a tract acquired by Livingood and known as Westover.

By March, four additional survey sheets for Mariemont were submitted by Livingood to Nolen, based on the discussions with Foster after his February visit and with Nolen in Cambridge. These were augmented by comments Livingood made for each sheet. His comments display not only his adamant notions about the new town that he felt was his, but also how persistent he could be with reminders. On the "Northwest" sheet, Livingood wanted Nolen's design to stress "various types of Group and Row houses, especially low-priced." The community house was to remain as he, Livingood, requested in its Plainville Road location adjacent to the stadium. Nolen was to preserve an intersection of that

road with Wooster Pike. Emphasized by Livingood, also, was news of acquiring the "Cresap Tract" to the west of the Harvard tract, thus adding to the village's acreage. On the "Southwest" sheet, directions were given for placement
in the bottom lands of the "garbage reduction plant" and "sewage disposal
plant." These facilities, like others hoped for by Nolen or Livingood in their
earliest discussions, were never built.

One of the most innovative elements ultimately built for Mariemont was a
central heating plant and its underground conduits, a system prompted by
Livingood, who suggested that the generating building should be constructed
in the "Northeast" or "Southeast" sections of town.

> Should we not *plan,* however, for an even more ambitious central heating plan,
> not only for the Institutional Tract but for the central properties and as much
> surrounding them as can be safely undertaken. I had always thought that a big
> boiler plant should go under the bluff, yet somewhat W. of your Pergola, which
> would [receive] coal (by rail) and water (Little Miami) close at hand. The time
> might come when we could [generate] POWER during the daytime for the shift-
> ing of cars [by steam engines moving coal cars to the generating plant?] thus
> eliminating that smoke. We might plan to make electricity for whole town. In
> general these are the only suggestions I find to add to those in my last letter ap-
> proving in the main of the colored sketch your Mr. Foster brought out with
> him on Feb. 8th and which we hurriedly discussed in your office later. I appre-
> ciate that you want to "get busy" but please consider all the above carefully (I
> may see you sooner than you think) before you get away on the wonderful trip
> abroad.[16]

Eventually the central heating plant was built in the southeast section of the village. It provided steam heat for the houses, apartments, and other buildings in
the original Nolen plan through an elaborate tunnel and pipe system. Deteriorating after World War II, it ceased operations.

Throughout April and May, Nolen revised his plans and prepared detailed
drawings in a "finished" scale of sixty feet to the inch, delighting Livingood and
providing him with "something to chew on in an architectural way."[17] Although Livingood wanted to think "intensively" about every aspect of Mariemont's plan, the project's estimated cost, in both land and construction, was
not mentioned in these early communications with Nolen. In the project's be-

ginning stages, no one could grasp the total investment that would be required from Mary Emery directly or through the Mariemont Company, which she formed in 1922.

In the spring of 1921, as Nolen drafted plans for Mariemont and sketched several color renderings for specific sections of the new town, Livingood prepared for one of his many extended trips abroad. The sketches, probably by Nolen's own hand, are tinted line drawings of the town center, farm buildings, the hospital group, and pensioners' cottages.[18] The drawings must have impressed Livingood, as the hospital and farm (eventually named Resthaven), when built, mirrored Nolen's delicate renderings. Presumably the drawings were passed to the assigned architects by Livingood, giving the town planner-artist the only developed examples of his designs for Mariemont buildings.

A month after dispatching his sketches, Nolen submitted to Livingood a long list of towns and villages that might be visited on his summer trip to England. The list was not conclusive, Nolen wrote, and it included some well-known stops, such as Wells, Saint Albans, Ely, and Chester, and the town-planned masterpieces of Letchworth, Port Sunlight, Bournville, Welwyn Garden City, and Hampstead Garden Suburb. Welwyn was suggested as "particularly worthwhile looking up as it would represent a revision based on expe-

This drawing and three others made in 1922 by John Nolen are the first known drawings illustrating Charles Livingood's ideas for buildings to be erected in Mariemont. An inn (at *left*), the square, and its fountain were eventually built.

Sketch for Mariemont farm buildings by John Nolen, 1922. The barn, silo, and farmer's cottage in Nolen's proposal were copied closely by Hubert E. Reeves, the New York architect chosen to design the farm buildings in 1924.

rience of the Letchworth idea." The letter ended with several pages of books Livingood might find appealing and the names of "persons interested in town and city planning and related subjects."[19]

Among the references recommended by Nolen were several with European town planning focus, material that Livingood might find helpful as he continued to study models at home and abroad. One of the books, Frederic C. Howe's *European Cities at Work*, extols the German practice of providing all services through a strong municipal authority but suggests a cooperative marriage among organizers. Livingood wanted Mariemont's services eventually to be in the hands of a municipal government. However, he answered only to Mary Emery, so the "cooperative marriage" between him and Nolen worked as long as Livingood's decisions were respected. Nevertheless, he must have agreed in principle with Howe's glowing words. "We are beginning to see the city as a conscious, living organism [where] the architect and the engineer, the educator

Sketch by John Nolen, a concept drawing made in 1922 for the Mariemont hospital, suggests a large Georgian Revival structure topped by a cupola. When constructed two years later, the original building, as designed by Samuel Hannaford and Sons, Cincinnati architects, was much smaller than Nolen's scale suggested.

and the artist, the administrator and the dreamer, can build and plan for the comfort, convenience, and the happiness of people, just as kings in an earlier age planned their cities for the gratification of their ambition and the glorification of their pride."[20]

Another recommended book was W. R. Hughes's *New Town: A Proposal in Agricultural, Educational, Civic, and Social Reconstruction,* from which Livingood might glean certain elements, later fulfilled in Mariemont, that could be likened to a "new Country-Town in England in such a spirit and on such a plan as shall stir the hearts of all who are seeking after freedom and fellowship."[21] Whether Livingood followed Nolen's lead and read these publications is unknown, but the latter's interest in broadening his patron's knowledge of the literature pertaining to town planning was as deep as his concern that Livingood visit many cities, towns, and model communities in preparation for the great exercise getting under way.

While Livingood prepared for his European trip, Nolen developed plans for an Indian museum that would be built on the tract once owned by Harvard University. This project was dear to Livingood's heart, probably in part because of his alumnus status and his love of prehistory. Nolen submitted a "Sketch for Museum for Indian Relics, Mariemont," to Livingood's delight.[22] Nolen's plan proposed an open-air pavilion of stone and rough timber, and Livingood suggested a display of body burials, cache-pit, utensils, and even a skeleton or two. He urged Foster to visit the Peabody Museum at Harvard University but not to "give yourself away when you go to the Museum. You must handle the situation with great care."[23] Concluding with a few suggestions for the proposed museum's tile floor and wooden uprights and cautioning Nolen not to prepare any more drawings, he urged his planner to focus on the village's plan. Livin-

The cottages proposed to house Emery estate pensioners in the Resthaven area of Mariemont were never built, although John Nolen's sketch illustrates his concept for them in 1922.

good was not only penny-wise with expenditures, but also properly on course toward the primary goal.

The Indian museum remained in limbo as Nolen and Livingood directed their attention to the general plan of the village, a masterfully drawn, final concept for Mariemont. Dated July 1921, it was entitled "A New Town" and bore Nolen's prophetic subtitle, "An Interpretation of Modern City Planning Principles applied to a Small Community to produce local Happiness. A National Exemplar."[24] Its creator wrote complimenting his client, "Some day I think we are all going to be proud of our joint enterprise."[25]

Nolen's plan of July 1921 served initially and throughout the building program as the preeminent guide for Mariemont's development. Livingood intended "to lay graphically before my principal a picture of the thing as it is to be finally, to show what we have yet to acquire, and in a measure how it will all look."[26] This plan, locating buildings and streets, parks and churches, gardens and stores, depicted a town covering 253 acres with 759 house lots. An eventual population of five thousand was envisioned. Tree-lined avenues radiated out from the town center, where shops, apartments, a bank, the town hall, a library, a hotel, a theater, a post office, and a community building were to be sited. Additional land purchases expanded the town's size to about 365 acres in 1922.[27]

The village as delineated in Nolen's master plan is dominated by the town center and the diagonal axes of streets radiating from this center and anchoring the town's core. Dotted around the plan are single houses placed arbitrarily on lots south of the main east-west artery, Wooster Pike. Row houses and apartments (the "cheap houses" for the workers) are clustered in the Dale Park section, following Livingood's suggestion outlined on the Punshon survey of 1918. The village's streets, many of their names already assigned, wind over the yard-square sheet. Most of Livingood's suggestions are incorporated, such as the pensioners' cottages and the hospital-convalescent complex at the northeast tip of the village, the stadium and football field with its adjoining tennis courts, and the allotment gardens tucked into open spaces behind apartments, following English garden city precedents. Dogwood Park sweeps along both sides of Whiskey Creek's ravines, inserting a finger of wilderness into a highly ordered design. Smaller parks abound throughout the plan, frequently assigned to street intersections.

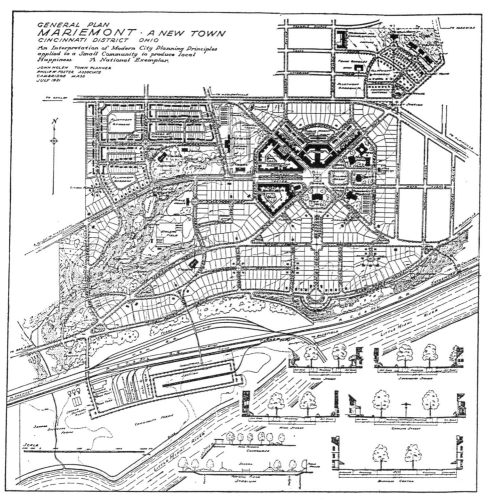

The "General Plan, Mariemont, A New Town," by John Nolen, July 1921. This plan determined the layout of the town before land was acquired for Westover, the industrial section, and the Indian View neighborhood to the right of the central square. Mature trees were illustrated along some streets and in Dogwood Park on a copy of the official plan that Nolen kept in his office.

Perhaps Nolen's most dramatic element was the handsome spine he called Center Avenue and Promenade (now Center Street), which led to a pergola and concourse overlooking the Little Miami River and the blue-hazed valley stretching to the south. As Nolen was keenly interested in the width of streets in his plans, the setback for houses, and the planting limits for trees, his Mariemont plan includes seven profiles, or cross sections, of street types, illustrating the variety required to avoid boring sight lines and repetitive borders.

Nolen responded cooperatively to Livingood's commission, accepting his patron's ideas with only minor changes. Where he digressed from Livingood's suggestions, Nolen refined, realigned, or expanded the plan with his own, more professionally conceived ideas. The Mariemont commission, unlike others for Nolen, came from an individual, not a committee or board, from a patron who was well informed about European prototypes, real estate development, and housing expectations. Nolen wisely read Livingood's desire to control the community's every detail, even though his "principal," Mary Emery, was the real force and foundation of the project. Without her there would be no Mariemont, Ohio, but without Livingood there could be no implementation of the scheme she supported so generously. Livingood was the entrée to the project's financial underpinnings and its de facto director.

Nolen followed his client's suggestions to the letter in most parts of the plan, such as the Dale Park section, where Livingood wanted "cheap houses," and the locations of church, pensioners' cottages, bluff overlook, and stadium complex. Nolen's proposed factory locations in the flatlands below the bluff, together with sewage and garbage disposal areas, amended only slightly the suggestions from Livingood as sketched on the surveyor's blueprint presented to Nolen's office by the "mysterious stranger" in 1920. Mariemont's industrial section, Westover, eventually was placed in the western extremity of the village on land acquired specifically for this purpose. This removed the sight and sound of factories from the residential sections. Other land to the east and west, some depicted on the 1921 plan, would be acquired in later years and added to the original acreage. At this stage in the planning, Nolen offered no suggestions for architects. Certainly, this was not required in his commission. Apparently, his plan was attractive enough to please Mrs. Emery.

After his summer abroad, Livingood returned first to Newport, then to Quebec, and on to Princeton, where Livingood's son Jack was enrolled. As Livingood conveyed to Nolen and Foster in a lengthy, handwritten letter, the Mariemont plan "projects my dream" and greatly satisfied him. However, Livingood sought more from his planner in 1921: the types of trees to be planted on streets, street and road surface materials, an opinion on sidewalk construction, whether or not brick should be used for all residences, and whether alleys should be planned for the community.[28] Livingood concluded his letter with an outline of the talk in downtown Cincinnati that would announce the Mariemont project to the public. This would be a well-staged, evening event to publicize what Livingood must have considered his best accomplishment in life. Members of Cincinnati's Commercial Club, then an all-male group of the city's foremost business leaders, would be fed and lectured with brief speeches by Nolen and Livingood. Slides of the city's slums and of housing developments in the United States and Europe were planned for the program.

Livingood reported in the same letter that his trip within England in the summer of 1921 had taken him and his family more than three thousand miles to cathedral towns, along the Roman Wall, and to the Lake Country. He had photographed at least four housing developments, finding that "conditions are so different" than those in America, and he had revisited the two leading garden cities. Letchworth he had found "rather drab and down at the heel; Ealing too old-fashioned and smugly prosperous . . . Welwyn was being built up very slowly. Croydon was the most interesting and helpful." Livingood signed off with comments on a rumored purchase by Henry Ford that might possibly affect the new town. That Ford would purchase the Cincinnati, Milford and Lebanon trolley line to carry coal along Mariemont's northern boundary to his Detroit factories was a rumor that never materialized.

Nolen was grateful for Livingood's letter, received after a "summer of silence," and he was anxious to hear directly more details of "English attempts to plan new towns" and to see his snapshots. Nolen hoped he would be included in the plans for the public announcement and offered to make slides of the plans, with some in color. Obviously, as town planner and designer of the scheme for the new town, Nolen wanted to be a major actor on the stage before the Commercial Club and ultimately before the nation. "If it should appear good," he wrote to Livingood, "let's say so frankly. In this case it is not personal vanity, for the product is a joint one in which we all had a part."[29]

Nolen was no sycophant in dealing with Livingood, but he cleverly chose his phrases and sentences, always appealing to his patron's self-importance and conscious that Livingood gave him his paycheck. The Cambridge town planner was well mannered, formal in his communications, and always eager to prepare for the next step in his business affairs. Nolen suggested in October 1921 that he develop an outline description of Mariemont that could be used in the Commercial Club presentation.[30] He thought that a synopsis or outline was essential before the presentation could be organized. Nolen had a busy practice, and he liked to look ahead as planner. The sense of urgency he conveyed often went unheeded. Livingood usually reacted more slowly to the project's needs.

A trip in November to several western states called Nolen away for eighteen days after his offer to draft an outline of the Mariemont project, but he returned fired with enthusiasm: "The more I saw of the big cities of the middle West (and often the small ones that are growing rapidly), the more I felt convinced that the solution of many of our most difficult problems connected either with the increase of wealth or the sharing of what makes life most worth while, [and] is to be found in the kind of town planning work and endeavor that Mariemont represents."[31] Not hearing immediately from Livingood, Nolen kept up his end of the correspondence and repeated his hope that a description of Mariemont could be prepared, perhaps with Livingood's ideas available before those by Nolen were delivered. That was not to be, as Livingood either recognized his own shortcomings or wanted Nolen's draft in hand to help him organize his own statement. He urged Nolen "to make a professional presentation" that would include such details as the number of lots in the 1921 plan that could be sold. Livingood wanted Nolen's point of view.[32]

As 1921 ended, Livingood continued to agonize over the Mariemont scheme and how it could be presented most effectively to the public. Nolen, not yet invited to participate in the presentation that would occur in April of the next year, suggested a national promotion and exhibition before the Architectural League of New York in February. Livingood would have none of it, wanting first to capture the hearts of his fellow Cincinnatians. Quite correctly, Nolen hoped to attract a wider audience for this amazing project about to begin in the Midwest. He wanted Mariemont to "have not merely a local but also a national and more dramatic public presentation."[33]

Nolen's worries that national publicity for Mariemont might be lacking proved to be groundless. There would be ample opportunity for publicizing the Mariemont venture in the press and in various professional journals after a public announcement was made in Cincinnati. Livingood devoted the first months of 1922 to preparing for this event. Not only would he herald a significant real estate and architectural project for Cincinnati and the nation that would serve, Livingood hoped, as an example for others to follow, but also he wanted to demonstrate his ability to conceive and execute a costly enterprise without all of the credit falling to another. Mary Emery never complained.

3 · THIS IS TO BE A MODEL TOWN

Mary Emery was seventy-eight years of age in 1922 and not in robust health. Her paintings and her summer home and gardens at Middletown, Rhode Island, were her special pleasures. She enjoyed frequent reports from Livingood on Mariemont's gestation, particularly on her increasing ownership of acreage. She saw in her representative, Livingood, a reflection of the Emery spirit and expertise in real estate evidenced by her late husband and oldest son. As Mary witnessed Livingood's excitement in developing plans for Mariemont, it became easier for her to write the checks that paid for it.

In mid-February, Nolen returned from a trip to Panama, Haiti, Costa Rica, and Cuba, stopping in Florida to oversee his planning projects. Mariemont was on his mind, he wrote to Livingood, and the report due his patron was begun. Nolen outlined only the divisions he intended to cover eventually in expanded, explanatory paragraphs, with headings such as: "I. Ideas back of the Plan, II. The Streets and Roads, III. The Town Center, IV. Recreation, V. the Homes, VI. Program and Policy, Appendix." Nolen added that the "work of professional men is irregular and spasmodic, and since the first of the year we have been pushed with one thing after another which clients considered urgent, especially the planning of the Babson Institute."[1] This excuse did not please Livingood, yet he himself procrastinated frequently in the ensuing years.

The physical development of Mariemont remained undecided in Livingood's mind in early 1922, even though Nolen's plan of July 1921 was in hand and accepted. Livingood sketched "A Plan for Improving Housing Conditions in Cincinnati," subtitling it "the 3rd worst congested city in America," to lay out what he considered advantages, features, and doubts and queries. He listed as advantages Mariemont's adjacency to Madisonville, Norwood, Oakley, and other suburban areas; its rail service into Cincinnati; its easy access to coal, lumber, and steel; the trolley line on the town's northern limit; the Little Miami River and its bottom lands for sewage disposal; protection from cold winds and storms; and its proximity to the cultural and educational opportunities of a large city. Mariemont's features, according to Livingood, would be its fresh air and fine views; initial cost of services, dwellings, and public places all borne by Mary Emery and the Mariemont Company (not yet formed but already in Livingood's thoughts); the houses and cottages, as well as the pensioners' and convalescent facilities; the possibility of individual ownership of property "under restrictions"; and the "final turning over of Company's stock to owners."[2]

A page of "Doubts and queries" raised concerns that Livingood should have addressed in first discussions with Nolen and engineers, but the latter were not yet contracted. Livingood wondered whether one thousand acres could be secured, and at what price? Would city water and gas be available? Would the Pennsylvania Railroad cooperate and sell land? And could transportation be improved? These questions and others, no doubt, haunted Livingood as he looked ahead to the announcement of Mariemont he hoped to orchestrate in the spring.

Writing from Lake Placid, New York, where he had gone in February "for a much-needed rest after a very hard winter," Livingood focused on the program to announce Mariemont's plan to the public. His exodus from Cincinnati was one of many trips taken to regain his health, he claimed, but their frequency and resort accommodations suggest a tendency to malingering.

Of course I understand the difficulties of meeting all professional demands, but sincerely hope that in due [course] a full plan may be evolved from your experience, for remember this is to be a model, and the opportunity is great. So much depends on the way the scheme is presented. We are still in the throes of securing the last vital pieces, and have a lot of detail to go through with to get the Harvard tract, but I am still in hopes that the plan to "blow the whole thing" before the Commercial Club, you as chief showman (with slides) to be pulled off this spring. Our City Planning Committee is keen for publicity, and under this guise I think we can "spring the thing" easily. But we must be *ready.* The newspaper sleuth *has the story,* discovered by himself in a way he won't divulge, but I have influence and he is sworn to secrecy until the night of your talk. My idea is this: you to start talking ostensibly on ideal city planning (and none is better fitted), then spring our sketch, explain it, and amplify with pictures of all sorts, real and imaginary. After which I will tell how the idea came to me and what I hope to see accomplished for my city *some day* in the near future.[3]

The date was set—Saturday, April 22, 1922—for announcing the founding of Mariemont to a patrician group of Cincinnati businessmen assembled at the Commercial Club's annual meeting and dinner. Livingood counted on Nolen's participation "from the professional point of view," and he expected Nolen to illustrate his talk with slides showing "how the town will look; for instance, typical street views in Letchworth, Port Sunlight, and in some American Model Towns with, of course, slides of those charming water color sketches made for the Mariemont project." Nolen's opinion was sought regarding another participant in the program, R. E. Miles, head of the Ohio Institute of Public Efficiency and a "Harvard man" known to Livingood for ten years. Nolen was also asked to provide suitable illustration of the town plan for the Sunday edition of the *Cincinnati Enquirer.* The title of the event shielded the real purpose, for Livingood intended to call it an "Evening on City Planning."[4]

Livingood plotted the program as he might for a stage performance. All the actors had their lines, and he was the director. By the end of March, Nolen had suggested a few points to consider for the Commercial Club presentation, such as a printed folder illustrating the general plan, publicity in the newspapers, and an exhibition of a set of plans. His suggestions were based on his experience as a town planner. Livingood responded by describing the intended audience.

But instead of answering categorically your questions, I take the liberty of sketching my idea of what should be said by us three speakers beginning at nine o'clock, after a long dinner in a stuffy room at the Queen City Club (our best) Saturday evening April 22nd. Remember that we should be speaking to Cincinnati's most representative citizens, financiers, lawyers, captains of industry, hard headed men of affairs, among whom chronic kickers, knockers, crass materialists, et al. We cannot afford to tire them nor antagonize them, but must forestall criticism even at the expense of losing the effect of presenting an "ideal."[5]

Livingood outlined Nolen's introduction by Commercial Club President E. W. Edwards and the steps leading through the program: general remarks and slides with Nolen's comments showing "a little technical detail," ten minutes for Mr. Miles on the "financial plan," and the final ten minutes for Livingood to "tell of the inception of the plan, my studies of the subject, the purchases of the properties and the part Mrs. Emery will take in the enterprise." Nolen was expected to emphasize "the ideal of a Model Town," strange advice from one who earlier claimed he disliked the term.

Cautioning Nolen that "we will meet sharp criticism if we exhibit pipe dreams at this time, for Cincinnati has yet to be educated," Livingood wanted to avoid too many specifics about the Mariemont project, leaving details to the newspaper's exclusive coverage, he wrote to Nolen. No brochure to distribute that evening was needed, and Livingood did not want to answer questions about the possibility of an architectural competition for Mariemont's buildings. Livingood promised only that the next months would be consumed with planning and constructing streets and sewers. He wanted the evening to be a "love feast and not a fight."

Throughout the month of April, other letters between Cambridge and Cincinnati ironed out the questions and confirmed Livingood's requirements for the April 22 program. Livingood urged Nolen to release the Mariemont story to Boston and New York newspapers after the *Cincinnati Enquirer* ran it on April 23. A bird's-eye sketch of the village by Nolen might be, Livingood argued, used in a slide as well as a future brochure. Certain details about Mariemont (number of building lots and miles of streets, houses and apartments to be built of brick, and steam heat from a central plant) Nolen was to note in his talk, in spite of Livingood's constant reminder that no specifics were to be mentioned.[6]

Nolen might have alarmed Livingood when he wrote that his remarks "probably will be impromptu and simply comment on the slides," but he complimented Livingood as a "town planner" and showered him with praise for "how fully you grasped the situation and what you wanted to do." He was obedient to his patron's demands for the Commercial Club event, but he looked beyond the matters at hand and questioned Livingood about issues affecting Mariemont's development and future. This inquiring nature persisted throughout his employment as town planner. In one letter written shortly before the April 22 lecture, he queried Livingood on the future government of the community and the maintenance of its property. That same letter enclosed the "Statistical State-ment" that Nolen felt would be "a test of the soundness of the plan, and the plan has stood the test most successfully."[7]

On the morning of the Commercial Club meeting, John Nolen arrived at Cincinnati's Winton Place station on the 10:50 train from Boston and was whisked away to Livingood's home on Baker Place. That evening, after an elab-orate dinner featuring jellied gumbo, filet of river salmon, squab chicken farci, and strawberry mousse, Nolen delivered to the tuxedo-clad diners his first ma-jor address and first recorded public statement on the new town. His im-promptu remarks were captured by a stenographer, who also noted that about fifty lantern slides were shown.

> Mariemont is an attempt not only to help the local situation in Cincinnati, but to do it on terms and conditions that can be duplicated wherever initiative, cap-ital and sound planning can be combined to support an enterprise of great pub-lic importance, namely, the building of new towns or suburbs, virtually com-plete communities, providing not only suitable homes, but also schools, recreation, amusement, shops, etc. for people of small means.
>
> My part in your program this evening is mainly to act as showman. I am to have the opportunity, in speaking on city planning as applied to home build-ing for workmen in Cincinnati, not merely to present what might possibly be termed generalities. It is also to be my privilege to show for the first time a concrete proposal, the successful execution of which is assured. For lovers of mankind this is in many respects, I believe, a dramatic moment. Once more we are to have a significant example of how widespread public welfare follows from persistent, well-directed effort combined with constructive imagination in busi-ness. In this instance it is your good fortune, and I hasten to congratulate you, that the man who sits modestly here at your board is a citizen of Cincinnati who has dreamed a dream so often and through so long a period, now nearly a decade, that that dream has come true.[8]

Following to the letter Livingood's guidelines for his "showman" duties, Nolen then discussed the site of Mariemont, the general street plan he had de-signed, the town center and its public buildings, comparisons with notable En-glish garden cities, and the density of families to an acre. He emphasized that costs initially would be borne by the Mariemont Company. The community was planned to cover 365 acres, Nolen said, with an eventual population of five thousand. Surprisingly, there was no recorded mention of Mary Emery in Nolen's talk and little to credit this generous lady in Livingood's remarks. It remained for the press to acknowledge her foundational role.

True to the editor's promise to Livingood, front page headlines in the *Cincinnati Enquirer* on April 23 blazed the news that a new community would be built east of the city, thanks to funding from Mary Muhlenberg Emery. In the United States no real estate or neighborhood development had approached this one. The public knew of the Emery fortune and charitable giving, but a project of this magnitude was unparalleled. "Millions to Be Spent in Dwellings for Workers' Mariemont" and "Lady Bountiful's Wand Is to Wave over Tract near Madisonville" announced the headlines alongside illustrations of Mrs. Emery in academic robes identifying her honorary degree from the University of Cincinnati. Columns of text lauding the news continued on two other pages.[9]

Now the secret purchaser of farmland was known. To the surprise, particularly, of dinner guest William Ellis, the Chicago real estate agent hired to buy the land, Mrs. Emery was the actual owner and Livingood the project's director. He had never met the latter until that evening. According to the news article, John R. Schindel, Cincinnati attorney and associate of Livingood, was responsible for developing the purchase scheme to hide the actual buyer's name. The local real estate agent handling details, William A. Hall, had not been aware of any owner other than Ellis during his negotiations with sellers. Land costs varied depending on the date of purchase and the parcel's acreage, but "the average price for the whole area brought the cost down to a figure quite within reason for the purposes of the enterprise," the article stated. Quoted one day later, William Hall said he had paid $700 per acre in the earliest stages of land acquisition, with later prices rising to $1,000 and $1,500 per acre. In 1921, he had paid $10,000 for the Stites home and three acres on Plainville Road. The last three parcels had been acquired one week before the Commercial Club meeting, when R. L. Houchins had sold his house and six acres for $30,000, the highest price paid for any one property.[10]

Although Nolen's remarks on April 22 were reported verbatim by the *Cincinnati Enquirer,* those of the two other speakers, R. E. Miles and Charles J. Livingood, were only summarized. Mary Emery's representative was well known in

Cincinnati, particularly in the Commercial Club setting, but Nolen was the celebrity and the one who unveiled the project. Livingood's points emphasized that Mariemont was not a scheme for profit, nor was it entirely a philanthropy, although private funds made it possible. When Mariemont was completed, proceeds from the sale of lots and buildings could be reinvested in other planned communities that would follow the Mariemont model. This project illustrated, Livingood said, that good housing and the benefits of a planned community could be "within reach of wage earners without carrying them too far from their daily occupations." As the dinner meeting ended, selected guests were interviewed by the newspaper reporter. Awed by the project's scope, William Cooper Procter, head of the Procter & Gamble Company, said in recognizing Mary Emery's crucial role, "It is a wonderful conception of service to the people. It is an ideally selected spot and has the support of every citizen of Cincinnati." Whether every citizen knew about it or even cared is debatable, but Procter clearly identified Mrs. Emery's heartfelt interest in service and charity, which characterized her life during her widowhood.

Nolen returned to Cambridge heartened by Cincinnati's reception of Mariemont, the new town, and on April 25 he recorded questions and answers discussed with his patron a few days earlier. Their tenor points to Nolen's thorough grasp of the many problems ahead, which Livingood did not yet fathom. Although the questioner and responder are not identified in each case of the eight sections of discussion, we know that Nolen wanted to complete the profile drawings of streets, prepare grading plans, and consult with engineers and architects. More than anything else, he wanted to be retained and "enter into another agreement with you to carry on these ideas for which you are to pay the office charges as before and so much for my professional services." Nolen hoped at this period to be involved in the selection of architects as well as to have some role in determining the style and character of houses. He offered to develop "two or three types of the workingman's home." Livingood questioned him further about this. Nolen immodestly stated that he was competent, adding his criticism of architects in general. Nolen felt that "architects don't know what to leave out. They are full of things that ought to be cut out." Both Nolen and his associate, Philip Foster, also criticized the Small House Service in Indianapolis as a development ignoring what working people want. "Foster and I went over the plans for small houses erected at Indianapolis," he concluded. "We are Site Planners—they are nothing but Architects. We give you the ideas of what can be done because we have studied all the work of all the architects."[11]

Livingood toyed in this same document with the idea of a competition for architects, but Nolen thought only the town center might benefit from this "to show a *tout ensemble* idea that really holds together." But he "would not mind having competition based upon plans for the various types of houses to be furnished by him." "Does this prevent my giving some of the work to local men?" Livingood asked, and Nolen's reply suggested a possible role for himself.

> Not at all. The method that you are going to employ is to secure ideas by a combined competition which would be outlined by the Town Planner in connection with town planning and with the competition you would not tie yourself further than getting the results and then the next step would follow from that and it could not be forecasted at this time. It would be part of the policy to use a considerable number of architects in connection with the work. You have a unified town plan and some unified effects through the general ideas of competition or some other way—perhaps by general consultants.

Nolen's rather hazy ideas of competition among architects and Livingood's apparent reluctance to follow this course combined to eliminate further consideration of this method of selecting the designers of Mariemont's buildings. A competition was never used, and direct commissioning of individual architects followed. But wisely for Livingood and the Mariemont scheme, Nolen was retained as consultant and town planner.

At the end of April 1922, Livingood traveled to Kingsport, Tennessee, to meet with Nolen. Under the auspices of the Kingsport Improvement Corporation, a commercial venture that owned most of the community's land before constructing, selling, and renting houses, a practically new community had grown from Nolen's plan. There were similarities between this bustling town of ten thousand inhabitants and what Livingood perceived for Mariemont. At this northeastern Tennessee town, he observed Nolen's planning accomplishments of 1919. He also wanted to see the houses and other buildings designed by architects Clinton Mackenzie and Grosvenor Atterbury. These two he would hire eventually for Mariemont.[12] As a prelude to that choice, Nolen wrote to Mackenzie before the Kingsport trip, encouraged that "at last we are to have a chance to build a new town practically from the ground up." He recommended Mackenzie to Livingood.[13] Although Livingood disliked the housing he saw at Kingsport, this did not deter his hiring of Mackenzie. Other Nolen projects, both in Delaware, were more favorably received by Livingood, such as Overlook Colony at Claymont and Union Park Gardens near Wilmington. Nolen was "much pleased with your [Livingood's] comment upon Overlook Colony and Union Park Gardens."[14]

These two planned developments resulted from demands created by World War I and the need to house defense workers then crowding into cities. For shipbuilders in Wilmington, Delaware, a new community flourished on fifty-eight acres of rolling farmland by 1918. Nolen used his favored design elements for Union Park Gardens, elements that would be used again in Mariemont, such as curved streets, varying sizes for residential lots, and a limited number of houses per acre.[15] Overlook Colony began in 1917, a company town financed and owned by General Chemical. It was a small community, encompassing only 196 dwellings, but with some group housing and the suburban amenities expected for Mariemont.[16] Among other things, Overlook's row houses appealed to Livingood, and he repeated their style and character in sections of Mariemont. Livingood based his search for architects on visits to towns similar to his dream, recommendations from Nolen and others, and friendships or acquaintances. He needed Nolen's continued services, and these were contracted for another year.[17] By the end of April, Nolen had received justified publicity for his role in Mrs. Emery's remarkable undertaking, and he continued as town planner, "cooperating" with Livingood, according to the press.[18]

As the muddy, wet spring began in Cincinnati, Livingood fantasized that a museum devoted to the American Indian and erected on the Harvard tract near the site of the ancient village and burials was in order. He loved archeology and the hunt for prehistoric man. Writing to Philip Foster, who apparently shared Livingood's interests, he urged him to help excavate some of the many mounds dotting the Mariemont fields and to plan a museum building.[19] Livingood loved digressions from work at hand, and the idea of an Indian museum fascinated him throughout the first decade of Mariemont's history.

Foster and Livingood shared an enthusiasm for pre-Columbian history, but Livingood hoped to gain some practical use from any excavations. Such incursions into ancient gravesites are not acceptable today and certainly were unfortunate at any time when conducted by amateurs. Nevertheless, Livingood encouraged Foster "that once you have completed the profiles therefore knowing just what can be done in the way of removing earth you should come out here, say early in June, and superintend for my laborers the removal of top dressing of certain high spots which probably are Indian Mounds." Livingood hoped that clay and gravel might be saved from excavated mounds "to stop erosion at various points which you yourself will at once see the need of. My point is that if we are to shave off some of these high spots that may be mounds we might as well save hauling material for the above purpose. At any rate I would like to have you on the property once this Spring before I leave for the season."[20]

Although Nolen made two visits to Mariemont that spring (on May 1 and 17, according to the records of his secretary), Foster journeyed out for an extended stay of five days (June 7–11). After this visit, presumably, plans were made for the earthmovers to level any mounds interfering with the street and town layout. Except for a few protuberances and ridges near the Madisonville Site and occupying the spine above the Little Miami River on the village's south side, no mounds are seen today within Mariemont's limits.

By the end of May, Nolen had drafted a change in location for the main artery through the planned community, the east-west highway known as Wooster Pike. This change had a dramatic effect on the heart of the soon-to-rise town and illustrated Nolen's respect for a town's focal point. "I was well pleased with my conversation with the County Engineer, and feel confident that he will approve of the plan submitted. The merit of this plan is that it keeps intact the features that we had in mind in connection with the town center, with good terminal views, and at the same time provides adequately for circulation directly to the east. Under this road plan there would be no confusion as to the main leads in and out of the town center."[21]

In laying out the streets of Mariemont, including the through highway, Nolen sensitively perceived the advantage of vistas and the relationships of one type of housing to another. Even the names of streets were important to him. But after receiving a list of proposed street names from Livingood, he tactfully put his comments aside to deal with grading plans. Livingood found it difficult during their partnership to recognize that Nolen had many commitments to other patrons, other cities to design, or lectures to deliver. Rail travel, in spite of good service, meant lengthy stays away from home and office. He crisscrossed the country many times while working on the Mariemont project, keeping his frantic schedule in balance and managing to satisfy every patron. Nolen seemed to love the pace and seldom complained. "I am trying hard to give this week to routine work, declining an invitation to attend the unveiling of the Lincoln Memorial in Washington tomorrow [May 30, 1922], and an important visit to Yonkers later in the week. I am on the program for the City Planning Conference at Springfield, Massachusetts, so I must be there the early part of next week. In the meantime, however, I want to see that Mariemont has whatever attention it needs at this time."[22]

By the end of May, with Livingood impatient to get away for the summer, Nolen was expected to do the spade work for the next important phase in Mariemont's plan: the search for an engineering firm to plan the sewers and water mains. The need to select competent professional help to design the village's infrastructure soon dominated communications between Nolen and his client. Correctly, both men delayed giving more attention to street names and types of houses. Livingood hoped to "obtain prices based on the opportunity for advertising on the part of certain people for if we succeed we have certainly put a real model before the world."[23] Early in June, Nolen could not resist returning to the question of street names, a subject that interested him, he told Livingood. Nolen thought Livingood's choices were "appropriate and attractive. Mariemont street names ought to have local color, and be, as you say, straightforward and simple. Of course, some names of streets, like the names of new babies, sound strange at first, but if they are wisely selected, one afterwards feels that no other name could have been used."[24]

The first article on Mariemont to appear in a professional journal was published in June 1922. Its single-page commentary accompanied a slightly retitled Nolen plan. Mary Emery as benefactor and John Nolen as town planner were given credit, but no mention was made of Livingood.[25] By the summer of 1922, when more information was available to the public, Mariemont had passed through two critical phases: acquisition of land and approval of Nolen's plan. The new town now moved forward rather tentatively into its third phase: the selection of engineers and architects.

A financial plan formulated by Livingood to forecast the use of Mary Emery's wealth and the outlay of her funds would come in July. First, however, Livingood and Nolen sought implementation of a carefully developed infrastructure. Choosing the Boston engineering firm of Fay, Spofford & Thorndike for this purpose over two other companies was wise; they were experienced and competent to design and build the entire water, storm drain, and sewer system. Livingood had wrestled with estimated costs, but he decided finally in favor of the Boston company and their winning bid of $322,250. Mary Emery's representative liked the firm's "pre-eminent standing" as well as their "elements of theory and practice in a happy combination, and I believe you have got them interested in Mariemont as an exemplar."[26]

Livingood regarded this choice as "momentous," yet he saw no need to receive firm bids from the contractor, stating that "his estimate will be largely a guess anyway." In the same letter to Nolen, he hoped to see the engineering work progress throughout 1923 while other portions of the project were started. But in late 1922, park areas were cleared, streets were roughly graded, and the nursery for trees and shrubs was planted. Livingood's intention in 1923 was to focus on organizing a holding company to manage and own the town, at least initially. Called the Mariemont Company, it would prepare plats and install an office force for selling lots. Livingood would then devote his time to selecting architects who would "be interested in developing certain types of homes." Additionally, he wanted to plan "for the erection of the important business structures at the town centre."

On July 21, 1922, writing from his summer vacation spot at Quebec's Manoir Richelieu, Livingood sketched out the first known statement on Mariemont's projected costs. He titled it "The Financial Picture of Mariemont." It was late in the planning sequence for so monumental a project. Furthermore, it was a tangle of speculation based on very tentative assumptions regarding both Mrs. Emery's required participation in the project's cost and the future purchasers of lots. Livingood's letter was written to his assistant, Thomas Hogan Jr., who was then with Mrs. Emery and her entourage in Newport. The letter's tone is therapeutic and introspective.

> The net result of my thought and calculations is that we have not got enough
> land available for lots, and that the carrying charges and overhead will be too

large to make the project a sure fire success from the financial point of view. But it is too late now to acquire more contiguous land. We must therefore keep repeating that Mrs. Emery has an ideal to express and that this will cost money.

Originally, when my idea crystallized, about 1913 my plan called for 600 A. [acres] on the plateau, which would have been more like it (now we have but 365 or 375 including the bottom lands which total some 70 leaving really only 300 A.). But upon investigating I discovered that to buy up the Plainville Road north to Madisonville as intended I should have to deal with some two or three hundred little owners, many already ready to build themselves homes (as they have done) so I had to be content, and it was trouble enough buying out the thirty or so owners of farms and dwellings. You know how costly the latter were.[27]

The letter then noted the acreages of other planned communities in the United States and England, with only Bournville (606 acres) and Letchworth (4,500 acres) exceeding Mariemont's holdings. Nolen had correctly assessed the lack of land and pointed it out, Livingood admitted. Hoping to explain to Hogan the financial future for the development and using the letter to visualize for himself a complete forecast, Livingood then listed actual costs and estimates for the work ahead. By April 1922, Mary Emery had spent about $391,000 for land purchases, fees, and Nolen's planning costs, plus about $175,000 for parks, the stadium area, and the institutional tract for the hospital and pensioners' cottages. Livingood's conjectured cost for Mariemont's completion included $1,026,000 for construction of utilities and streets and operating expenses; $3,100,000 for erecting houses and buildings; and $1,125,000 for improvements to Mrs. Emery's tracts and an endowment to run the hospital. The total $5,817,000 was daunting for Livingood to contemplate, even recognizing Mary Emery's wealth. His estimate was surprisingly close to the total cost that Mrs. Emery assumed during her lifetime.

Livingood acknowledged to Hogan in the same letter that the Mariemont Company, soon to be formed as the holding organization, "will probably have to undertake the building of everything about the town center to insure coherence of design," and "for the same reason it must construct groups of houses to set a standard and to provide homes for the lowest wage earners who may never be able to buy a home, these groups to be scattered throughout the property." Foreseeing that the sale of 700 lots might provide income of only $439,000 or $539,000 to replenish the coffers, he turned negative on the future. He commiserated to Hogan: "Indeed as I see it now, we shall never build that Hotel, nor the Post Office nor any churches or schools, nor that East End recreation center shown on Nolen's plan. The Town Hall will provide all the space needed for library, art exhibits, police station, post office, public comfort rooms, once we come under Cincinnati government."

The financing of Mariemont, for both land purchases and working capital for the forthcoming Mariemont Company, was Mary Emery's. As she owned the property, paid all the bills from the beginning of the Mariemont project, and provided the working capital for the Mariemont Company, sales and exchanges between her and the corporate body in which she was the sole stockholder were paper transfers. Livingood, in his hoped-for financial plan, although somewhat convoluted and complex, intended at this date to sell common and preferred stock to investors. He would sell building lots, of course, to potential home builders. His estimates of income derived from the sale of lots were questionable. He concluded his letter to Hogan with rhetorical questions, indicating his indecision at this late stage in the planning process. He queried: "Will we sell lots under the Cincinnati suburban market? Will we enter extensively into building of houses? Can we count on occupancy of so many front feet of property? We must remember that Cincinnati's big stores will always attract the general public which will want to go to town. Shall we make a builder's profit on houses built? Can we meet the 6% interest on the $1,000,000 Pfd? What is the likelihood of paying dividends on Common?"

Sultry July passed as usual for Mary Emery at Newport and Charles Livingood at Pointe-a-Pic, Quebec, where he consulted with Nolen on staff leaders for Mariemont, particularly a resident landscape architect and a resident engineer. Nolen thought that an experienced nurseryman was needed for two or three years at a salary of $3,000 per year. He also wanted to work with the person selected to help choose nursery stock, attesting to Nolen's continuing interest in landscape architecture and the total appearance of the village when built. He cautioned Livingood to "pay men what they are worth, and if men are worth it, they really earn it, and the work is cheaper than it would be with a lower salaried man."[28] In August, Livingood engaged the Boston architectural firm of Ripley & LeBoutillier, a firm used for the Mariemont project, to design his summer home in Quebec near the Saint Lawrence River.[29]

Livingood's absence from Cincinnati did not deter his activity on behalf of Mariemont in the summer of 1922. He convinced the Hamilton County Commissioners to permit a relocation of Wooster Pike so that highway could pass through the center of Nolen's planned village in a new alignment. Also, he began acquiring property "rather wildly," he feared, in the Indian View subdivision to the east of town, adding about fifty-five acres to Mary Emery's holdings. Nolen thought that the property, with its narrow streets and existing buildings, might be a menace to Mariemont's town center. Livingood concurred, and the small subdivision was purchased through a confidential agent, C. C. Mand.[30]

Although Livingood appointed Fred E. Peck as resident nurseryman and Clarence B. Fancy as resident engineer, any staff added to the payroll made him apprehensive, as he had complained earlier in the summer. Salaries for staff totaled $20,000 per year at this point, an amount that Livingood cautiously thought might "handicap the project with too much expense."[31] But Livingood expected expenditures that would greatly exceed these salaries. Successful negotiations ended weeks of interviews with candidates for the critical engineering of sewer and water lines when Nolen, acting on behalf of his employer, arranged for Livingood to sign the contract with the Boston firm of Fay, Spofford & Thorndike. Livingood's response to Nolen not only emphasized his important role as Mary Emery's agent, but he wanted him

> to convince that firm of my right to sign for [Mrs. Emery], and obtain the privilege to transfer this Agreement to the Mariemont Company of which I shall be President when it is incorporated. Mrs. Emery, in writing, pledges to carry out anything she undertakes, indeed has a clause in her Will to this effect, directing her executors to continue and complete any such undertaking, provided it can be accomplished. I have a Power of Attorney, but not here, to act as Mrs. Emery's Agent, and have been in sole charge of her estate since the death of Mr. Emery, from whom she inherited it, in 1906. Will you not urge Fay-Spofford to take up with you at once the matter as a whole, and push the preparing of the plans to completion as early as possible, so that in the Spring the actual work may commence.[32]

As Livingood busied himself in preparing to leave Quebec for Cincinnati, where he arrived in early October, he approved the street names selected for Mariemont, groused about Hubert G. Ripley's drawings of the town center, and asked Foster for some help in building his summer home.

> Now that you are returned from what I hope was a restful vacation, I am wondering if you cannot ink in the street names we have definitely adopted for Mariemont. You will recall that you and I went over them on the ground, Mr. Nolen approved of them on June 17th, after consultation with you, and on June 28th Mrs. Emery expressed her approval.
>
> After considerable delay I am at last in receipt of the colored plan representing the Town Center, with its buildings, but regret to say that in my judgment the artist made the Square entirely too large. It gives a false impression. The buildings themselves are good looking, but I feel also that he has not properly shown the diagonal streets. The theatre block appears to be much too long. It is only 200 feet front.
>
> If you are carrying out my instructions to have this Center and the buildings around it drawn in lead pencil like the sketches you submitted my office, please see that he makes these corrections before attempting another view of the Town Center; all of these sketches to be used in our booklet on Mariemont, merely.[33]

Livingood's fascination with the "bold, free manner" of the sketches stemmed from his deep interest in urban architecture, long fostered by his association with Thomas Emery's Sons and his many European trips. His ideas for Mariemont's architecture were not firmly explored, however, until Nolen's plan was in place. Livingood visualized Mariemont as a somewhat quaint English village, and only in 1922 did he make his first official contacts with prospective designers. His letters to Nolen sought his advice, but Nolen never was very interested in architects or their designs. Nolen knew historic styles and was acquainted with many architects, yet his writings and his lectures focus wholeheartedly on town planning and its structural basis. He mentioned architects, styles, or architectural requirements only occasionally and then in connection with a town plan he devised. His priority was clear as he urged the design of buildings "with reference to the plan rather than the plan studied with reference to the buildings it is to make conspicuous."[34]

Livingood determined to make the choice of architects his own. He absorbed himself in this next phase of the town's progress, sharing his worries with Nolen. Livingood wanted certain districts of Mariemont to have "character" but not "absolute uniformity of design." He queried Nolen on the idea of inviting proposals from "architects of distinction," naming Wilson Eyre as an example. Clearly, Livingood enjoyed this activity, as he wrote to Nolen,

> I know they are expensive men and promulgate fanciful ideas, but they set a standard and give a certain cachet, which the average architect does not give. Now don't turn me down too cold on this suggestion. I want to have some fun, and I get my fun in seeing a dream realized. Of course I do not want to set too high a standard, but I believe these men, now that they have learned their lessons, will be glad to make their contributions to our exemplar. I have had a number of applications. Indeed one architect came here to see me, a bully young fellow from New York named Reeves [Hubert E. Reeves, later employed to design the Resthaven group] who has done some dandy workmen's homes.[35]

In the autumn of 1922, after his return from Canada, Livingood began his search for architects. His architectural taste was conservative. Revival styles inherited from European models impressed him, as did the settled quaintness of English country villages. Livingood did not appreciate, apparently, the modernist movement in architecture, and there is no mention in his papers of the leading architect-exponents of modernism. Contemporary movements were distanced from tradition, he felt, and tradition is what he exploited for Mariemont.

Livingood wavered as to how his choices should be made. A competition seemed to appeal to him at one point, but that translated rather quickly into "suggestions" or "proposals" that architects might make to him. Finally, he opted for a personal interview that he would conduct with each architect-candidate. Whatever the selection method, Livingood was to remain in charge of the process. His explanation to Nolen is illuminating.

> I do not pretend to be an expert and moreover I am only human and must protect myself against details but I am vitally interested and wish to have a finger in the pie all along for this is my dream. If I am wrong in my plan to have a number of architects compete against each other as it were in evolving the best type of group housing, well, other men indulge themselves in other things,— fool enterprises, bad business ventures, elaborate homes which they will never

occupy, so I want the joy of seeing ideals expressed, not in foolish fancies but the best work of the best men on their special lines. Therefore I would write them briefly right now so that I can interview them when I come east next time of my plan to enlist the interest of such men as McKenzie [*sic*], Coffin & Coffin, Ballinger & Perrott, Grosvenor Atterbury even. They all charge the same commission, 6%, but the total amount involved will not be very great in any one case excepting perhaps that of McKenzie and the Coffins who have specialized on the cheaper home for workmen; and I believe that when they know that their plans will be studied closely in competition with their competitors they will give the project serious attention. A bright young architect named Reeves came all the way to Murray Bay on his own hook to show me what he can do and has done. My idea is to have these fellows work the coming winter after this first rush is over and make their suggestions next spring, for buildings to be erected in 1924, although it is possible we can do some building in the north-west section before this.[36]

Before the architects were chosen, Livingood announced he had made good on an earlier interest: to purchase trees from Mount Vernon, George Washington's estate on the Potomac. "For I want to buy from sentiment," he wrote in September to Nolen, "the 1,000 or 1,500 trees from Mount Vernon." His arboreal interest equaled his admiration of the first president of the United States, noting that such purchases of trees "will be a good advertisement as well as a great satisfaction to Mrs. Livingood who is the Vice Regent of Mount Vernon from Ohio. Peck thinks well of the idea, and as he will have his Nursery ready for babies about the middle of October, if all goes well, I see no reason why we should not go ahead, but, of course, I want your advice and help in ordering the rest of the trees, not only for lining the streets but for planting in the Institutional Tract."[37] During his 2,000-mile return trip by automobile to Cincinnati, Livingood stopped at the Virginia estate to act on his whim. In his October 6 letter focusing on choosing architects, Livingood indicated that he had made his purchase.

Just as Livingood completed the acquisition of the Indian View subdivision properties, extending the village to the east and permitting the new alignment of Wooster Pike as the main east-west road, he placed his order with the Mount Vernon custodian for 650 trees. He hoped the order might be increased to 1,000

VIEW IN

A·VIEW·IN·THE·RESIDENCE·SECTION · MARIEM...

Drawn in November 1922 by Hubert G. Ripley, a Boston architect who later was one of the designers of Mariemont buildings, this sketch is an early, imagined view of residences and the church in the Dale Park neighborhood, then titled the "industrial housing section." This drawing and three others were the second visualizations of buildings for Mariemont.

NOV· 1922 ·

An imagined view of Mariemont residences drawn by architect Hubert G. Ripley in November 1922.

𝒜 · VIEW ·

· VIEW · OF · THE · 𝒯𝒪𝒲𝒩 · 𝐻𝒜𝐿𝐿 · AND · ℬ𝒜𝒩𝒦 · MA

TOWN · CENTER · MARIEMONT · OHIO ·

Hubert G. Ripley's drawing of the town center of Mariemont, probably done in November 1922, followed Charles Livingood's proposed placement for an inn, shopping arcade, square and fountain, and town hall (*far left*). Of these buildings, only the Mariemont Inn was completed by the Mariemont Company, but not in the style suggested by Ripley.

Several public buildings of impressive scale, such as the town hall and bank proposed for the south side of the town center, were suggested by Hubert G. Ripley. This drawing probably dates from November 1922. These elegant structures were never built.

specimens at seventy-five cents apiece.[38] From this beginning with saplings and whips, Mariemont's leafy splendor grew. Cultivated farm fields became streets and greens, residential lots and commercial buildings, each area to be land-scaped and lined with a variety of trees.

Livingood's method of selecting architects received a boost when the famous British town planner, Raymond Unwin, partner with Barry Parker at Letchworth and Hampstead Garden Suburb, visited Nolen in his Harvard Square office. Nolen naturally shared with Unwin his plans for Mariemont and told him of the possibility of a competition to pick architects. Unwin disliked competitions and told Nolen that "the best thing to do with competition drawings, in his judg-ment, is to put them in the scrap basket." He thought competitions, however, were a successful means of discovering the qualifications of architects.[39]

Many architects and certainly most town planners admired Unwin's philoso-phy and teachings. They recognized his seminal role in the evolution of town planning and his major publication, *Town Planning in Practice,* as a Bible of sorts. It was first published in 1909, and Nolen knew it well. He endorsed completely Unwin's theses on architects and buildings, such as the importance of the "site planner" in supervising architects. Unwin contended that, if the architect was required to produce "a symmetrical, picturesque, or other special treatment," the town planner "should be able to suggest this treatment to the architect or builder who is responsible for the building on the plot. By such suggestions, wisely made, very much may be secured that will be helpful to the total effect."[40]

It is not surprising that Livingood never reacted to Nolen about Unwin's com-ments. The choice of architects obsessed him, and in mid-October he wanted support from Nolen more than anything else. Livingood's assumption that Nolen would offer his guidance evidenced once again the patron's hazy planning, his lack of organizational forecasting. He wrote to Nolen, criticizing him.

> I appreciate your good wishes, etc., but I fear you did not get the full import of my request for *advice.* What I want is your approval of my plan to ask selected architects of my own choosing to undertake to submit plans for *types* of houses that would be suitable for our project, assigning to some of the best such definite localities for grouping as Hopkins Place, Sheldon Place, etc. It is not a competition but a distribution among competitors for fame. I think it is a good idea especially if we can get the architects to see the importance of putting their

best thought into the opportunity. I want this advice quickly because I must get out my lines so that when I go east this winter I shall know whom to see personally and explain the matter more in detail to. In brief I would be committing myself to the selection of a number of outside architects but this I am willing to risk because we must have *some* of the work of a *special* distinction. Our local architects are all right and will be given an opportunity; only as I stated in my last letter I want the joy of carrying out this pet scheme of mine unless of course it meets with your absolute disapproval.

We have excellent architects here and to each of my personal friends I intend giving an important piece of work and in addition an opportunity also to submit for purchase plans for small houses.[41]

Before that letter reached him, Nolen had inquired about "the progress of Mariemont since you returned to Cincinnati" and particularly about the program for the autumn and winter. He proposed more trips to Mariemont by either Nolen or Foster.[42] Nolen announced in the same letter a long southern trip for several weeks in late October, and this, plus the lack of advice, upset Livingood and his plans to visit Nolen in Boston toward the end of the month. Livingood whined that this news "is a blow between the eyes," as he feared that Nolen erroneously thought that progress with Mariemont's infrastructure was under way. Only a contract was in hand with the Boston firm responsible for the major task of designing and providing sewers, water lines, and other underground utilities.[43]

True, little had been done on the Mariemont site by October 1922 except to fell a few trees. Livingood had received a report from Fay, Spofford & Thorndike delaying plans for sewers and water lines until February. He expected Nolen to provide the thrust, telling him, "Now it is up to you to say just what further can be done physically during 1923." For his part, Livingood mapped out the next direction for himself: organizing the Mariemont Company during the winter, perfecting plans for its operation, negotiating with architects, and developing a scheme to sell lots.

Correspondence between Livingood and Nolen shows that mail delivery was rapid in the 1920s, with overnight service from one major city to another considered normal. Their letters often crossed in the mail, with two or more concurrent documents ripe with questions and answers. When Nolen responded on October 20, he was as yet unaware that Livingood was upset with him for planning a lengthy southern trip. Nolen's response on that date included his first list of suggested architects and guidelines for their employment.

> I am entirely in sympathy with your general idea as to special architects and special work in connection with Mariemont. There are three points, however, that occur to me as of importance. The first is the necessity of having some reliable method of harmonizing (I don't mean "monotonizing," if I may use such a term) the whole of the architecture of Mariemont. This, of course, can be done in a variety of ways, but some individual or group of individuals must have authority to review and finally pass upon the work of the architects from the point of view of the plan as a whole. If you are willing to give the time to it, perhaps you can do this yourself. Of course we are at your service. The second point of importance in connection with the dwelling house planning is that the architects selected shall know through and through the planning requirements, including cost, of the small house. The third point is the choice of qualified architects for this particular part of the work.
>
> All of the special men with whom I have talked—I mean men like C. H. Cheney of California, H. V. Hubbard of Harvard University, A. C. Comey here in Cambridge, and Raymond Unwin of London—have asked me what was going to be done about the control and harmonizing of the architectural work of Mariemont. I could give you many illustrations—of course you know them as well as I do—of the general failure of the architectural work due to lack of control from the architectural point of view.[44]

As suggested in that letter, Nolen as town planner expected to have a role in the choice of architects for Mariemont's buildings. He imagined that he might at least be a reviewer, if he did not participate as a selector, of the architects. He did not press his position too forcefully, but five of the fourteen architectural firms he recommended to Livingood on October 20, 1922, were chosen ultimately. Nolen's suggested architects were drawn from only three cities: Clinton Mackenzie, Coffin & Coffin, Grosvenor Atterbury, Bertram G. Goodhue, and Richard H. Dana Jr. (in New York); Ballinger Company, Emile G. Perrot, and Rankin, Kellogg & Crane (in Philadelphia); Kilham, Hopkins, & Greeley, Ripley & LeBoutillier, Frost & Raymond, Lois L. Howe & Manning, William H. Cox, and Andrew H. Hepburn (in Boston).[45]

Passing through Boston on his way to Newport in late October to bring

Mary Emery back to Cincinnati, Livingood hoped to meet with Nolen to discuss a range of concerns, including land shortage on the concourse's perimeter,
a new location for pensioners' cottages, grading problems, a review of letters
"about a controlling group under whom architects of my selection with your
aid shall work," and a rail siding on the Dugan tract. Both men were disappointed that their train schedules did not mesh, but Livingood settled for Foster, who would meet him at the Harvard Club. Nolen again urged that a "program" prepared by his office from time to time would assist the assignment of
work for Mariemont. He also wanted "one of the office men" to make a field
visit as a prelude for additional meetings, held regularly on site, between Nolen
and Livingood.[46] By November 1922, Nolen had issued to Livingood his first
"program," a monthly list titled "Work to be done." It became an outline for
future work schedules, noting general needs (such as regular visits from Nolen's
office) and specific ones (the preparation of planting plans).

November was a busy month for the Mariemont project. Without waiting
for any formal groundbreaking ceremony, Livingood ordered the earthmovers
to begin their work. By the tenth of the month, he wrote to Nolen that "we began yesterday morning actually to make the dirt fly on Mariemont proper by
the use of five tractors which are taking off the top of the high knoll overlooking the river."[47] After a summer of little accomplishment, the project jumped
to life. Livingood met with Nolen and Foster in Cincinnati on November 25–
28, and they tramped over the rutted fields where their new town would emerge.
They met with representatives of Fay, Spofford & Thorndike to plot the essential work to be completed in 1923, including the specifications for sewers, water mains, storm drains, and the sewage treatment plant. Nolen also submitted
a lengthy list of nursery stock, recording both Latin and familiar names for the
shrubs and trees that might be grown in Mariemont's climate.[48] By Thanks-
giving, twenty-five hundred trees had been planted in the nursery under Fred
Peck's care. Livingood called his happy little garden the "Mt. Vernon Nurseries."

Livingood envisioned a corporate entity for Mariemont that eventually
would hold the property acquired by Mrs. Emery, receive financing from stock
owned almost exclusively by her, sell lots, and erect homes and buildings
through a subsidiary building and loan company. By late autumn he and his
lawyer had drafted a statement to guide the Mariemont Company. This cre-

ation of Livingood, with Mary Emery's authorization, had a singular purpose: to plan, build, and operate Mariemont "for the benefit of wage earners of different economic grades . . . affording the best housing and community conditions possible, consistent with sound principles." Livingood's prospectus decried city expansionism, but he noted that Mariemont could not emulate Letchworth and its efforts to counteract similar growth. "This country is still individualistic in its attitude and action," he wrote in the prospectus, adding that the Mariemont Company was "not intended as an experiment in social organization, but proposes to make use of familiar methods which have been tested in American experience."[49] Dividends for the newly formed Mariemont Company would be limited. The virtues of planning principles could be demonstrated in the "orderly and adequate development of the suburb of Mariemont." Once all homes and lots were sold, the company would withdraw from ownership and management in hope of repeating the process elsewhere.

On December 1, 1922, the Mariemont Company was incorporated in Ohio, initially for "half a million," with its trustees becoming the fiduciaries of the development project. Besides Livingood, who served as president, the incorporators were Frank H. Nelson, Thomas Hogan Jr., Bleecker Marquette, and John R. Schindel. All were well known to Mary Emery and closely involved in the Mariemont project, except for Nelson, who did not participate in planning the new town.[50] Although Mary retained ownership of stock in her name, her personal control of most of the land was transferred to the Mariemont Company. It could not be overlooked, however, even in the new corporate entity, that her wealth had made possible the land purchases and the financing of the company's stock, both initially and throughout the life of the company.

December's gray days did not inhibit a motion picture crew from roaming over Mariemont's site and recording "eight tractors and a plough at work with scoops bringing the Concourse up to its level . . . a skyline view of the tractors returning to the top of the hill . . . and Young Bob Fancy [son of engineer Clarence B. Fancy] hunting for Indian relics and calling his father's attention to his 'finds.'" Livingood hoped that Pathe News might distribute the footage he had commissioned, and Nolen liked the idea of recording the action "of these first days when the dirt began to fly and when young Bob Fancy was hunting for Indian relics."[51]

Choosing the architects, a task greatly enjoyed by Livingood and guarded jealously by him, began in earnest in November. The selection process started with a letter to the candidate, followed usually by an interview and a contract. A typical inquiry on Thomas Emery's Sons stationery is the letter Livingood wrote to the Boston architects Lois L. Howe and Eleanor Manning. Probably the letter's wording was used with each architect under consideration, amending it only to insert particulars about the specific commission.

I am wondering whether you are interested enough in the housing problem in the middle west to be one of the architects to be employed by me in the development of certain "groups" of ideal homes in Mariemont for people of small means? Your name has been given me by Mr. John Nolen, whose plan for this new community adjoining Cincinnati has been accepted and upon which we are now actively engaged. Of course I realize that generally speaking you do work of a much higher grade than would be required, yet the problem catches the imagination and a number of architects have asked to be represented.

As I see it now I should like to see groups of houses go up in certain strategic neighborhoods in illustration of what we should like to see in various centers to set the proper standard. If you will read the enclosed articles (which were hurriedly written and are not authentic in many points) you will observe that it is the intention to form a subsidiary building company of which I shall be the President, to carry out many of the building projects.

If you can answer the first question in the affirmative please advise me whether you would undertake to furnish complete working plans and specifications and on what percentage on a group let us say of eight or ten houses to comprise Denny Place on the plat to cost say $5,000 to $6,000 each. The property at this location is level and as you will at once note in a retired, yet very accessible, location as regards the Town Center and Wooster Pike, which is the main boulevard (a state road) running east and west through Mariemont. It is my own idea that this group will appeal to artists who desire to live in the country in a really attractive neighborhood. This group will be separated by the boulevard and park system from the workmen's homes and yet be some distance from the more expensive neighborhood which of course is that overlooking the Little Miami River on Bluff Drive.

Mr. Nolen has given me to understand that you take especial pride in design, that you have learned much about the needs especially of women, and should be admirably equipped to produce a homogenous grouping of attractive cottages, possibly of frame to give greater flexibility of design. Of course the difficulties nowadays is to keep down costs.

I am writing similar letters to this to others like yourselves whose working design has been distinctive and hope they will be glad to be contributors to this "National Exemplar" (I do not like the words "Model Town") not merely as an illustration of what they can do as architects but because of the certainty that this project at least, of the many attempted, is going through.

Luckily for me we have selected a tract within reasonable distance of a great factory colony. But we shall be obliged to cater to all classes though our intention still is to build homes for and to sell to people of modest means.

I have of course seen most of the model towns both abroad and here, and know the pitfalls and discouragement but I am prepared for them. I believe we can make a contribution to the problem of housing by the erection of many real homes about a small center near enough to a large city to satisfy the ambitions of the average American citizen—the kind who loves his home. Naturally I am asking the assistance of local architects and have gotten them interested in the big problem of proper planning on the assumption that they too want to see "better housing" here in the middle west.

As to the "period," if any, which should be attempted in these "Places," I am leaving to the individual architects though I hasten to say that all plans both for Places, group housing and public buildings erected under our care must be submitted to a supervising architect who will be a man of distinction in the profession.

If this interests you and you would like to undertake a commission please let me know at once and I shall endeavor to call when next in Boston, which may be about the 15th or 20th of this month. There will be no haste however in the acceptance of the plans or the erection of houses for we have not yet even completed a comprehensive plan for the sewer system, water supply, etc., which will take all of 1923. What I am trying to do now is to enlist the cooperation on a business basis of such people as yourself, Wilson Eyre, Grosvenor Atterbury and others in the proper architectural development of Mariemont.[52]

Livingood's rambling but background-packed letter was enough to excite any architect willing to design buildings within a framework by such an eminent town planner, John Nolen. Some knew that Nolen had recommended them to the town's director and were expecting an inquiry. Others approached by Livingood had no prior notice and perhaps had only sketchy news about Mariemont's beginnings. A few contacted Nolen for more information, giving him an opportunity to plant an idea or two with the prospective designers. Nolen wrote Livingood about a contact from Howe & Manning, resulting in the town planner's recommendation that their houses for Mariemont should be built "of the local hill stone and be quite simple in design, perhaps some of them being semi-detached houses, or smaller groups."[53]

Nolen's letter enclosed three colored diagrams to guide Livingood and the assigned architects.[54] The first diagram designated "Architectural Groups," where housing in "each separate color group should be designed as a unit" and "have the same general architectural characteristics." The second Nolen diagram plotted "Valuation Groups," with house values of $2,500 to $15,000 segregated into eleven categories. The final plan illustrated "Material Groups" and the four "areas in which one material should predominate"—brick, stone, stucco, or wood. Nolen's restrictions, geared to protect the integrity of the town plan, were self-explanatory, he felt. He recognized that property valuations might be revised upward, but they reflected existing real estate conditions in Cincinnati.

As each architect was selected by Livingood, a set of blueprints of the assigned location for the houses or buildings and topographical plans were sent to the successful candidate, who also received a completed contract, a copy of the Cincinnati Building Code, and a wage scale for construction workers for 1923. As recorded in his letter to Howe and Manning, Livingood did not dictate the style to be followed for the buildings assigned to an architect, but he expected a harmonious relationship to other buildings in the area. His taste was as conservative as his choice of designers. He risked little in the free rein he offered, as expressed in his instructions to Richard H. Dana Jr., when he expected "a pleasing variety yet coupled with durability and low costs." The design of townhouses assigned to Dana was left to the architect, but Livingood urged him to consider the nearby church and school for a harmonious relationship, as well as the "very large Recreation Hall, to be designed by Garber & Woodward of this city, of brick probably in the *colonial* style." Livingood hoped to review Dana's final plans before he drew them and suggested three-room apartments for a corner building "flanked by compactly designed groups of houses all to harmonize, but the details of room sizes, allotment, etc., must be worked out later."[55]

Early in December, Nolen spoke in Hanover, New Hampshire, on "New Ideals in the Planning of American Towns and Cities," with Mariemont as the expected focus in the part devoted to "New Towns." Nolen's practice in re-planning existing cities equaled his work designing new towns, but he enjoyed the challenge of the new over the burdens of the old.[56] With the holiday season approaching, Livingood selected a "jury" of local men "to whom plans for individual houses by purchasers of lots must be submitted." Alfred O. Elzner and Frederick W. Garber, both Cincinnatians, were chosen, and a third would be added later. To monitor and approve the various public buildings and the town center, Livingood picked a respected, nationally known architect practicing in Philadelphia, Paul Philippe Cret (1876–1945). It is not known whether this eminent designer was asked to provide any plans for housing or public buildings in Mariemont in addition to his assignment as consultant or reviewer, but his involvement with the village was slight. Livingood believed that an architect was needed to review the plans of others, but only for the town center and its public buildings. He and Nolen could pass on other areas and their intended structures.[57] By the end of the month, Livingood wrote Nolen that "Paul Cret writes me that with such talent there will not be much need of his co-ordinating mind on the various groups at least."[58]

On December 20 Livingood met with Nolen in Philadelphia to discuss a proposed steam plant that would provide heat for a large section of the village. Nolen was expected to "investigate steam heating plants of this magnitude, especially the Girard College plant" and "secure an efficient landscape architect," submitting his name, qualifications, and expected salary first to Livingood. The latter was to draw up guidelines for the architects already commissioned and to point out to the architects, the two men agreed, that houses would have no more than five rooms, planting areas would be indicated, garages could be within the house or alongside, and cellar spaces would be under kitchens except in the northwest section.[59] These conditions were modified or exempted frequently, as many houses were larger than indicated by Livingood.

By December 23 Livingood had engaged sixteen architects. These he discussed with Mary Emery, "who listened with eager interest to the story of my travels among the architects."[60] On December 28 the list expanded to twenty names. These he supplied to Nolen with a diagram "showing my allotment of commissions to date." Of the listed architects, twelve had their designs built in Mary Emery's new town.

Elzner & Anderson, Citizens Bank Bldg., Cincinnati, Ohio
Garber & Woodward, Union Central Life Ins. Bldg., Cincinnati, Ohio
Samuel E. Hannaford & Son, Dixie Terminal Bldg., Cincinnati, Ohio
Herbert Spielman, Merc. Libr. Bldg., Cincinnati, Ohio
Jos. G. Steinkamp & Bros., Merc. Libr. Bldg., Cincinnati, Ohio
Zettel & Rapp, Merc. Libr. Bldg., Cincinnati, Ohio
Howe & Manning, 101 Tremont Street, Boston, Mass.
Allen W. Jackson, 25 Arch Street, Boston, Mass.
Ripley & LeBoutillier, 45 Bromfield Street, Boston, Mass.
Grosvenor Atterbury, 139 E. 53rd Street, New York, N.Y.
Richard H. Dana, Jr., 350 Madison Ave., New York, N.Y.
Louis E. Jallade, 129 Lexington Avenue, New York, N.Y.
Clinton Mackenzie, 119 Broad Street, New York, N.Y.
Henry O. Milliken, 4 East 39th Street, New York, N.Y.
Hubert E. Reeves, 4 East 39th Street, New York, N.Y.
Arthur E. Brockie, 1713 Sansom St., Philadelphia, Pa.
Robert R. McGoodwin, 1422 Walnut Street, Philadelphia, Pa.
Mellor, Meigs & Howe, 205 S. Juniper Street, Philadelphia, Pa.
Wilson Eyre & McIlvaine, 1003 Spruce Street, Philadelphia, Pa.
E. B. Gilchrist, 1618 Latimer, Philadelphia, Pa.[61]

4 · WORK BEGINS

The year 1923 began with Livingood's earnest pursuit of architects for the Mariemont project. He relied on Nolen for advice and liaison with his choices, but authorized commissions came only from Livingood. Meetings among patron, town planner, and architects were scheduled in New York and Boston, as well as at the Mariemont site, as Livingood sought to jell his ideas. Livingood enjoyed bringing his chosen people together for conferences, apparently unconcerned that professional jealousy might cloud the results. Some contacts he left in Nolen's hands, at least initially, such as those with Clinton Mackenzie, Richard Dana, and Hubert Ripley. Livingood expected Nolen to join him in New York and Boston as conferences were held with the chosen architects. He reminded Nolen that only "suggestions which can be worked up during the summer were expected," as final plans would be approved at a later date.[1]

Nolen concurred in Livingood's wish to see only "suggestions" at this time and proposed the Harvard Club in New York for the planned meeting on January 22.[2] Livingood intended that the chosen architects would submit rough ideas or suggestions for the buildings assigned to them, allowing him time to study their appearance and place in relationship to other parts of Nolen's scheme. Approval for final working drawings and blueprints followed questions and changes, and usually each architect visited the assigned site before submitting any drafts.[3]

Livingood's cautious moves from one stage to the next in Mariemont's development slowed progress but ensured adherence to his concept. However, his long absences from Cincinnati, as during summer vacation trips, often slowed the project's momentum. Always tactful, Nolen did not display much concern about this. He remained optimistic and excited about the project in all its aspects, even when he suggested in his letter of January 9 that there were many difficulties with the installation of underground utilities and wires. Both Nolen and Livingood hoped that wires and utilities could be placed underground. Their persistence provided Mariemont with one of its lasting achievements: elimination of the visual pollution of above-ground wires.

Although his approved plan was the basic framework for the construction of the English village imagined by Livingood and his initial role as town planner thus was concluded, Nolen pursued his future involvement in the project in letters to his patron. Early in January 1923 he submitted to Livingood his request for an increased stipend along with a "Program of Work to be Done—Office and Field." The latter was an agenda of sorts for expertise and supervision, updated month by month, that he and his office should provide. Nolen recalled that the drafting cost, correspondence, field work, and conferences with Livingood for himself and Foster in 1922 exceeded somewhat those charges in 1921. Looking back on the results, Nolen was pleased with the progress, considering 1922 "a year of substantial achievement. I have a conviction also that we have been working on practical lines, and that our general planning has proved sound. It stood most successfully its first severe test in the contracts and plans for the public utilities, and is now meeting the second test in the general arrangements for the architectural work."[4]

Nolen's tentative program listed fourteen tasks to be undertaken by him and his staff, including the drafting of plans for plantings, grading, and construction details; investigation of underground utilities and a steam plant; review of architectural work "from the general planning point of view"; and regular visits to Mariemont for consultation. All of these recommendations were valid in view of his role as town planner. They were well conceived to assist Livingood and were characteristic of Nolen's thoroughness. Some were accepted in the years ahead; others were neglected or ignored by Livingood. Nolen concluded his letter with a request to increase his monthly stipend of $200, an amount set in the first encounters between Nolen and Livingood, to $300. The increased stipend was approved by Livingood at the end of January.

Meetings with architects began shortly after the first sketches for the village church by Louis E. Jallade and for the recreation hall by Frederick Garber were presented to Livingood. The Harvard Club in New York was the setting for a round-table discussion in late January. In the autumn of 1922, Livingood had received pencil renderings by Hubert G. Ripley of the Mariemont square and its buildings, an elegant concoction of Colonial Revival and English half-timbered structures evocative of Chester, England, and buildings suggesting Palladian villas near Venice. Ripley's drawings proposed a mix of styles that might appear jarring to one wanting architectural purity. Perhaps reflecting his interest in neoclassical architecture or perhaps in an attempt to depict a prosperous English town with buildings in various styles, Ripley's renderings were inventive and fluid. However, Livingood was upset that Ripley's drawings imagined too much. They expanded the intended size of the square and its projected buildings, he told Philip Foster, Nolen's associate.[5] Nevertheless, Livingood did not refuse the suggestion of neoclassical buildings. The village center was cast as an elegant Hollywood motion picture set, not exactly a workingman's usual environment.

The New York meeting on January 22 was hosted by Mariemont's leader for Nolen and the commissioned architects. It was the first of ten meetings in New York or Mariemont in 1923, the busiest schedule of conferences during Nolen's tenure. Hoping "to coordinate and crystallize the ideas for group housing in the North-west section of Mariemont," Livingood invited designers Clinton Mackenzie, Richard H. Dana Jr., Edmund B. Gilchrist, Hubert G. Ripley, and Addison B. LeBoutillier.[6] Upon Livingood's return to Cincinnati, he agreed to Nolen's requested stipend and added a bonus. Nolen's son, John Jr., an engineer then employed by Fay, Spofford & Thorndike, was accepted as a field representative for the Mariemont project. Livingood's trip to New York had ended with "a very satisfactory interview with Mr. Paul P. Cret," he wrote to Nolen, "with whom I have come to terms in the matter of his taking the general architectural supervision of plans and designs."[7]

January's meeting and one on February 9 in New York were the last for many months between Nolen and Mrs. Emery's representative. Livingood's peripatetic nature carried him away to Europe for another extended vacation, this time one that lasted from February to October. He excused himself because of stress and overwork, enlisting a physician to restrict his activities while resting at various spas and elegant hotels. Nolen was chagrined at this handicap, for major decisions could be made only by Livingood. Just before Livingood sailed from New York, Nolen was pleased to hear that a brief meeting could be arranged at the Ritz-Carlton Hotel. Little did the Cambridge planner know that this would be the last personal encounter for many months. Livingood wrote to Nolen in preparation for the meeting, stating that all of the architects save one Philadelphian had accepted their contracts. He expected Nolen to prepare lists of trees and shrubs, and he added that "Mr. Jalade [*sic*] has prepared a beautiful model in clay of the chapel for the northwest section, and Mr. Hubert E. Reeves has been here for several days and finally finished a plan acceptable to me for the Community Barn, Superintendent's Cottage and Milk Barn, all most attractive."[8]

Nolen wanted to see Jallade's clay model of the church and Garber's plans for the "Community Buildings," he wrote to Livingood before the New York meeting, enclosing with his letter the requested list of trees, shrubs, and plants prescribed as nursery stock for the village.[9] He also noted that the pergola and wall for the concourse overlooking the valley and the Little Miami River had been done as a "preliminary sketch" (actually the work of Philip W. Foster) and "of course is subject to revision." Nolen's enclosure, a twenty-four-page report, is elaborate and detailed, recording Latin and common names, the number of each variety to be ordered, a list of streets and their assigned tree types, and the American nurseries where stock could be purchased. Probably the list's most curious feature is the wide range of trees and plants, a botanical garden of specimens more expansive than might be expected in suburbs in the 1920s. A limited range of saplings (primarily elm, maple, and oak) were the usual planting materials in new developments. Gardens of flowers and shrubs were seldom contemplated.

An addendum assigning certain trees and shrubs by type and quantity to the Dale Park section, the first portion of Mariemont to be constructed, expressed Nolen's expertise as landscape architect. He had been contracted for these skills, in addition to town planning, for he was expected to draw up planting designs and supervise installations. His talent in this field had been recognized long before he had gained fame as a town planner. Livingood may have been surprised at the size of the planting program, but he could not fault Nolen's thoughtful concern over the future of tree-lined streets and landscaped homesites. Although the eventual wooded appearance, green spaces, and shady streets of the village derived from Nolen's plan, there is no record that Nolen's extensive list of plant materials was ordered in its entirety.

As the architects prepared their first renderings of the buildings assigned to them, referring to them as "sketches" or "suggestions," they corresponded frequently with Livingood and occasionally with Nolen. Eleanor Manning and Hubert Ripley wrote to explain their sketches, now lost, typifying some of the queries expected from architects working many miles from their sites. Manning, assigned a group of houses closely bunched and facing a green or close on Denny Place, explained her design proposal and sketches as

> very tentative, subject to revision when we get working at a larger scale and to criticism, particularly from the landscape architect. The garage presents difficulties which may be solved later. The plans as we show them are all more or less conventional and for persons who would like the conventional living room and dining room with a very small kitchen, three bed rooms and bath, or two bed rooms and bath. We are trying some other ideas for living room, kitchenette, and two bed rooms and bath in group houses. We are continuing to study the problem, but we thought it might be well to get some criticism from you as to the special requirements, if any have developed, from the people who are likely to live in this locality.[10]

Livingood had not given Manning enough information, apparently, about the intended residents of the new town. Her commission did not carry the same designation as the Dale Park section, where wage earners were the expected renters.

Ripley's commission, unlike Manning's, focused on the northwest, or Dale Park, section of Mariemont, the region assigned to apartments and low-cost townhouses. One intersection was bordered by Jallade's church, a range of detached houses by Cincinnati architect Charles W. Short, and Ripley & LeBoutillier's apartments above street-level shops. Ripley's two buildings on either side of the intersection at this square mirrored each other. His suggestions for two different designs met with Livingood's approval, but as Livingood indicated no preference or guidance for further changes, Ripley wrote for clarification. This sort of clarifying exchange must have been frequent between Livingood and his architects as they worked up their suggestions for his approval and comments. Ripley asked, concerning the apartment buildings he designed, whether there should be two different buildings on the same square or two buildings on the corners that would be substantially alike. He wanted variation in detail, but with the mass of the two buildings approximately the same. After a site visit in the spring, drawings would be ready for final approval in the summer.[11]

Ripley's sequence of events to meet his contract terms with Livingood was followed, with occasional changes in the order, by all of the retained architects: tentative drawings or suggestions submitted to Livingood, a conference or two in New York or Boston, a site visit, an exchange of letters, and approval of final drawings. More often than not, Nolen did not review the final drawings, nor was he involved beyond a few consultations he earnestly desired.

Mariemont's winter hibernation ended with the warmer weather of March. Livingood remained in Europe, and plans for the underground utilities and streets were finished. Nolen worked briefly in Florida on his other commitments, and the public began to grasp the magnitude of Mariemont through laudatory articles in various journals. Two of these appeared in March, one written anonymously but certainly with information and illustrations provided by either Nolen or Livingood for the account in *Survey* magazine.

> One of the most important of American community developments at the present time is Mariemont, the town projected near Ohio's second largest industrial city. Important for more than one reason: it is, probably, the largest garden suburb so far attempted on this continent; with sites for industrial plants and complete provision for self-sufficiency, it comes nearer than any other American settlement to the model of the English garden city as exemplified at Letchworth and Wellwyn [*sic*]; much of it is being built at one time, a fact which makes possible an economy in construction and in the provision of public services as desirable as it is rare. Lastly, the plans have been made by John Nolen, of Cambridge, Massachusetts, a town and city planner whose work is always of more than usual interest.[12]

Neither that unidentified author nor Nolen, who wrote a lengthy article appearing in the *National Real Estate Journal,* mentioned Livingood and his major role in Mariemont. This omission would bring, a few months later, a reprimand from Mary Emery, passed on by Hogan. But the *National Real Estate Journal* published the largest number of illustrations of Mariemont to date, lavish drawings by Hubert Ripley and simpler watercolors from Nolen's hand.[13]

Shortly after Justin R. Hartzog, one of Nolen's staff members, visited Mariemont on March 12–14 to confer on the busy schedule planned for the spring
and summer, the Mariemont Company experienced its first personnel problem,
which threatened the project's smooth continuance. Foster's report to Nolen in
Florida explained the situation involving Clarence B. Fancy, resident engineer,
who had difficulties with county and city officials. Hogan wanted to discharge
Fancy and make what arrangement he could about his year's contract.[14] Foster
was noncommittal about Fancy's abilities, but he strongly urged the employment of a project engineer "on the job to take Mr. Livingood's place" to accommodate his frequent absences. He thought that no one would be hired to
take Fancy's place, however, until Livingood returned from Europe, "knowing
Mr. Livingood's personality."

This tale never reached Livingood in France, but Nolen and Foster realized
more than ever that the day-to-day management of building a new town required more than the sporadic attention received from Livingood when vacation called. Nolen submitted to the Mariemont Company his "Scheme for Organization," which placed him between Livingood and all other personnel in
the chain.[15] In this plan, Nolen would supervise not only the architects and engineers hired by Livingood, but a project manager for construction as well. The
project manager would answer to Nolen, who would direct all of the resident
personnel in this proposed scheme. On April 13, Hogan wrote Nolen that Fay,
Spofford & Thorndike were "engaged to undertake the complete engineering
management." He filled in with more news concerning the project's problem
with the resident engineer. Clarence Fancy resigned on April 30, 1923, but was
permitted to occupy his rent-free house in Mariemont (one of the frame farmhouses on the land when it had been purchased by Mary Emery) until his children finished the current school year.[16]

Nolen's organization scheme was ill fated. When he visited Mariemont on
April 18 to witness the opening of bids for construction work on roads and utilities, his proposed chain of command was ignored because it lacked Livingood's
opinion. Livingood's controlling hand and guidance were essential, for he was
the decision maker, but his extended absences disrupted the project's progress.
Months passed before a project manager was hired, and this position was not
answerable to Nolen.

A train from Boston carrying George L. Mirick and one of the partners representing the engineering firm of Fay, Spofford & Thorndike arrived in Cincinnati on April 12 to prepare for reviewing the bids. Joining this duo from Springfield, Massachusetts, was Warren W. Parks, a twenty-seven-year-old engineer working for the same company but now recruited by the Mariemont Company as resident engineer to replace the dismissed Clarence Fancy.[17] Parks remained for twenty years, through Mariemont's transition from privately owned town to incorporated village. Hogan called April 18, when the bids were opened, "an auspicious day,"[18] yet a more celebratory event was just ahead. Livingood missed these, however, enjoying instead the sights and pleasures of Italy and France while writing Nolen to praise the planner's efforts.

> A second letter from you, and so welcome, the last bringing the good news that plans have been accepted by all concerned. Now for action! Of course I have always been interested in your success (probably would not have settled upon you otherwise; nothing succeeds like . . .) but I am today especially proud of "Success!" What a wonderfully inspiring life, to others if not to yourself who had to endure and persevere against such odds. The great thing is you have always been doing the constructive. I congratulate you.
>
> Here I am eating the lotus, revelling in Beauty and cussing myself for having overdone, for my old Doctor here says my whole system is in a pretty bad way. But I shall pull through and return ready for the interesting work of *building* with so many ideas, if only Labor will let us carry them out. Please, in the midst of technical work, don't forget that we should soon have a sales plat, numbered lots etc. on *the very latest* system for quick disposal. I want to engage an experienced local subdivision operator to help me this Fall fix upon proper prices. Then begin to sell. Forgive this brief note, but believe me, with best wishes from all to all. Please send me the name and a plan, if possible, of the model French town nr Paris. We saw the plan you recall at Harvard.[19]

Moving into northern Italy and then to Monte Carlo, Livingood and his family reached Provence for an extended tour that stopped at Aix, Arles, Nimes, and Dijon, among many other cities. His diary records a visit to the Pont du Gard, the Roman architectural marvel, on April 23, 1923, when another ingenious wonder thousands of miles across the ocean was begun: Mariemont.[20]

On Monday afternoon, April 23, 1923, Mary Emery's limousine brought her

The Old Ferris House · Plainville Pike

Near the center of Mariemont is one of the oldest buildings in Hamilton County, Ohio, the Eliphalet Ferris house, begun about 1802. Shown as it appeared in the John Nolen scrapbook, July 1922, the Ferris house became the headquarters for Mariemont Company field work. The roof provided a triangulation station for surveys.

The arrival of founder Mary M. Emery on April 23, 1923, at the Ferris house on Plainville Road before the groundbreaking ceremony for Mariemont (*left* to *right:* Thomas Hogan Jr.; Helen Baird, Mrs. Emery's nurse; Mary Emery; Rev. Frank Nelson; and Bleecker Marquette).

More than one hundred officials and guests attended the groundbreaking ceremony for Mariemont on April 23, 1923. In this panoramic view photographed at the Ferris house, Mary Emery (*center,* near granite marker) holds a silver spade and a bouquet of roses.

and her nurse, Helen Baird, to the old Ferris house on Plainville Road, then serving as field headquarters for the Mariemont Company. Mrs. Emery's chauffeur, Charles Singer, always resplendent in his brass-buttoned livery and puttees, as Elizabeth Livingood McGuire recalled, drew the car up to the hedged enclosure just east of the brick building where generations of Ferrises had been reared. Mary Emery stepped out on a path of planks laid for her and other distinguished guests. Her minister, the Reverend Frank H. Nelson, and Thomas Hogan Jr., John Schindel, and Bleecker Marquette greeted her as a beribboned, silver-plated shovel was placed in her hands. Soon a crowd of more than one hundred employees of the Mariemont Company and of Thomas Emery's Sons, together with their wives and children, gathered behind Mariemont's donor and faced the Ferris house. A three-foot shaft of granite, a marker to be placed where the silver shovel entered the ground, lay near Mary Emery's feet. This marker became the official elevation for the entire town. A still camera took photographs of the event and the well-dressed group, while a motion picture film captured the spry donor lifting the shovel and smiling to the crowd. This film is the only known live-action document of Mary Emery.[21]

The groundbreaking, missed by both Nolen and Livingood, not only marked Mariemont's official beginning, but also celebrated the first anniversary of its announcement. Nolen's visit on April 18 for the opening of bids had precluded another trip west so soon after his return to Boston, and Livingood's unfortunate breakdown kept him in Europe for treatment. Thus, both men were denied the well-deserved applause they might have received at Mary's side. Cincinnati's newspapers reported extravagantly on the event and the brief reception that followed, expanding the accounts with numerous illustrations. Two days later the event's significance was heralded on an editorial page as "the cynosure of all sociological eyes . . . a great experiment . . . born of a silver spade in its mouth . . . its future seems assured."[22]

Writing two years after Mariemont's groundbreaking, a reporter from Rhode Island correctly but somewhat impertinently assessed Mary Emery's character and the magnitude of her Mariemont project.

> Twenty-one of the leading architects of the United States, given virtual carte blanche, are building on the outskirts of this Queen City by the Ohio a model town. Back of this unique and truly remarkable experiment in town construc-

tion and attempt to solve the housing problems for persons of limited means is
one of the most delightful old ladies imaginable. One calls her old because you
are told she is 81, but as she stood there a few short months ago, at the turning
of the first spadeful of earth at "her town," Mrs. Mary M. Emery held her immense bouquet with all the self-consciousness and shyness of a young bride.
Mrs. Emery has no particular quarrel with the modern flapper or the modern,
bob-haired and short skirted grandmother, but she belongs to the old school—
the old school of gold-rimmed spectacles and black bonnets with strings on
them and a bit of white ruching around the front. Mrs. Emery is in her own
right one of the richest women in the United States, but about her are none of
the pretensions of the wealthy. It is estimated that her fortune reaches all the
way from $30,000,000 to $40,000,000.[23]

Neither Nolen nor Livingood registered any complaint about missing the
ceremony at Mariemont on April 23, but Nolen, tactful as always, wrote his employer to urge the hiring eventually of a project manager who might steer day-
to-day operations. Livingood's prolonged absence delayed important decisions.
Nolen reported that "everything is going nicely, and although we miss you, we
can get along, especially if we can count upon building up soon after your return the right local organization, headed by a well qualified project manager.
That is the great thing, however, and I am sure you will agree with me that when
action is taken we should get the right man." Nolen added that he was alarmed
at the cost of sewer and water contracts but admitted that these concerns "must
be talked over with other big questions when you return."[24]

Livingood apologized to Nolen that he was "not to come home this summer!" His illness or breakdown somehow prohibited his return to Cincinnati
and his responsibilities there, yet his health did not retard an active travel schedule throughout Europe, including a stop at Lake Como. Thomas Hogan attempted to carry on in Livingood's absence, albeit tentatively. He and Schindel, always seeking Livingood's opinion before action was taken, planned to
meet Nolen in June in Cincinnati. On May 18, Mrs. Emery drove out to Mariemont in her chauffeured limousine; she "watched the operation of a trench dig-
ger and backfiller on Elm Street then visited the nursery and quarry," according to Warren Parks's diary. Later in the month, Hogan escorted Mrs. Emery to
Newport and then returned for the meeting with Nolen, first acknowledging

receipt of "an attractive article" on Mariemont.[25] Written anonymously, "A Demonstration Town for Ohio" is the most thoughtful and extensive publication on Nolen's new town to that date. After crediting Mary Emery, Livingood, and Nolen, the article waxed philosophical on "social discontent" and the "higher Bolshevism" of big business. The author praised Mrs. Emery's altruism in providing a town planned for working people but came perilously close to condemning the merchant princes, like Thomas J. Emery, the source of Mary's fortune, for their commercialism.

> Town planning is not a decorative luxury; it is an attempt to bring order out of social and economic anarchy and to restore home owning to the common people. Nearly all of the residential building that is producing the optimistic figures of real estate records is taking the shape of mansions or apartment houses. The building of cottages does not "pay" anywhere except in town planned garden cities where it pays enough to satisfy a civilization that is not obsessed by greed and knows something of the values of the riches of the spirit, beauty, order, justice, contentment, education and friendly service and co-operation for the common good.[26]

Nolen was quoted throughout the Canadian article, and his assumption that rentals of apartments "will be as low as $15 a month" incurred Hogan's displeasure. Hogan was ever aware of the commercial needs of the enterprise, and he and Livingood were "convinced that it will be impossible to construct apartments and semi-detached houses of even the most modest type that will permit us to rent them for such a low figure. Here in Cincinnati, the Adams Building, which is one of our tenements, is occupied almost exclusively by the foreign element and yet four rooms in this building rent for $15 a month; for three room flats we receive $10 and $12. This building was erected many, many years ago and is far from modern."[27] Nolen aimed too low on more than rents. Quoted in the article's last paragraph, he predicted that "a new town can be built for $1,000,000." By the end of 1923, Mary Emery's expenditure for Mariemont's land and initial infrastructure already exceeded that amount, and much more would be needed when construction of houses began.

As Livingood wended his way from the Continent to England, his postcards and letters to Nolen recollected earlier visits to garden cities while comparing them to his dream of Mariemont. "His" village eventually met with some of the problems, sadly, that he saw and disliked in English prototypes, but at this stage he proudly urged Nolen and the architects to make the project a success. He had seen Letchworth ten years earlier, in 1913, but the visit in 1923 disappointed him. He had hoped to meet Ebenezer Howard, crediting Howard's book as "my first real inspiration," but the eminent town planner eluded him. Livingood viewed Letchworth as run-down, sparsely settled, and with a "slimy mark" on new buildings. The architecture was successful, he wrote, but commonplace. He feared that the proprietors were in need of money and were "selling to anybody." This latter comment underscored Livingood's hauteur and support for Mariemont's rentals to a class he deemed acceptable.

To Livingood's eyes on this trip in 1923, Letchworth looked abandoned. It compared unfavorably, he wrote, to Forest Hills Gardens in New York. Some commercial success was apparent, however, in the one hundred shops he saw in the business section. Another planned community on Livingood's itinerary was Welwyn Garden City, not very far advanced in its building program beyond Mariemont's. However, Welwyn boasted five hundred occupied houses in 1923. Livingood's report to Nolen concluded with compliments, a complaint or two about English models, and a plea.

> You are a greater town planner than all of 'em put together. All depends now on our success with the American architects (who are so much better, thank God), for we must escape the dull monotony and heaviness of their brick and stucco "groups." It's really most depressing, the uniformity of style and material, the eternal (I might say infernally) red roofs. I note though with interest that there are neighborhoods and *neighborhoods*. We are right in that. And the site of Welwyn is superb, though right in the open. But think of it, all those people, and not an industry started as yet. And 21 miles from London! Please, please make Mariemont a *success*.[28]

Toward the end of May, Nolen was invited to participate in a major meeting, the International Cities and Town Planning Conference, in Gothenberg, Sweden, scheduled for August of that same year. Hopeful that Livingood could attend, as he was to remain in Europe for his recuperation and seemed to thrive on travel, Nolen wrote to encourage his client to join him. The world's leading town planners were expected to attend, and Nolen intended to arrange an exhibition of his commissions, Mariemont included, at the conference site. It was a rare opportunity, Nolen pleaded with Livingood, to present Mariemont to a gathering of renowned urban designers. The pleas went unanswered.[29]

Although Nolen looked ahead eagerly to his European trip in July and August, in the spring he worked closely with Fay, Spofford & Thorndike on the major engineering needs for Mariemont. Fay's Boston firm was responsible for carefully plotting the grading and utilities for a town that existed only on paper. Foster and Nolen looked over their shoulders constantly, with the Mariemont Company team of Schindel and Hogan hosting reviews in Cincinnati, such as the one held June 18–20.[30] This team recognized the wisdom of providing an essential infrastructure before construction began for the houses, public buildings, streets, and parklands. Much of the success in completing this stage of development is due to the competence of Nolen and his vast experience. Frederick H. Fay's collegial spirit and the supervisory abilities of George L. Mirick from Fay's office were important factors as well. Fortunate, too, was Livingood's agreement that utilities should be placed underground, at least in most areas of Mariemont. He wrote in June that some of the neighborhoods might be served by overhead electric lines, as "low-priced property cannot *stand* sinking wires." But he knew that Mary Emery approved the additional cost of underground utilities as "a gift she could make to her citizens."[31] Ultimately, the concept of requiring underground placement for all utilities was followed. This part of Mariemont's fabric remains one of its most treasured assets.

During the summer, Mary Emery rested in Newport, Livingood bustled around Europe and England, and Nolen relished the postcards he received regularly, always finding some comment to make in response to Livingood's observations. In mid-June Nolen readied himself for his trip to the International Cities and Town Planning Conference in Gothenburg, and he selected a candidate for resident landscape architect for Mariemont. Glenn Hall had been employed initially by Nolen as a draftsman in the Mariemont office, at no extra cost to the Mariemont Company. The position of landscape architect was important, Nolen knew, in supervising the first plantings on streets and lanes.[32] Nolen apparently was able to hire needed workers to expedite the planning process for Mariemont, at least when his office absorbed the costs, but he skillfully maneuvered his choices into key posts that Livingood might agree to hire as Mariemont Company employees. By the end of June, Glenn Hall had established himself at Mariemont in a small office in the Ferris house, or field headquarters, as it was then called. He promptly set to work drawing subdivision plats with lot layouts and their dimensions, as Livingood was eager to outline a procedure to sell lots. Nolen opposed any premature action for sales until a substantial number of buildings had been erected, but the company's intention moved ahead regardless of Nolen's objections.

Nolen was a businessman given to careful, step-by-step outlining of a project's needs. He was neither impulsive in his assessments nor temperamental in dealings with clients. His copious records, memoranda, lists, and correspondence illustrate the work patterns of a cautious, eminently qualified designer for hire. A typical memorandum, one prepared by Nolen on July 16 in preparation for a meeting in Cincinnati on July 16–18, lists seventeen points to discuss with Hogan, Schindel, and others. He knew that certain decisions had to be made without delay, such as the "Murray Street Layout, Relocation for Wooster Pike, Street Construction on edge of Bluff, and Map for recording and sales." Although Nolen did not note this in his memorandum, some of the items probably would be left for Livingood to approve, such as "Concourse, Submit drawings" or "Acquisition of Norfolk and Western Property."[33] Nolen returned to his Cambridge office in time to write Livingood before he set off for Scandinavia, offering his strong recommendation against permitting overhead lines. He also subtly inserted himself as a reviewer of architects' plans, writing that he had received sketches and plans from Richard H. Dana Jr. and thought that he had "caught the spirit of Mariemont and worked out the practical problems."[34]

As Nolen set sail for Europe, Livingood continued his "cure" while feeding suggestions on Mariemont back to Nolen's office. A set of six postcards in Livingood's neat penmanship, sent to Philip Foster and crammed with comments on his travels and hopes for Mariemont, illustrates Livingood's persistent focus on details, even at his great distance from the actual site.

> I was amazed at the building that was done about Glasgow and Edinboro because of the War. Then of course you know that I studied Letchworth (for the fourth time) and Welwyn. Finally, we motored through Normandy and Brittany, the Loire Valley, up again into Normandy to see some developments, and through the Battlefields and France under reconstruction. My impressions as to

housing must wait—I am unequal to the task of writing—but in brief European housing has nothing for us. We must develop our own *naturally*. As for the work being done outside Paris it is either still on paper or else a dismal hodge-podge and a crime. But then the French never have understood what we , excel in—domestic architecture. They run to the grand.

Of course Mariemont was in my mind (pleasantly) all the time, but in general I have merely had reports (no problems) from Mr. Hogan, and you too have been most considerate. John Nolen's letters were so sympathetic, especially his last suggesting our meeting either in Sweden or in England, both alas, absolutely impossible for we sail from Cherbourg on the Mauretania on Sept. 8th. This means that I shall drop in on you at your office about the middle of the month, and you must come down to Newport, too, to meet Mrs. Emery who, I am happy to say, has been in splendid health (for her) all summer.

I did so enjoy your excellent article on the *first page* of "The Modern Hospital," so full of good common sense. I have sent the number to Hannaford's who are to design our hospital, though did you know that my old friend and associate in many building projects, the head of his firm, has just passed away. A great personal loss to me, but his brothers and son still carry on. I have enjoyed studying your more recent (May 1923) study for a portion of the Stadium which you must surely send to Fred A. [*sic*] Garber, Union Central Life Bldg. Cinti, for him to be mulling over. Although please change from "Field House" to "Reception Hall." Also, I am still hopeful that you can squeeze into the East of the Running Track, near Murray Ave as you choose, an *indicated* (at least) Swimming Pool, say 40×90. Spectators seated on the concrete seats and grass can see the kids disporting and yet not be *too* near. I should *think* the bathers could run around to dress in the shower room and beneath the central bleachers. I trust it will be possible this Fall to begin grading and perhaps start to lay streets in the N.W. section, the demand for Workmen's homes being so great. The others can wait. But I am beginning to feel that ordinary asphalt will be too hot and too soft in mid-summer. We must be on the look-out for a suitable, easily kept clean surface. Are you sure that the distance from curb to curb should not be reduced? I hate to think of the cost should we be compelled to lay anything like concrete. And please remember that in my eyes Cherry Lane [the street directly in front of the projected church] should be a lane, meandering between rows of cherry trees with grass growing under them right up to the somewhat irregular, New England coal-tar & sand sidewalk.

You see how my mind runs on. I see the whole project *finished*. Mr. Jallade has instructions to present *finished* plans for the little English Norman church upon my return, for I do want to lay its foundations this Fall. Much of the stone is already on the site. If only we could afford to import the roof-stones from England. I know a man who can secure as many as 100 tons, he says.

Now good bye until we meet. And send my Greetings to Nolen. Also my best to all the workers in the office. How long ago that first interview seems![35]

During Livingood's month-long recuperative stay at Engelberg, Switzerland, John Nolen appeared at the Swedish conference on planning (August 3–10) and delivered a lengthy address reviewing city and town design in America and the "exceptional interest" presented by Mariemont in alleviating housing problems. Nolen emphasized American contributions to town planning, including parks, playgrounds, large residence lots, and zoning; he stated that garden cities and garden suburbs by English town planners have slight influence. While this last observation might be argued, Nolen's review of America's discontented workers who "are mere renters, and therefore drifters and floaters—at least sixty per cent of us," led to a brief account of Roger W. Babson's prescient statistics, the coming growth of suburbs, and the curse of unplanned sprawl. Leading to his outline of Mariemont's design, Nolen advocated an urgent hunt for accessible sites that have good railroad lines, are within fifteen or twenty miles of cities, and have suitable roads for the automobile. He applauded Mariemont's "terms and conditions that can be duplicated wherever initiative, capital and sound planning can be combined to support an enterprise of great public importance, namely, the building of new towns and suburbs, virtually complete communities, providing not only suitable homes but also schools, recreation, museums and shops for people of small means." Nolen prophesied that Mariemont "will not remain alone in Cincinnati, but will spread through the country, bringing relief and blessings in its wake."[36]

By August's end, Livingood began to tire of his European stay, and his letters to Nolen were full of questions and concerns for Mariemont. While preparing for his return to the United States, he wrote to Nolen, who had just finished attending the conference in Gothenburg, to encourage an early meeting between the two men. He requested Nolen's presence in Newport about September 20, 1923. There, he and Nolen could discuss the Gothenburg conference and their shared interest in better housing, he said. It was clear in Livingood's letter that some crucial decisions had been delayed during his absence of many months.

> Our only hope then is careful planning, watching the corners, close control of architectural impulses, and wholesale intelligent building *ourselves*. So do urge men like Ripley to look after the details in his specifications. I shall want to go over their plans at once. Tom Hogan's letter telling of the wonderful contracts made for putting everything underground, even in the N.W. section, has just been read, with great satisfaction, and I see that we are up against quick decision about our roads and streets. We must not be precipitate, however. I have much yet to say and *learn*. Also, I want your opinion first on the lay-out presented for the street lighting, type of lamp, standards, etc. This is to be a *model*.[37]

In this correspondence, Livingood's defining term for Mariemont was *model*. When he first had contacted Nolen, however, in 1920, Livingood disliked the term and did not want the community to be known as a *model* village. The word had become a battle cry by 1923, apparently. He intended it to inspire those involved with the project, but he firmly believed that the concept and methods of Mariemont would be repeated elsewhere. He decried the use of state assistance (and probably any other tax-based support or administration) but did not recognize at this stage that Mary Emery's financial backing was unique and unlikely to be replicated.

Nolen returned to his Cambridge office on September 4, dug into accumulated correspondence, and discussed with Foster his observations on the European scene. He advised Foster to visit Cincinnati and oversee the progress at Mariemont, a three-day trip set for September 11–13, as "the best arrangement, for many reasons." One reason, of course, was the breathing spell Nolen needed to review all of his planning projects, and he knew the call to Newport later in September was not to be denied. He wrote to Hogan that he was

> full of impressions from abroad, and realize more than ever how essential it is for me professionally to keep in personal touch with what is going on in different parts of Europe. It is not because we can duplicate their work here. Conditions are too different. But there is so much to be learned, nevertheless. I was

astonished to find that a number of cities in Holland had recently built as many as 5,000 or 6,000 workmen's homes; and in England since the war the municipalities, with the government's co-operation, have constructed over 200,000 houses, almost all of brick. It makes Mariemont seem very small in comparison.[38]

He concluded by praising Mariemont as having "more significance than we have heretofore attributed to it."

Nolen journeyed to Newport to meet Mrs. Emery and confer with her, Livingood, and Hogan. The latter recorded questions and answers they discussed on September 25–26, focusing only on the practical matters needing attention back at Mariemont, such as extending Wooster Pike, piping water from the Little Miami River for fountains, a plan for the Concourse, paving of streets and alleys, and street lighting issues, among others. These were issues to be settled before houses were constructed, but the chosen architects for Mariemont were impatient for more guidelines.

Some architects, like Robert McGoodwin, plunged ahead with recommendations to Livingood. The Philadelphia architect asked for approval of several points critical to the appearance of the commission he had received, and he specified the costs of his houses. First, he thought twelve houses, not ten, should be built on Albert Place, the cul-de-sac assigned to him. Next, each house should be 22,000 cubic feet in size (an unusual way to measure the size of a residence), costing fifty cents per cubic foot, or about $8,800 per house as a minimum estimate. Garages and closure walls would average about $650 per building, with an average total cost of about $9,450 for each of the houses. McGoodwin added that he preferred service drives in the rear of Albert Place properties "in order to keep the front entrances from being entirely crowded up with driveways which will detract enormously from the general effect of the Place."[39] These drives for the dozen houses were completed as he requested.

On September 29, Livingood, as president of the Mariemont Company, issued "General Instructions" for architects of "Group Housing" and "Places," spelling out twenty-four detailed requirements "to enable them to draw up Plans and Specifications" for the exteriors and interiors of the buildings.[40] This document, the first noting design requirements for the commissioned architects, reflects Livingood's experience in home and apartment building with

Thomas Emery's Sons. He may have received advice from architects or contractors employed by that firm and well known to him, but Nolen seems to have been consulted only after the instructions were issued. The twenty-four points are very specific, requiring, as examples, consideration of types of downspouts, brick or fieldstone sills, toilets with no lids but set on marble slabs, and rooms with stock doors and picture molding. Architects named in the first category of "Group Housing" were Clinton Mackenzie, Edmund B. Gilchrist, Richard H. Dana Jr., Hubert G. Ripley, and Mellor, Meigs & Howe. The second category, for "Places," included Howe & Manning, Robert R. McGoodwin, Grosvenor Atterbury, and Wilson Eyre & McIlvaine. Of those listed, the last-named firm in each category did not complete any dwellings or public buildings at Mariemont.

In early October, Livingood sent "General Instructions" to Philip Foster and questioned the plans of Richard H. Dana, already in hand, which placed only four rooms in each unit. "Don't you think this would be a mistake?" he asked. "A tenant likes his neighborhood. His family increases. The house will soon be too small and he must move farther afield, and at a greater cost than if simply into the next group. I think there should be variety. Please let me know your views at once from a Town Planning point of view." The enclosed copy of "General Instructions" was to be sent to the architects that week, Livingood noted.[41]

Foster's clear-sighted response to Livingood's query summarized the virtues of variety and the "problems of subdivision work," referring to Dana's houses in the early plan he had submitted. Foster liked an "assortment [of design] to meet different needs." Such variations, he felt, will bring different kinds of families into the housing groups and thus will tend to make a more democratic neighborhood. Foster spelled out for Livingood his simple, direct conclusions about architects' designs, and these echoed Nolen's.

> From the planning point of view the variety and size and character of the houses is well worthwhile and is what keeps a street from being monotonous. The "builder's row" is deadly because the houses are all of one size and shape. The ornamentation and color varies but that counts for little as compared to the bulk and outline. The old New England village, which was decidedly attractive, was usually all in one style of Colonial architecture, painted white with green blinds. Mansion and cottage, store and church, all followed the same gen-

eral architectural characteristics, yet there is little that could be called monotonous.[42]

After Nolen's visit in late September to Mary Emery's estate in Rhode Island, he sent his patron a book by Edgar Allan Poe in appreciation for her hospitality. This elicited Mary's dignified response and a word or two on her new town.

> In spite of your admonition not to acknowledge the graceful compliment you pay me by suggesting that I would like the story of Poe's Domain of Arnheim, I must express my appreciation and thank you for giving me the inspiration it suggests. A marked book is more intimate than a conversation and I have taken to heart one of Poe's conditions of bliss, viz, "to have an object of unceasing pursuit"—of course that is what Mariemont represents and therefore I must be in a "condition of bliss!" Many thanks to you for opening up the vista.[43]

Nolen received Mary's gracious letter about the same time as the arrival of Livingood's "General Instructions" and an organizational chart for Mariemont drafted by the resident engineer, Warren Parks. The latter was "merely a record of the present working forces," Nolen hoped, but Parks's chart incorrectly listed Nolen, the Mariemont Company, and Fay's engineering firm as equals, a troika that Livingood never would condone. "So far as I know," Nolen added in his letter to Livingood, "you still approve the general idea of building up at the right time a local Mariemont organization." Only one brief paragraph recorded three comments on Livingood's instructions to the architects. Tree planting schedules for lots should be delayed, he urged, as he wanted some fences in front of selected properties. Fences were useful for "utility, interest, and variety," he wrote.[44]

Defending his instructions, Livingood responded to Nolen's contentions and disavowed Parks's organizational chart. "It is our intention," he wrote, "to create an Organization by the first of the year so that we can in earnest begin the erection of homes on the coming of Spring." He acknowledged Nolen's criticisms but did not change his stance. Livingood added that the architects themselves approved the instructions. In view of Livingood's unchallenged direction of the entire project, it seems unlikely that the architects had much room for disagreement.[45]

In that same letter, Livingood signaled to Nolen the beginning of Mariemont's church, based on architect Louis E. Jallade's references to prototypes he had visited and the inspiration he had absorbed during a summer trip in 1923 to England. Jallade produced a clay model to visualize the height of the tower and the actual location of the building to be erected alongside the old Ferris cemetery. Otto Kadon, Cincinnati's best stonemason, was retained to lay the stone for the church, a project carried out with great skill and sympathy for the medieval appearance of the church. Livingood insisted on specimen walls to be put up adjacent to the cemetery before any construction of the exterior walls of the church could begin. James Griffith & Sons, a company often used by Thomas Emery's Sons, handled the construction.

Nolen sent Jallade a grading plan for the church land, adding in a letter that "Mr. Livingood has written very enthusiastically about your design for the church, and I hope before long to have an opportunity to see it. Perhaps I can come to your office sometime when I am in New York." Jallade wrote to Nolen on the same day, telling him he had met his son in "Marriemont" and that he was "putting everything that I have got into the little church for Mr. Livingood and I think you will be interested when you see the efforts that we have put into the study of this building."[46] Jallade's church was to be the first building constructed in the new town. This decision almost certainly was Mary Emery's, but she did not attend the groundbreaking ceremony on November 12, 1923. Wielding the silver spade Mary had used in April to begin the project, Livingood acted in her stead. He also marked the boundaries of the church by walking behind a plow and two white horses. No single building or part of Mariemont excited Livingood as much as the proposed church. From its beginning, it was the architectural gemstone of the community.

Mary Emery was a staunch Episcopalian and the major patron of Cincinnati's largest Episcopal church, of which Livingood was also a member. From its beginning, the Mariemont church was to be nondenominational, although any churches erected subsequently in the village could follow the religion its members desired. Nolen's plan placed several churches on assigned plats, but none was ever built.

It is remarkable that Livingood, for all of his dedication to creating an English village characterized by half-timbered houses, pedimented classical doorways, and pastoral greens, sought antique building materials only for the church roof. The church must have an authentic medieval roof, Livingood decided, to set off its Norman-style architecture. Although Jallade may have suggested this special effect to him, it is known that Livingood explored the possibility of acquiring authentic roof stones from an English source in 1923. In a letter seeking the help of an English friend in acquiring old roof stones similar to those in Malmesbury, England, Livingood wrote that he wanted to use Cincinnati-area stone for the church walls and tower. A woods near Mariemont was commandeered for the rough-hewn timbers to support the roof, the porch, and the lich gate on Wooster Pike.[47]

Livingood's approach to an English acquaintance in Malmesbury produced no answer, apparently, and Livingood then wrote to Nolen asking to enlist Raymond Unwin in the quest.[48] The search for authentic roof stones was unsuccessful with Nolen and Unwin, but eventually Jallade discovered a source for the fourteenth-century materials Livingood desired so earnestly. That Livingood cared deeply about the visual effect of church and roof is apparent in his closing words to Joseph Moore, the Malmesbury innkeeper, whom Livingood contacted to search for lichen-covered roof materials.

> In brief I want the church roof to look like the roofs of Malmesbury whose charm I shall never forget. This is my one chance of making a thing of beauty in this little industrial village. We have a good beginning. In the cemetery which has perhaps 30 or 40 small monuments, tombstones, etc., which are placed in the charming irregularity so much desired to get the effect. Even the enclosing wall though built nearly 100 years ago is still there, and it is this wall we shall imitate in the walls of our church.

Livingood's wish was fulfilled eventually, when medieval roof stones were acquired in England to crown Jallade's church.

By Nolen's and Foster's visit to Mariemont on November 15–17, 1923, Livingood still had not decided on the organizational structure that would build and develop the village. Warren Parks's chart was in hand, but Livingood wisely sought Nolen's perspective, and he wrote after the visit to explain his objectives.

> Soon after your delightful visit I was called East on business to Philadelphia and New York, and as I was away a week returning but yesterday, saw a lot of Architects and "sich" and was brought face to face with the immediate need of an organization for our building campaign next Spring. I met especially a contractor, one of the big men in New York, who at a round table discussion pictured just what we should have and I am flabbergasted.

The Ferris Cemetery

The Ferris family cemetery, preserved by the Mariemont Company, is shown as it appeared in 1922. Members of the pioneer Ferris and Stites families were buried here throughout the nineteenth century, and the Mariemont Memorial Church was built adjacent to the cemetery.

I wish you would prepare me a chart showing how the organization would head up to me as you did for the development; but in foot notes tell me exactly what [here Nolen has underlined the two preceding words and penciled a question mark in the margin] from your experience each man's duties would be as fully as you can take the time. Now mind, I do not agree that I will agree with your picture but I know you have had experience or at least contact with other big enterprises and you promised to help me.

This contractor, by the way, after going over the whole project with the blue prints before him agreed that I must have the best help, especially in the Business Manager but upon careful reflection gave it as his opinion that I could get such a man for from between $6,000 and $10,000. This is exactly my own idea.[49]

Livingood's inability to assess the magnitude of the Mariemont project and its requirements plagued the enterprise from its initial concept to its partial fulfillment. In this example, his rather late recognition that an organizational chart as well as a business manager might be needed displays this weak perception.

In early December 1923, Livingood sought not only the "picture of the Organization we will require to build in Dale Park early next Spring" but also a resident landscape architect to replace Glenn Hall, who had been engaged temporarily from Nolen's office. Another of Nolen's colleagues, Justin Hartzog, was proposed by Nolen, but this obtained no approval from Livingood, as he confided to Foster. Hartzog lacked "the pep that we are used to having around our office at least. I am myself writing to several men, especially in the hope of finding a good landscape architect but if you think that Mr. Ashley will do to *start* our landscape work this coming Spring let me have some further data about him if he is still available."[50] Nolen helped in the hunt, suggesting Joseph F. Whitney as landscape architect, a recommendation also endorsed by Henry V. Hubbard, a Harvard professor and landscape architect once associated with Olmsted Brothers and who had helped design Mrs. Emery's estate in Rhode Island.[51]

The Mariemont Company sent out its first Christmas card in 1923, picturing a quaint coaching scene and an imaginary half-timbered English inn on its cover, perhaps suggesting Livingood's vision for Mariemont. Its cheery message credited the new town as "A National Exemplar, an interpretation of modern city planning principles applied to a small community to produce local happiness." Christmas brought a few fears, however. Livingood's lengthy letter to Nolen, written the day following, filled four pages with questions and misgivings. The project required daily decisions, and these bore down on Livingood. He was considering Joseph F. Whitney as resident landscape architect, and he appreciated Nolen's recommendation of him. He had some doubts, however, for he thought that

> we do not now need as you would indicate in your most recent letter, a real first-class resident landscape architect, unless he is to be the Town Planning representative at the same time which would be fine. . . . I hope we can find a young fellow willing to come and work his way up but with the understanding that eventually "a first-class resident landscape architect" will be put over him, unless he is a wonder himself. It seems to me that Whitney should have had more experience to be the final landscape architect.[52]

The letter further spelled out Livingood's concerns about street surfaces and curbs, as well as setback of residences, details that frequently concerned him. Referring to Cincinnati regulations, he told Nolen that setbacks of thirty feet, not twenty, were acceptable.

Livingood expected Nolen's plan for the lagoon, a small lake south of the Dale Park section and adjacent to Nolen's planned Dogwood Park, to be a "reflecting basin," but its cost staggered him. He urged Nolen to visit Chicago on his way back from a trip to California to inspect "that wonderful display of 59 varieties of road surface undertaken a few years ago by the State of Illinois." That Livingood had not estimated construction costs and types of housing very carefully before he had committed to the architects' plans is shown in his closing words to Nolen. Livingood was frightened by the number of group houses to be built and their "imposing" appearance.

Seldom did Nolen fail to respond to Livingood's concerns, if only to clarify an issue or two or perhaps to suggest an obvious solution. His responses invariably were tactful and as succinct as he could be while explaining technical and artistic points. To concerns about the candidacy of Joseph Whitney as resident landscape architect, Nolen replied that this position should also be the town planning representative and that "he should be at least as well qualified a man as Whitney. I should prefer a man who had more experience than Whitney, but I doubt very much whether we can find one." He defended the varieties of curbing he suggested, agreed that the lagoon was expensive, and questioned the justification of its cost. Nolen's longest defense was reserved for his proposed setback of buildings in the Dale Park section; fifteen to twenty-five feet, not the thirty feet Livingood advocated. Finally, he urged simpler, less expensive buildings.[53]

An active year of construction lay ahead, awaiting decisions and the completion of underground utilities begun in 1923. Livingood focused on the Dale Park section for the first assault. After absenting himself most of 1923 in Europe, he ruminated with Nolen over his choices of architects, the rising costs of building, and guidelines for the Mariemont Company, as well as the designers of the new town. Already selected were the architects named by Livingood in 1922, and to these he communicated his hopes and demands. Allen W. Jackson of Boston was not among those recommended by Nolen earlier in 1922, but

Livingood added him to the list. As Jackson's forte was a revival style for half-timbered houses, he was assigned a group of freestanding units to be built on Mariemont Avenue close to Dogwood Park. Nolen correctly offered advice to his employer about Jackson's commission, suggesting that a specific building site be assigned to him and not left open. As town planner Nolen rightly knew that certain streets, intersections, and grades helped define an architect's designs.[54]

Nolen's comments, resulting from a meeting with Jackson in Boston, concluded with advice sure to captivate Livingood. Jackson hoped to design "a 'string' of houses, either in detached or possibly group houses, along the concave side of a street, making an informal irregular, picturesque group such as one sees so often in England," using half timber and stucco in a Tudor style. Jackson enclosed three photographs (now lost) with his letter to Livingood as examples of what he might design.

Jackson followed Nolen's urging by writing to Livingood to settle some still undecided issues about the three houses he was to design. Because the appearance of his assigned buildings was "conspicuous," Jackson expected a favorable hearing. In his letter to Livingood, he stated that Nolen agreed with him in "the matter of grouping several houses together, either separated by party walls or making them actually separate, but linking them all together by walls, garages, or something to make them all of a piece. This sort of thing can be done better in this style of architecture than any other."[55]

Both Livingood and Nolen fretted as the architects prepared to begin construction in 1924. Livingood's usual hand wringing about the Mariemont project was expressed frequently in dealings with architects, as with Allen Jackson. Through it all, Livingood remained in control. The busiest year for Mariemont lay ahead.

5 ⋆ ARCHITECTS AND
BUILDINGS

One writer, observing winter's grip on the filled utility trenches and the un-graded streets crisscrossing Mariemont, thought that "a giant had loosed his strength for a trial effort and then rested for a while as he prepared for the or-deal to come."[1] By January 1924 the assault on construction had been ordered. Fay, Spofford & Thorndike submitted to Livingood and Nolen a practical as-sessment of the armies of workers needed for construction. If the Mariemont Company intended to build four houses per week (i.e., townhouses or multi-family units, but not apartments) at a cost of $6,000 to $10,000 per house, la-bor costs estimated at 40 percent of house costs should be added. Three hun-dred to five hundred men earning average wages of thirty-three dollars per week were required, Fay noted, adding that an office force of "about 30 people" was needed for purchasing, expediting, and timekeeping. An additional corps of two hundred laborers "of much lower grade than artisans required for building construction," who would live "in makeshift manner about job, and in manner which no artisan would consider," should be added by the summer of 1925. And in that year, fully eight hundred men should be employed on the con-struction of residences, public buildings (including stores and apartments), the Resthaven barn and units, and streets and miscellaneous work. Fay's report con-cluded that the construction of 759 houses, not to mention the other building requirements of Mariemont, required 190 weeks. That is, from the spring of 1923 to the end of 1928 (considering time off for bad weather).[2]

As the New Year began, Livingood anguished over Boston architect Allen W. Jackson's determination to design a range of half-timbered houses he was com-missioned to undertake south of Wooster Pike in a section reserved for single homes, more expensive than the "workingmen's" units in the Dale Park section. Livingood resisted Jackson's plea for assigned sites, and he expected to receive drawings for houses "in timbered work" in the Tudor style. He wanted Jackson to visualize for him "two or three typical houses bearing the imprint of your serious study of this topic, to be used as illustrations of what can be done, these to be placed perhaps at strategic points. Of course, the great trouble is that this style of construction calls for larger money outlay than is usual for the class of occupant that we are trying to serve." Livingood thought the designs were "perhaps a little *too* plain, that you were cutting too close to the bone. What I meant to convey to Mr. Nolen was, when we looked them over together that I wanted to be assured that these were the best that you knew how and that you had carefully considered the matter of plan and design as well as costs." The letter was concluded haughtily, telling Jackson it was immaterial as to the placement of the houses, and their location would receive the attention they deserved.[3]

Livingood's vision of an English village focused occasionally on details that seemed minor to the grand plan. Once he pondered sidewalks, hoping they could be the "coal tar" type "much in use in that most beautiful town [Williamstown, Mass.] perfectly feasible even here in hot Cincinnati."[4] He disliked "glaring cement" and clung "tenaciously to the New England coal tar sidewalks wherever possible, believing that they should widen out and wind about trees (even if we have to plant them out of line)." Curbs for Mariemont's streets concentrated his attention, too, especially for the Dale Park area, the section to begin in the spring. On January 21, Livingood wrote to Philip Foster that the stone from Mariemont's quarry was particularly adapted to polishing ("just like Tennessee marble") and that it could be crushed for use in foundations. The same letter carried news of Livingood's commissions to the last of the architects for the Dale Park section, Charles Cellarius, "who is going to do some cheap homes on Beech Street," and A. Lincoln Fechheimer for the school building, "the best local architect of Jewish name hereabouts with quite a good deal of experience in this kind of work."[5] Several days later Livingood wrote Foster again to thank him for his "colored sketch of Dale Park" and its landscape scheme, likened to a formal English garden.

I can see that you put lots of loving care into this sketch and that you have very definite ideas as to how the Park should look. Now I cannot say offhand that we shall adopt all your ideas but in the main they are certainly most interesting. My imagination is caught especially by the circular recreation lawn. This I take it will be the site for church festivals in the summer evenings.

Then there is that delightful sunken play field, if I read the topography correctly, which can be viewed from Plainville Pike and from the Overlook attached to the formal garden. I suppose the formal garden is all right if it can be well policed. Certainly the design is good but I doubt whether an open garden like this filled with flowers will survive on so public a road; yet we must have faith in our people.[6]

Two issues nagging Livingood, he confessed in his January 28 letter, were specifications for the architects and the appointment of a general manager. A postscript told Foster that interviews for this position ended with the hiring of Joseph H. Peterson, an engineer from Cleveland, Ohio. Peterson's seventeen years' experience as an engineer; his direction of engineering projects in Colorado, Wyoming, and California; and his work with Brooklyn's Botanical Gardens seemed to present a man well qualified for the job. He began his new assignment in February, ready to take on the burdens of day-to-day management of construction. Livingood's presence and decision making could not be denied, however. Apparently, the "General Instructions" given to architects in 1923 were insufficient (and perhaps too simplistic), forcing Livingood to provide more detailed directions. Livingood was pestered by the assigned architects for more guidance, and he acknowledged his tardiness in providing specifications for building materials, plumbing fixtures, and furnaces for the houses in the Dale Park section on and around Chestnut Street.

In February, Livingood quibbled with Nolen over fees charged in addition to his professional retainer. Such disagreements can be frequent between patron and planner or architect, as shown here when Livingood began feeling the pinch for Mariemont's costs. He objected to additional charges for Foster's revised plan for the Dale Park section, as he thought the retainers paid to Nolen's firm would cover such drawings. "Surely all the engineering, platting, contours, etc. have all been paid for by our Company when you turned over the block plans. I ask you frankly whether if you are to lay out walks along the bank and indicate the shape of the Island [part of the boathouse complex and lagoon area, which was developed later] we must pay for your experience as though we were hiring a landscape architect," Livingood complained to Nolen. Pinchpenny with some costs, Livingood was extravagant with others, such as the boathouse project.[7]

Nolen's response to Livingood's complaint, written a month later because of the planner's trip to San Diego and other business commitments, was a three-page defense of the planner's responsibilities in general and his work for Mariemont in particular. The text of Nolen's letter comprises a brief overview of the usual time involvement of a town planner with his client.

Let me state first of all that we are ready to accept whatever arrangement is in your judgment right and best, all things considered. However, we should like to state our preference, namely, that whatever the amount of the annual or monthly fee is, it should cover only our services as professional consultants. This would include all time that I give to Mariemont both in the office and the field. In other words, there would be the personal visits to Cincinnati; conferences with you or other officers of the Mariemont Company in Cincinnati or elsewhere; consultations with engineers, architects, landscape architects and other designers, contractors, etc.; office time in the study of all the various Mariemont problems, both general and detail, that arise in connection with the town planning—in fact, the consideration of Mariemont in every way and at any time. This professional consulting fee would also cover Mr. Foster's services in so far as they were of the same character and of course on all important problems that come to us for study or decision we go over them carefully together and give whatever amount of time is necessary.

We believe from experience in other places that it is better not to try to separate the charges for Mr. Foster's time for what might be called "design," strictly speaking, from the rest of his time in the drafting room used in services other than design. The line is a difficult one to establish, and the decisions must necessarily be rather arbitrary. Of course we could not afford to include all of Mr. Foster's time in the monthly payment for professional services as consultants, because the amount for his drafting supervision of plans, etc., would be as much as or more than the professional fee, and would allow nothing for field visits and other consulting services of a professional character for either of us.

To return to my first statement, we are quite willing to submit the matter for your consideration and decision. On any basis that we are accustomed to use or by comparison with the charges of others, we believe that three hundred dollars a month, the present fee, is not too large a sum for professional services as outlined above. The office fee for the Mariemont work of the first years, two hundred dollars a month, was less than the sum we have usually been paid for similar work.[8]

No adjustment was made in the charges for Foster's work, as Livingood merely acknowledged "gratefully [Nolen's] very important letter of March 21," and submitted to Foster the sample copy for a new flyer, or "bulletin" as he called it, advertising Mariemont. Nolen was then on another excursion to California but expected to stop at Mariemont on his return to the East Coast. Livingood's copy was recycled from an earlier statement, with certain parts corrected (such as acreage, from 365 to 415 acres; that construction was in progress; and that Thomas Hogan's name as secretary of the Mariemont Company was added to Nolen's for those seeking information).[9] The town plan of July 1921 again appeared to illustrate the new town springing alive with laborers and steam shovels, mule teams and tractors, carpenters and bricklayers.

The spring of 1924 brought Mary Emery's nephew, John J. Emery, her brother-in-law's oldest son, from New York to Cincinnati to inspect the Emery interests and holdings. And there on April 1 he joined Livingood and Hogan at the groundbreaking that began construction on Mariemont's Chestnut Street for the village's first residential buildings, the group houses of Richard H. Dana Jr. Mrs. Emery did not attend.[10] The town site was a sea of mud as the construction crew, soon to number more than a thousand men, began to build 325 dwelling units in the Dale Park section.[11] To orchestrate on-site activities, especially the supervision of hundreds of laborers, the mule teams with their loads of lumber, and the steam shovels scraping out foundations, a special team was needed. The resident architect, engineer, and landscape architect joined together to supervise, reporting regularly to Livingood and Nolen. While Nolen could not give the project the frequent, often daily, inspections rendered by Livingood, he visited Mariemont at least four times during 1924.[12] Important decisions, always referred to Livingood for final approval, usually were made after an exchange of letters between Nolen and his client.

Throughout April, Livingood badgered Foster about the latter's designs for the swimming pool and the tennis courts adjacent to the recreation hall, and he sought advice on advertising the new industrial area of Mariemont, called Westover, a tract of forty-five acres immediately west of the village.[13] But after

Aerial views of the landscape were rare in 1924, when this first known photograph of Mariemont was taken from an airplane. In this view to the northwest, road grading at the town center has begun and the framework of streets emerges.

the inauguration of the Dana units, Livingood perceived the usefulness of an outline, his "wish list" for 1924, which he delivered to Nolen as a two-page document, the most complete assessment to date of his dreams and hopes for the year. His list was divided into several categories: construction accomplishments, formation of a building organization, acquisition of machinery and equipment, establishment of a sales and rental staff, and commencement of several public buildings. It was an awesome recital of the task ahead.

For the first time, Livingood seemed to appreciate the need to outline the project's work schedule for the year at hand. Nolen's encouragement was rewarded. Livingood's hopes for construction accomplishments included installing underground all utilities by July 25; finishing Dale Park streets and alleys by October, with tree planting soon to follow; erecting the stone wall of the concourse overlooking the Little Miami River valley by June 10; dredging the lagoon and completing its concrete dam by June 10; planning the landscaping of Dale Park sites; and most important, "that the Commissions of Dana, Gilchrist, Ripley, Mackenzie, Ziegler, Cellarius, Kruckemeyer, and possibly the houses (frame) by Elzner and by Short will be ready by October 10—an ambitious program but worth striving for."[14] Thus, the Mariemont Company's work for the summer and autumn of 1924 was presented and given a benediction by Livingood after the first few paragraphs: "The future as to construction of houses is in the lap of the Gods."

The company's building organization, Livingood thought, was "pretty well established," as it had engaged a plumbing company and agreed to purchase forty thousand barrels of cement as well as one million bricks and lumber for joists and flooring. He intended the company to provide the manpower and to control all of the construction in 1924, except for the elementary school, which would be contracted, "and possibly the houses by Elzner." His array of equipment included fifty wagons and their mule teams as well as uncounted trucks, tractors, and scrapers. Livingood hoped to perfect a plan with his lawyer Schindel for governing the village and simultaneously to "institute a plan of sales: terms, restrictions, re-capture clause, use of Building Association methods, etc." Hopes were high to pour the foundations for the stadium and recreation building, prepare the Resthaven barn for its livestock, and ensure the completion of the steam plant by August 1, 1925. Finally, Livingood noted that he "must complete his selection of architects for development of Town Center and adjacent public buildings." That is, although the residential architects and a few public building designers had been chosen, the town center remained unassigned. Livingood's intentions were good, but only the Mariemont Inn at the town center ever progressed beyond the drawing board.

Laborers and craftsmen by the hundreds came to Mariemont in the spring. Livingood's attention was then focused on the architects. He was not only the arbiter of all matters pertaining to their designs and assignments, but also the final authority on personnel, at least for the senior positions. In late April the general manager, Joseph H. Peterson, resigned under pressure, and George L. Mirick assumed this important post as deputy for Livingood.[15] Apparently a clash of personalities had resulted in Peterson's departure, which underscores

Photographed in 1924, the first residential units under construction in Mariemont were the townhouses (*center*) designed by New York architect Richard H. Dana Jr. The stone walls of the Mariemont Memorial Church (*center right*, near grove of trees) by New York architect Louis E. Jallade are near completion.

the authoritarian nature of the president of the Mariemont Company. Peterson confided in Nolen that "right or wrong if one is unable to fit in with Mr. Livingood's peculiar personality he can no longer operate successfully with Mr. Livingood. Have heard that George Mirick is to be my successor. That is indeed a surprise from more reasons than one."[16]

Nolen was queried occasionally for his opinion of the architects' submissions, but Livingood never consulted collegially with him as an equal. Allen W. Jackson, preparing plans for a group of half-timbered houses south of Wooster Pike, wrote Nolen that "Livingood writes me that he is pleased with [the plans], but wants to consult with you 'the last of this month' when you are there about them." Nolen had recognized early in this relationship that architectural decisions were not his, but Livingood's, as he wrote to Clinton Mackenzie: "Mr. Livingood is handling the house matter largely himself."[17] This control continued throughout the life of the construction project.

Livingood sometimes relied on his membership or trusteeship in Cincinnati institutions to help resolve problems with Mariemont. He enjoyed a special relationship with the Cincinnati Art Museum as Mrs. Emery's representative. He had known the museum's directors from the institution's inception: Alfred T. Goshorn, the first director, and Joseph Henry Gest, its second leader. Although Livingood worked with one of the two subsequent directors, Walter Siple, and knew the fourth, Philip R. Adams, it was Gest who shared the years when Mary Emery's Edgecliffe Collection of old master paintings was formed and when Mariemont began. That town's development needed Gest's expertise at least once, when Livingood sought Gest's help in finding an art teacher for Dale Park School. Livingood's insistence on finding the right teacher for the new school seemed tempered, however, by his admonition that the "salary cannot be very large at least for the present, but the position affords great opportunity to help us really develop the School System of a much bigger enterprise than we are planning this year, so please do your best for me and oblige."[18]

Livingood recognized that an elementary school was essential to attracting families. The school would be free to all children residing in Mariemont, for its operations were supported by the Mariemont Company. In its initial home before Dale Park School was completed, the school was housed in a frame building, a kind of one-room schoolhouse in an urban setting.

As the steamy days of June settled on Cincinnati, Livingood made arrangements for his vacation in Canada, writing to Nolen that "my health is such that I must leave *now* and when I shall get back I really don't know." He urged Nolen to meet with Hogan "to go over the situation financially and otherwise" and to discuss with the new general manager, Mirick, the many details demanding the town planner's counsel: construction of roads, sidewalks, and alleys; standards or posts for streetlights; and street numbers and names. By June 1924, Livingood had decided to print a brochure to promote Mariemont, engaging the Russian-American artist, Andrew Avinoff (1884–1948), to illustrate the cover. Livingood visualized the cover as

> a picture as through a window, of the Church, Cemetery, Dale Park, Dana houses, and a few houses on Cherry Lane with a lovely background of the hills behind, and on the back of this cover which we shall use a jacket for future publications there will be a "black print" (only it will be in colors) showing the com-

plete layout of Mariemont, including Westover with many buildings spotted including the layout of "Places." It will make a very interesting-looking cover, with Rest Haven peeping over the top of the front page of the cover. Within we shall have the complete story of Mariemont, historical, as well as the possibilities of the Town, method of Government, control, restrictions, etc., with reproductions of the various Architects' plans as submitted.

The brochure, filled with black-and-white illustrations, was to be distributed free of charge to interested parties.[19]

Livingood's brochure, the most important publication to be issued by the Mariemont Company for use in attracting renters and eventual lot purchasers, finally was under way. Nolen earlier had urged a similar project, and Livingood rightly perceived the usefulness it might have during the busy days of construction. When published eventually in 1925, the sixty-four-page brochure was a guidebook rich in illustrations, both photographic and rendered by architects, as well as an account of the village's prehistory, twelve reasons for living in Mariemont, Nolen's philosophy of town planning, Livingood's detailed overview of the new town's advantages, and charts and statistical lists. Entitled *A Descriptive and Pictured Story of Mariemont—a New Town: "A National Exemplar,"* the brochure was punctuated with paragraph headers announcing "Really cheap houses and many small flats," "Town Center is easy of access," or "Mariemont is not mere experiment."[20]

By mid-June, the Mariemont Company had moved away from its integration with Thomas Emery's Sons by revamping its letterhead, dropping the Emerys' office address at 115 East Fourth Street, Cincinnati, and noting its new and separate location at 1 Baker Court.[21] General Manager Mirick expected all correspondence with Nolen and the architects regarding Mariemont to be channeled through him at the new address, yet communications still made their way to the field headquarters in the Ferris house or to the landscape architect's office, frustrating Mirick's hoped-for control. Keeping artistic decision making to himself where Livingood's approval was not necessary, Nolen carefully guided those who turned to him for advice, giving wise counsel. For example, the young resident landscape architect, Whitney, fretted over the color of stone to be used for the concourse, and Nolen's response allayed his fears: "If there is no need for an immediate decision regarding the stone wall at the Concourse, I should like to

A Descriptive and Pictured Story of
—MARIEMONT—
A New Town

"A National Exemplar"

Mariemont's primary promotional brochure, *A Descriptive and Pictured Story of Marie-mont—a New Town,* published in 1925, was written by Charles Livingood and John Nolen, with the cover illustration by Andrew Avinoff (1884–1948).

leave the matter open until my next visit to Mariemont the latter part of this month. My opinion now, and Mr. Foster concurs, is that the local quarry stone as it comes will be satisfactory, the pergola to be some shade of brown."[22]

As Livingood and Nolen had expected, 1924 sparkled with construction activity as fourteen architects, not counting Jallade and his church already under way in 1923, launched their assigned buildings. Livingood confirmed their assignments and listed them among twenty-one who were commissioned to design buildings. He also determined, probably with Nolen, the types of building materials (brick, wood, stucco, and stone) to predominate in each section where unsold lots were set aside for private homes. An additional assignment listed on a colored chart the architectural groupings and the comment, "Groups having the same color should have the same general architectural characteristics."[23]

Mariemont in 1924 was an anthill of energy, including the church site, where Louis Eugene Jallade (1876–1957), New York architect, translated his plans into the Norman-style stone edifice recollecting innumerable English parish churches. Born in Montreal, Quebec, Jallade had been educated in New York and Paris and had attended the École des Beaux-Arts in 1901–3. With the Boston firm of Allan & Collins, he supervised construction of the Union Theological Seminary, New York, in 1906. After he began his own private practice that year, his designs for churches, temples, clubs, and hotels demonstrated his eclecticism and keen ability to replicate earlier styles. He was selected by Mrs. Emery to plan the Army-Navy YMCA donated by her to the City of Newport and dedicated in 1911. Known to both Livingood and Mary Emery, he was forty-seven when chosen to plan the first building for the new town. Nolen did not suggest Jallade on his list of proposed architects in 1922, but Livingood included him on his first roll prepared in December 1922.

During Jallade's initial inspection of Mariemont on August 1, 1923, he walked around the hillock abutting the pioneer cemetery, the setting for his church. The surrounding terrain was wooded and hilly, with just a bare skeleton of Nolen's layout evident in the surrounding streets and utilities. Before the groundbreaking on November 12, 1923, Jallade traveled through the English countryside absorbing the look of Norman churches that would determine the character of the nondenominational chapel he would create in Ohio. Throughout 1924 and 1925, the stonemasons under Cincinnati craftsman Otto Kadon worked slowly but expertly to cut and cement the stones for nave and side-aisle sections of the 295-seat church. Jallade understood Livingood's desire to create a centerpiece for his village: picturesque, rooted in the past, mellow, and lichen covered. Livingood's intention to secure old roof stones from England was made known to Nolen and Raymond Unwin, but nothing came of it until the summer of 1926, when Jallade hunted the Cotswolds for the proper, aged stones for the church roof.[24] By this time, the church structure was essentially complete except for its roof, and the first service was held within it on July 11.

A page from *Gentleman's Magazine*, 1795, illustrates the tithe barn at Calcot, near Tetbury, England, and its foundation stone, dated 1300. Roof stones from this medieval building were used to complete the Mariemont Memorial Church designed by Louis E. Jallade.

Little did the Cistercian monks of Kingswood Abbey realize that their tithe barn at Calcot, not far from Tetbury, Gloucestershire, would lose most of its roof to a midwestern American church centuries after they had laid the cornerstone in 1300. Nor do many visitors to Mariemont, while viewing what seems to be a transplanted English-Norman church, recognize the stones on the purposely sagging roof as authentically medieval. Writing for the *Cincinnati Enquirer* and awed by the roof's antiquity, a reporter coupled his description of the tithe barn and its history with an illustration of it from an eighteenth-century rendering.

> The church, when finished, will be, throughout, one of the most remarkable pieces of architecture in America, and of all its many unusual features the roof is most interesting, probably one of the oldest roofs in the world and by hundreds of years the oldest in America. To enhance the medieval architectural style of the church and to bring to it added atmosphere of true antiquity, Charles J. Livingood, President of the Mariemont Company, has brought from England the roof of a building which once belonged to the Cistercian monks.[25]

Calcot tithe barn, near Tetbury, England, source of the roof stones for Mariemont Memorial Church, photographed in 1988.

Jallade sought in the summer of 1926 what others had never found, authentic roof stones, finally locating them at Calcot. Jallade's hunt through the Cotswolds, visiting the towns of Malmesbury, Tetbury, and Gloucester, brought him to Calcot farm. A winter storm preceding Jallade's summer visit in 1926 had damaged the roof of the medieval tithe barn, and the owner willingly sold a large section of roof after the architect explained his project, a church for the new town of Mariemont. The barn's roof stones are rectangles of various sizes (most are 5 by 12 inches), each pierced with one or two holes for hanging on pegs inserted in the roof's trusses. Locking over each other like scales when installed, the roof is impervious to rain and the elements. Moss and lichen cover the stones, adding the appearance of antiquity so relished by Livingood and Jallade.[26]

Romantic allure attached itself not only to the roof, but to the design of the edifice as well. Published reports on the Calcot tithe barn also likened Jallade's church to the Saint Giles parish church at Stoke Poges, between London and Oxford, made famous by Thomas Gray's immortal "Elegy in a Country Church Yard." The Norman-style architecture used by Jallade, however, derives from dozens of churches built in the twelfth and thirteenth centuries and dotted across the south and west of England. It does not replicate the Stoke Poges church. Norman influence is reflected in such details as Mariemont's squat and crenelated tower with its flèche, the pointed-arch windows with lead tracery, and the sawtooth motif encircling the door at the east end. Heavy oak trusses and whitewashed walls distinguish the simple interior. A tiny wooden porch leads into the nave at the church's northeast corner, while a quaint lich gate introduces the path up the hill from Wooster Pike to the cemetery and church.

Mariemont's first constructed housing was Richard Dana's two-story apartments in the Dale Park district. Begun in 1924, they inaugurated the so-called wage earners' residences that Livingood so anxiously sought to complete and rent. Richard Henry Dana Jr. (1879–1933), New York architect, belonged to a well-known literary family. His ability to adapt the Georgian style, with its pedimented roofs, red brick, and shuttered windows, appealed to Nolen when he first suggested his services to Livingood in 1922. Dana understood from the start that Livingood wanted economies in construction and in the apartments themselves. Most apartments in the rank of Dana's buildings have five rooms. The

Interior of the Mariemont Memorial Church nearing completion in September 1925. Modeled after English-Norman parish churches, c. 1200–1300, the nondenominational church was the first building under construction in the new town.

Mariemont Company's brochure described them as "small . . . cozy . . . home-like . . . very compactly arranged."

Balanced and symmetrical, the Georgian-style façade and plan of the Mariemont school was designed by the Cincinnati firm of Fechheimer, Ihorst, & McCoy; building began on April 25, 1924. The school's style echoes that of the Dana apartments across Chestnut Street, the main east-west axis designed by Nolen to bisect the Dale Park district. The Mariemont school's principal architect was Abraham Lincoln Fechheimer (1876–1954), member of a prominent Cincinnati family. He had been born deaf and had earned a degree in architecture from Columbia University in 1894 and a diploma from the École des Beaux-Arts, Paris, in 1904. After working in Chicago and Cincinnati, he had associated with Benjamin L. Ihorst and P. L. McCoy, both Cincinnati architects. Fechheimer's two-story, red brick building breaks no new aesthetic

Dale Park School (*left*) and townhouses by New York City architect Richard H. Dana Jr. border Chestnut Street. The columns and pediment of a two-story apartment building designed by Cincinnati architect Charles Cellarius close the vista photographed in 1931.

Dale Park School, designed by Cincinnati architect A. Lincoln Fechheimer and begun in 1924, was operated by the Mariemont Company for residents' children in the elementary grades. In the first years after its opening, three hundred children in ten classrooms were taught by teachers employed by the company.

ground, but harmoniously blends into its setting and English village backdrop. In this neighborhood school, operated privately by the Mariemont Company, children in kindergarten through the eighth grade were offered free education.

Starts were made on May 5 and 8, 1924, on two more Dale Park sites, the paired, three-story apartment buildings adjacent to the neighborhood's square, followed by group housing at the northwestern gateway to the village. The Boston firm of Ripley & LeBoutillier designed the former, and New York's Clinton Mackenzie developed plans for the latter. Hubert G. Ripley (1869–1942) was trained at the Massachusetts Institute of Technology, graduated in 1890, and worked on the Columbian Exposition in Chicago in 1892. A talented draftsman and artist, Ripley was retained originally by Livingood in 1921 and 1922 to prepare a set of renderings illustrating the neoclassical buildings and certain residential units in the proposed village of Mariemont. These imaginative, facile drawings were reproduced frequently in various periodicals. Addison B. LeBoutillier (1879–1951) joined Ripley's practice in 1919. Their Mariemont commission required the linkage of commercial shops on the ground floor with two floors of small apartments above in two brick buildings, providing residents with convenient access to marketing and services. While many older city neighborhoods offered similar commercial-residential combinations where owners or renters lived above the shops, Ripley and Livingood submerged the commercial ground floor into the building's mass. The shops do not stand out from the upper floors, having no special lighting or blatant signage.

Livingood did not intend the Dale Park square, with its "few shops about the village church, the nucleus of one of the many neighborhood centers," to compete with the larger town center, "for here will be found the throbbing, busy life of the community."[27] The town center, according to Livingood, was to be filled with fifty shops, a theater, and an inn, all clustered in half-timbered structures near the town hall, public library, and post office. None of these was realized on the level imagined by Livingood and Nolen. A Cincinnati firm, Joseph Steinkamp & Brother, which had long associations with the Emery interests, drew plans for an immense block that echoed The Rows of Chester, England. The Tudor-style structure and arcade were approved by the noted Paul P. Cret, hired earlier as a consultant to the Mariemont Company for public buildings, but Steinkamp's grandiose concept, handsome as it is, stretched beyond the ultimate abilities of the Mariemont Company and was never built. Only the illustration in the company's promotional brochure suggests the architect's ill-fated intention.

A large apartment building and group houses containing thirty units along Murray Avenue and Beech Street were begun on May 8, closing the northwest corner of the Dale Park section and forming a sort of gateway to the community. The architect was Clinton Mackenzie (1872–1940) of New York City. Educated at Stevens Institute of Technology, Columbia University, and the École des Beaux-Arts, his association with Nolen at Kingsport, Tennessee, made him a likely candidate to be one of Mariemont's architects. He was among the first group of designers suggested by Nolen to Livingood in 1922 and "was chosen because of his countrywide reputation in constructing reasonably-priced group housing."[28] Mackenzie styled his three-story apartment building with Tudor Revival motifs, a half-timbered façade, and stuccoed exterior walls. Only the Ripley & LeBoutillier structures equal it in number of floors. Mackenzie's steeply roofed, two-story group houses combine, somewhat unhappily, surfaces of brick and stone. Some of these four-family units are unattractive rectangles, barracks-like, with wood siding. At the rear of the apartment building, Nolen set aside a large area for "allotment gardens," providing space for home gardeners. In advertisements, the Mariemont Company touted the gardens as lending "a touch of country" to the apartments' location."[29]

Charles F. Cellarius (1891–1973) enjoyed special status with the Mariemont Company from the time he was selected to design a rank of flats on Beech Street and the village's fire and police station. Although his obituary called him the "supervising architect of Mariemont," no doubt because of his semiofficial role in reviewing contractors' plans for the village long after the Mariemont Company had ceased its operations, he is listed as "Resident Architect" in promotional materials in 1925.[30] Cellarius graduated from Massachusetts Institute of Technology and Yale University before opening his office in Cincinnati after World War I. His specialty was Georgian Revival, or "Colonial"-style architecture, as a newspaper reporter labeled it. He exploited this specialty in numerous academic buildings for Berea College, Ohio State University, and Miami University in Oxford, Ohio. His fire and police station for Mariemont, a kind of Hansel and Gretel cottage, was begun on June 12, 1924, along with thirty-one residences designed either as two-family units or four-family townhouses. Verandas and pillared porticos distinguish the Saint Louis flats, as the former were called, while the townhouses resemble the Dana apartments in their uncomplicated classical balance and placement on the lots.

The Mariemont Company broke ground on June 12, 1924, for forty-seven units bordering both sides of Maple Street, an interior, narrow roadway hemmed in by the Dana and Gilchrist houses on adjacent streets to the north and south. Nolen conceived of Maple Street as quiet and sheltered. The Cincinnati architectural firm of Kruckemeyer & Strong was assigned this part of the housing project. Edward H. Kruckemeyer (1886–1965) had been educated at Cincinnati's Ohio Mechanics Institute, the University of Michigan, and the Massachusetts Institute of Technology. He first worked with the Cincinnati

MARIEMONT · CINCINNATI · DISTRICT · OHIO · AP.

TORES AND GROUP HOUSING RIPLEY AND LE BOUTILLIER ARCHITECTS · BOSTON MA

The Ripley & LeBoutillier apartments and stores were placed at the old town square to form a shopping and residential center for the Dale Park neighborhood. In this drawing by Hubert G. Ripley, done in 1922 or 1923, gabled roofs, well-proportioned fenestration, and fine brick masonry distinguish these buildings, which face a small park and fountain.

Although the Mariemont Company intended in 1924 to erect this block of shops, offices, and apartments at the town center as "the principal structure in the village," the building designed by Joseph G. Steinkamp & Brother, Cincinnati architects, was never built. Paul P. Cret, the well-known Philadelphia architect hired by Charles Livingood as consultant for public buildings in Mariemont, lent his name to Steinkamp's project but was not responsible for its design.

Group houses on Beech Street, begun in 1924, were designed by Clinton Mackenzie, a New York architect, who had worked with John Nolen at Kingsport, Tennessee, before his Mariemont commission. Rounded arches, porches, setbacks, and changing roof heights provide variety to the Mackenzie houses.

At the northwest edge of Mariemont, the broad and angled façade of stucco, stone, and half timber of the three-story apartment building designed by Clinton Mackenzie formed an impressive entrance to the village at this point. Only the paired apartment buildings of Ripley & LeBoutillier vied with it in size.

firm of Garber & Woodward and joined with Charles R. Strong (1890–1968) in 1915 after traveling with him in Europe during the prior year. The two architects knew each other from their studies at MIT, where Strong also graduated in 1911. Their collaboration produced "a little village all to itself," as the Mariemont Company's brochure stated, with "no stiff curbs and glaring sidewalks to spoil its charm as a village street." Kruckemeyer & Strong's rather large rooms attracted the attention of renters, and their reliance on an old architectural device, a forced perspective, registered favorably with Nolen and Livingood.

The architects succeeded in drafting "an architectural scheme when the space is such that one cannot back off far enough to take in the effect at a comprehensive glance. To see this group, as a whole, it must be viewed endwise so to speak. So the architects resorted to an illusion as old as the Egyptian Temple of Karnack; they exaggerated the perspective, giving the idea that the street was somewhat longer than it really is." Kruckemeyer decreased the setbacks of each building along Maple Street, with front yards gradually diminishing by about

Pillars, porches, and the occasional pediments form impressive façades for the so-called Saint Louis flats designed by Charles Cellarius and begun in 1924. These two-story build-ings contained two or four units each. Metal roofs for residences were not commonly em-ployed by other architects in the Cincinnati area.

six feet from east to west.[31] This architectural subtlety enhanced Nolen's plan for the Dale Park section, endorsing Livingood's persistent efforts to create a contained, cozy English village.

The first construction start outside the Dale Park section occurred on June 23, 1924, with a group of twelve freestanding single and two-family houses, strongly echoing the whitewashed residences at Letchworth, with hints of C. F. Voysey's house at Bedford Park, London. The two-story brick houses by one of Philadelphia's finest architects, Robert R. McGoodwin (1886–1967), were set in a "close" or cul-de-sac, called Albert Place, named for the Emery's youngest son. Peaked roofs, narrow windows emphasizing the verticality of the houses, and a lack of any ornamentation distinguish these buildings. A service lane behind

Albert Place, insistently recommended by McGoodwin, removed garages and trash collecting to the rear and out of sight from the main approach.

McGoodwin had graduated from the University of Pennsylvania with bachelor's and master's degrees, traveled and studied in Rome and Paris in 1907–9, and entered practice with Horace Trumbauer in Philadelphia. Livingood selected McGoodwin in 1922 along with other architects from four major cities (Boston, Cincinnati, New York, and Philadelphia), who would be involved in the new community. Although Nolen did not include him on his initial list, McGoodwin's known appreciation of the English garden city model may have appealed to the Mariemont Company president, even as other Philadelphia architects, such as Gilchrist and Ziegler, were sought for Livingood's own reasons. By approving construction for the McGoodwin group, Livingood moved out

Townhouses on Maple Street, designed by Cincinnati architects Kruckemeyer & Strong and begun in 1924, were photographed shortly after their completion by the noted photographer, Nancy Ford Cones, a member of the Pictorialist movement in American photographic history. Her architectural studies of Mariemont in the late 1920s were invested with a rich atmosphere.

Houses under construction on Albert Place, a cul-de-sac named for Mary and Thomas J. Emery's younger son. Philadelphia architect Robert R. McGoodwin designed the houses and provided them with a rear lane, out of sight from the street, for service and garage access.

from the wage earners' neighborhood to provide the first of several pocket or satellite areas that would anchor Mariemont across its width and depth. Four such satellites were planned, providing evidence to prospective lot purchasers that the development was under way in all its parts.

A few days after McGoodwin's group began, "Small English houses," as Livingood called them, were under construction by June 27 across from Jallade's church on Oak Street. Charles W. Short (1884–1954), their architect, was an ardent Anglophile and a dedicated student of English architecture who maintained offices in Cincinnati, primarily, but also in New York and London. He worked in the office of Ralph Adams Cram in Boston and with the U.S. Department of Labor during World War I. By the 1920s he was in practice in Cincinnati. The Mariemont Company, feeling the burden of maintaining a large labor force of carpenters, masons, plumbers, and roofers to undertake all of the construction in 1924 except the church and school, opted to bring in an outside contractor for the Short houses. Stucco and fieldstone, half-timbering on second floor façades, deeply recessed windows, and curiously flaring roofs define Short's group of four buildings that close the western edge of the church lawn.[32]

One of McGoodwin's Philadelphia colleagues, Edmund B. Gilchrist (1885–1953), adapted the Philadelphia row house he knew so well to his thirty-nine units along the northern border of Mariemont. Begun on July 8, 1924, Gilchrist's two- and three-story houses have varying setbacks. The warm red brick in Flemish bond pattern is articulated by heavy wood cornices at the gutter line, shuttered six-over-six windows, and tiny entrance porches. Gilchrist spoke of the difficulty in designing his assigned group, hoping he would not "string his houses out like a train of cars."[33] The Gilchrist group's elegant and refined Georgian Revival style, harking back to influences abounding on the eastern seaboard, is the most sophisticated architectural expression among Mariemont

Charles W. Short, Cincinnati architect and ardent Anglophile who once maintained an office in London, planned a group of four houses on Oak Street. Begun in 1924, the houses with half-timbered, stucco, and stone façades provided the desired effect in their position facing the church.

Several commissioned architects produced elevation drawings in pen or pencil showing the placement of their buildings on Mariemont streets. Edmund B. Gilchrist drafted this vignette of the townhouses that were begun in 1924 and modeled after eighteenth-century row houses in his native Philadelphia.

Only a few original drawings by architects for Mariemont Company commissions, like this one by Edmund B. Gilchrist, exist. American architects in the 1920s usually were experienced in rendering finished drawings for their clients, and Mariemont's architects were no exception.

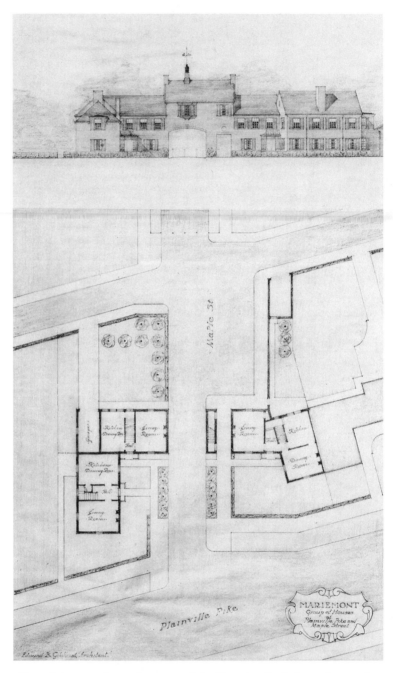

One of the most interesting parts of the Georgian Revival townhouses designed by Edmund B. Gilchrist is the Honeymoon Cottage, a small apartment built over the archway of Maple Street.

Townhouses by Edmund B. Gilchrist were built along Plainville Road and on Murray Avenue, the northern boundary of Mariemont. In 1925, they were nearing completion.

commissions in the 1920s. It has none of the quaintness or rural English village character Livingood sought, but recollects the Georgian townhouses of London's squares or Philadelphia's closely bunched blocks of eighteenth-century residences. Gilchrist's practice seldom left the Philadelphia area, where he had studied at Drexel University and the University of Pennsylvania before working with Horace Trumbauer and Wilson Eyre. His own practice was established in 1911, and in 1922 Livingood listed him among the architects he would sponsor.

At the northeastern extremity of Mariemont, where the lowlands met the higher elevations of Indian Hill, a suburb of multiacre estates that developed about the same time as Mrs. Emery's new town, the hospital was under way by July 1924. It was designed by the prestigious Cincinnati firm of Samuel Hannaford & Sons and abuts Resthaven. The hospital occupies the highest point in the town. A four-story brick, stone, and concrete structure, the symmetrical

Mariemont Hospital, begun in 1924, overlooked Mariemont from a hill near the Resthaven section of the village. Designed by the Cincinnati firm of Samuel Hannaford & Sons, its imposing and symmetrical façade was later extended and partially hidden. The cupola is a recurring element in Mariemont's public buildings.

façade was to be balanced by two wings that were built years later. Expectations exceeded accomplishments with the hospital, for its service to Mariemont and the surrounding eastern suburbs did not materialize until 1942. Hannaford's cupola, a Georgian-style motif similar to that decorating the roof of Dale Park School, is the only eye-catching element in the otherwise restrained, conservative appearance of the building.

Samuel H. Hannaford (1835–1911), a contemporary of Thomas J. Emery, was born in Devonshire, England, and emigrated to the United States in 1844. He was educated in Cincinnati's public schools and formed an architectural partnership with Edwin Anderson in 1858. By 1870, he was independent, attracting his two sons, Harvey Eldredge and Charles Edward, to join him. They became full partners by 1887. Hannaford's important buildings in Cincinnati before 1900 were Victorian expressions, ponderous and medieval looking, quite unlike the neoclassicism displayed in his Mariemont Hospital. The firm's work for the

Emery real estate interests was extensive, and Samuel Hannaford is remembered as the architect of Mary and Thomas Emery's Cincinnati residence, Edgecliffe. Hannaford also designed the Palace and Emery Hotels and the Saint Paul Building, among others in Cincinnati, for Thomas J. and John J. Emery.

The final group housing in the Dale Park section was entrusted to the third, and last, Philadelphia architect to be employed in Mariemont, Carl A. Ziegler (1878–1952). He had studied at the University of Pennsylvania and formed a practice with Herman Duhring and Brogniard Okie in 1899. Ziegler worked independently when he undertook the Mariemont commission on August 5, 1924, for the handsome row of eight houses facing the Ripley & LeBoutillier buildings on Chestnut Street. Ziegler's relatively spacious interiors improved on those in neighboring buildings, and this became a factor in advertising these units, originally rented by the Mariemont Company. Heavy stone chimneys

The last group housing in the Dale Park section, begun in 1924, was a row of eight units by Carl A. Ziegler, Philadelphia architect. Sturdy chimneys, stuccoed walls, narrow windows, and steeply pitched roofs suggested the appearance of Cotswold farmhouses. Like all other houses or apartments in the Dale Park section, these were built initially to rent.

and steeply pitched roofs dominate the streetside and offer additional variation in architectural styles in Dale Park.

When Mariemont was launched, there were only a few American architectural firms headed by women. One of these rarities was the Boston office of Lois L. Howe (1864–1964) and Eleanor Manning (1884–1973). Both were graduates of the Massachusetts Institute of Technology, the trainer of many of the Mariemont architects. Howe was on her own from 1896 to 1912, and in 1913 Manning joined her. Manning was the leader of the two architects in advocating the garden city model for the United States.[34] This advocacy and their many commissions in New England for private residences as well as public-use buildings recommended them to Nolen. They were among the six Boston firms proposed by Nolen and one of two ultimately selected by Livingood in 1922.

Howe & Manning were commissioned to execute designs for nine buildings (eleven residences) on Denny Place, a charming close across from Dogwood Park's playing field and woods. Denny Place was intended by Livingood as a special group of homes for artists. His insistence on English village quaintness is fully realized in the fieldstone exterior walls, the pedimented classical doorways, and the imposing placement of the homes around a central green. The close captures some of the character of England's Blaise Hamlet, near Bristol, an eighteenth-century group of cottages facing a green and one of the first planned communities in England. Howe & Manning paired their nine buildings so that double residences match each other; single dwellings in stucco are the close's bookends. By today's standards of construction, the materials are luxurious. Livingood's economic hierarchy for renters and owners clearly meant Denny Place (named for Mrs. Emery's mother and using her maiden name) for families with higher incomes than those in the Dale Park section. The Mariemont Company intended the Denny Place houses "as guide posts." The buildings, along with those on Albert Place and Sheldon Close, were "nucleii [sic] to show what the ultimate trend of development in their respective regions would be."[35]

Livingood called on two well-known Cincinnati architects to design small, individual houses to anchor the western extremity of the village's original boundary. Twelve structures were planned to be erected in a string stretching along Wooster Pike and around Linden Place, a cul-de-sac, by Alfred O. Elzner

The Boston architectural firm headed by two women, Lois L. Howe and Eleanor Manning, was commissioned to design a group of houses for Denny Place, one of three areas south of Wooster Pike where the Mariemont Company elected to show desirable building styles to prospective home builders. Using stone native to the region, the houses were the largest single-family dwellings constructed by the Mariemont Company.

(1862–1933) and George M. Anderson (1869–1916). Elzner had received art instruction from Cincinnati's most notable painter, Frank Duveneck, before studying at Ohio Mechanics Institute and the Massachusetts Institute of Technology. In 1885, he was associated with H. H. Richardson in Boston and acted as superintendent for construction of Richardson's Chamber of Commerce building, Cincinnati. About 1896 he and George Anderson joined in partnership. Their most important and renowned commission was the Ingalls Building, regarded as the first reinforced concrete "skyscraper." Other clients included many socially prominent Cincinnatians, partly because of Anderson's heritage as the son of Larz Anderson and Emma Mendenhall. He had studied at Columbia University and the École des Beaux-Arts, Paris, and with Louis Comfort Tiffany in New York.

Anderson's sophisticated Beaux-Arts style and Elzner's modified Victorianism are not apparent in the simple frame, two-story bungalows in Mariemont begun on October 31, 1924. Livingood apparently considered these houses as

The "Frame Cottages" advertised in 1924 on the large sign in front of nearly finished houses were unusually simple residences on Wooster Pike, near the western entrance to the village. Elzner & Anderson, Cincinnati architects, provided communal garages to be shared by the residents.

models for subsequent homes in the neighborhood, and as early as 1922 he had proposed the two architects for the pensioners' cottages in the Resthaven section. Economy of materials and inexpensive construction costs guided Livingood's appointment of the two architects for the Linden Place houses.[36]

In the extreme northeast section of Mariemont, the last project to be initiated in 1924 began with the highest hopes but ended a failure. Mrs. Emery intended to create a small portion of the village as a retirement neighborhood of cottages for pensioners, a working farm, gardens, and a nursery to provide trees and plants for landscaping the new town. In Resthaven, Mary Emery hoped "to retire superannuated employees on a small pension for life," living in "a colony of small houses gathered around the farm group and an allotment garden as a nucleus, where employees of the various Emery interests grown old in service may have a comfortable home amid pleasant surroundings for the remainder of their lives."[37]

A bright, young architect from New York, Hubert E. Reeves, aggressively pursued the Resthaven commission and won Livingood's approval, a fact he mentioned to Nolen. Reeves developed an ensemble of buildings that would appeal to any gentleman farmer. The barn and connecting stalls, the dairy room, and the tenant's cottage were recognized as part of a suburb, not a rustic agricultural station in the country but one that needed pristine maintenance. Although this part of Mariemont was decidedly rural when Mrs. Emery purchased it and chickens and cows were raised at Resthaven along with crops in the adjoining fields, the farm's original appearance and its proposed service as a retirement community complete with tiny cottages evaporated within five years. In February 1929, the acres surrounding the barn and allocated for pensioners were divided into residential lots for private purchasers and sold by the Mariemont Company.[38] The nursery and greenhouse disappeared, and the pensioners' cottages were never built. Only Resthaven barn remained intact. Its elegant architectural integrity eventually was compromised when it became a

Resthaven barn and farmer's cottage (at *far right*) were part of the plan that included small homes for Emery estate pensioners. Designed by a young architect from New York, Hubert E. Reeves, Resthaven was the last construction project in 1924. The pensioners' cottages were never built.

parking lot for trucks and tractors as well as the headquarters for the village's maintenance department.

Mary Emery's missing presence during Mariemont's construction in 1924, according to the paucity of news accounts or records, must not be misread. She received frequent reports from Livingood on the new town's progress and trusted his executive abilities. Her health was poor, and she continued to reside in Newport for half the year. And, although the family fortune was based on housing and land ownership, Mary's focus during her married years and as a widow never was entrepreneurial. She was deeply committed to the project and intrigued by its progress, of course, but for several reasons she had little to do with the day-to-day operation. This was left to Livingood. Mariemont was but one of her many philanthropies.

The long reach of Livingood, vacationing in Quebec during July, was felt in lengthy letters with queries and commands for Mariemont's progress. From his new summer home at Pointe-a-Pic, called Penteaves, where he was "obliged to take a complete rest" under doctor's orders, he wrote to Nolen about the program for the remaining months of 1924. Nolen's outline for his part included drawing up sales plat maps, preparing planting lists and plans for the streets and public areas, drafting deed restrictions, consulting with the architects (naming only Paul P. Cret), developing a policy statement for Mariemont's administration, drafting plans for Westover (the industrial section), and making bi-monthly field visits to Mariemont for consultation.[39] Livingood's response deferred Nolen's work on some points and pushed for others. The Mariemont Company, he noted, would develop its own sales plats. A sales and rental agent, William A. Hall, was retained for this purpose. Livingood reinforced his role, certainly well recognized by Nolen, of controlling the architects. Livingood admitted that the architects "are carrying out my definite wishes. So please forgive me if I overstep now and then. I have been on the ground daily for a number of months, and have long had a picture in mind of how the buildings will look if properly placed according to their structure."[40]

In the same letter, Livingood criticized himself for approving the "perhaps foolish house-over-the-street by Gilchrist with three posts and a chain blocking the entrance to Maple Street." This was the Honeymoon Apartment, a tiny residence arching over a narrow roadway, charmingly capped with a cupola. He urged a delay with Nolen in determining the "social welfare organization" in 1924, meaning a scheme for the governance of the village after the Mariemont Company ceased its control. He wanted Nolen's advice, however, because of his experience in "the form of deeds, restrictions, re-purchase clause, etc. about which I have a lot of data, although see how badly it is all working out at Forest Hills." Livingood was uneasy with any administrative responsibility or duty that pressed him beyond a time schedule he concocted. Thus, he deferred responsibilities on more than one occasion. His delays and inaction were costly errors soon felt by Mrs. Emery's purse. Lengthy vacations or rest cures were not conducive to good management, but Livingood seemed oblivious.

The closing paragraphs in Livingood's letter of July 12, 1924, recorded the progress in growing nursery stock. More than eighty thousand trees, shrubs, and plants had been planted, he noted, and the "imaginative, good sense and a high ideal" in Whitney's efforts improved Dogwood Park. He also touched on the work of three architects.

The first was Paul P. Cret (1876–1945), commissioned by Livingood to approve designs for the town center and public buildings. Cret lent his name to the illustration of the Steinkamp theater block in the Mariemont Company's promotional brochure. Livingood's remarks to Nolen defended his commitment to architectural styles in keeping with Mariemont's resemblance to an English village. "I have already submitted to Mr. Paul P. Cret the design for the Village Inn, on that point at the Town center—a fine piece of work by my friends, Zettel and Rapp, old English in style but very simple, and he approves, after some modification, although I pointed out that he was thereby giving the keynote to the Town center development. Frankly I see no other style possible. Colonial is out of the question where there are so many stores and a theatre involved." Steinkamp's three-story arcaded building in half-timbered style, reminiscent of the commercial center of Chester, England, was the most monumental structure conceived for the new town. Never built, it was as unrealized as the town hall that was first suggested in illustrations by Hubert Ripley. Livingood concluded,

> When it comes to the Town hall, which is not urgent, I shall in a like manner submit to [Cret] the suggestions by the architect selected, Mr. Henry O. Milliken, a distant relative of Mrs. Emery's, in whom she is very much interested.

The Mariemont Inn, as drawn by Cincinnati architects Zettel & Rapp, was designed in the Tudor vernacular as a large V-shaped building of shops and hotel rooms. Begun in 1925, it never attained the full dimensions indicated in the drawing. However, the inn remains the dominant structure on the town square.

> I know that he does not lean towards the Colonial, but have not approved any design by him. Mr. Cret was lately in consultation at my suggestion with Mr. Jallade, whose plans and elevations for the English Norman stone church now under erection, he approves in every particular. So you see we are making progress.

Nolen appeared in Mariemont for a three-day inspection on July 17–19, to see firsthand the seven construction sites begun since his last visit in May. The summer heat and humidity only intensified the effervescence evident everywhere as the laborers swarmed over grading equipment and the skeletal streets laid out by Nolen. General Manager Mirick had tried to discourage Nolen's visit, noting in a telegram quite correctly that "the only one who can make decisions is not here and I do not know just when he will be here."[41] Livingood, the decision maker, returned briefly to Cincinnati at the end of the month but too late to encounter Nolen. Before he left again for his summer home in Canada in early August, he expressed to Nolen his concerns about the concourse, Philip Foster's splendid pergola and overlook across the Little Miami

River. Livingood wanted the embankment submerged, disagreed with Nolen's suggestion for a fence to protect walkers from slipping over the precipice, and pumped up his hope for this "wonderful view" to the distant blue-gray hills. Livingood wrote that the concourse was "to be one of the show places in the United States, if I am a judge. I had no idea myself how beautiful the Little Miami Valley is in mid-summer. This Concourse will be unique—it will be the center of the greatest gatherings and towards evening will be a delightful spot for the inhabitants to congregate, for it has this great advantage—the sun does *not* set in the eyes of the visitor."[42]

Mid-August brought more fussing from Livingood about the concourse. "I should make it clear that to my mind, and I have thought of this hundreds of times," emphasized Livingood in a letter to Nolen, that he expected a "smooth lawn (with some planting of course) upon which tired men and women, after their day's work can lie full length away from the noise and bustle of the concourse which will be full of people, especially children."[43] He wanted Nolen to give advice on the finish of the concourse wall, "a practical matter not architecture," and worried over the materials used for the pergola's columns. Usually, Livingood's letters covered many topics, and this one was no exception, for he pleaded for Nolen's instructions for street lighting and told him that a model apartment in the Dana group was completely furnished "at a cost of about $550.00 for a five-roomed house." He ended the same letter, signing himself as "Your sick friend," with comments on two architects whose buildings were not yet under way.

> When on the spot please look over our assorted piles of newly cut timbers, only don't take any of my hickory (for which I have an especial use) nor too much of the oak, as architects such as Atterbury are counting on this for timbered work on their English houses; also Mr. Jackson, no doubt, whose houses we may start this Fall. We were all enamored of his designs, and Atterbury's layout is simply lovely. He by-the-way is questioning still whether a Buick can make a turn at the round end of Sheldon Place. We may have to let him enlarge the radius.

Among the articles on Mariemont published in 1924, none attracted a wider audience, especially away from Cincinnati, than one published in the *New York Times Magazine* on August 24, 1924.[44] Illustrated with Hubert Ripley's imagi-

John Nolen's associate, Philip W. Foster, designed a graceful stone and wood arc to over-look the bluffs above the Little Miami River valley. The concourse at the southern edge of Mariemont punctuates the end of Center Street, one of the major axes in the village. It was eventually planted with wisteria.

native and romantic renderings, the author spread an abbreviated history of a city before the reader and presciently addressed the growing problem of traffic congestion, inadequate roads, and the automobile's effect on cities. His assessment of Mariemont's promise, however, recognized its virtues and the vices of suburban developments without "a real community scheme." The *New York Times* writer lauded Mariemont as "a consistent and well-thought-out under-taking in the way of a town deliberately planned with an eye to the present and the future."

Nolen is recognized in the well-written article as "the planner of Mariemont" and even quoted, while Livingood is acknowledged only in the concluding paragraph. This he probably regarded as a slight, for he wrote to Nolen, "Did you ever read anything more prosy and uninspired than the article on Mariemont which *finally* appears in N. Y. Sunday Times of the 24th." In that same letter he bemoaned his health and labor troubles, stating that "we may see the Mariemont project dropped entirely." Contrary to Livingood's opinion, Nolen liked the article and wrote to its author on August 27, "My congratulations on the excellent form in which you have presented 'The City Set at the Crossroads.' It is a fresh, accurate, and interesting story."[45]

In his August 26 letter to Nolen, Livingood turned earnestly to the publication of the Mariemont Company's brochure, which would serve as the village's principal promotion vehicle. He urged Nolen to read over the text he had written for the brochure and asked him to write a section. His request initiated many months of nagging before Nolen finally obliged him, but Livingood correctly saw the need to include a statement from the planner of the National Exemplar and hoped to get a "thesis on housing" from him.

Nolen seldom missed an opportunity to write an article for publication. He was a prolific author, preaching the cause of town planning and defending its importance. But reflecting on Livingood's request he demurred tactfully while pointing out the weaknesses in the draft sent to him. His reasoned response noted his questions and criticisms while illustrating, more than Livingood realized, Nolen's knowledge of his field and the practical necessity of how to promote a major planning project. Nolen wondered whether the brochure's message would be "sufficiently interesting." How would the brochure be used? What was its purpose? To whom would it be sent? Nolen proposed "clearness and interest" in its writing, and he thought Livingood was the only author needed. Probably Nolen wanted to distance himself somewhat from the brochure if it was poorly received. "It would be better for you to do it all," he stated.[46]

Nolen then bombarded the draft. "Is it correct to say that Mariemont is simply a real estate development on normal American lines, except that it employs the limited dividend principle? Do you think the reference to the Indians (which you have told very well) is the best way of beginning? It seems to me that the first statement ought to be directly about Mariemont. I should hesitate myself to put into print that municipal and governmental housing schemes in this country have seen their day, considering the present tendency in practically all the other countries of the world." After citing nearly a dozen questions or complaints about the text, Nolen stepped on thin ice by suggesting to Livingood that he consider employing "an experienced writer and publicity man for this kind of a job, one who would be capable of taking your paper and your views and putting them forth in a special way to serve the purpose that you have in mind." Livingood prided himself on his writing abilities. He was not easily dissuaded.

Nolen's arguments were answered one by one in Livingood's response. Although he explained the new brochure's intended audience and its tenor, Livingood did not surrender his authorship. His response indicated the importance he attached to the brochure.

> You ask what the final Brochure is for. To my mind, it is intended not for publicity around Cincinnati (that will come otherwise and through a much simpler folder to be given away in quantities) but first for those who are in earnest about settling there and want to know everything possible to help make up their minds, and secondly, to *answer questions*. This Brochure is being asked for every day. One man is interested in one phase of it, another in another; as it will be presented under headings we will simply have to refer to them in reply. It will have a handsome cover because worth keeping and to maintain the dignity of the project. This cover is being made now in colors by Country Life Press with a sketch showing a view of the Memorial Church and its neighborhood as through a window on the front page, and on the back a full black print with a lot of reading matter for the man who wants a quick picture of the project.
>
> I note your suggestion that a professional writer be employed. I fear this unless it be someone like yourself who understands the subject in addition to being a good writer. See how badly the information furnished the N. Y. "Times" turned out. Newspapers have their own special writers to whom they toss morsels confident that the writer knows what the "Times" public wants. This man, whoever he was, to make space at so much a line gives an *academic* discussion of housing to show his knowledge and then tacks on a few unilluminating details about Mariemont, drawn largely from your facts. Other professional writers I notice merely used our project to exploit cherished opinions, usually sociological. Such is not the purpose of our Brochure. It is to tell the story with enthusiasm, yet with truth to everyone who might possibly be interested. Now I appreciate that this should be done more logically perhaps, and

with greater dignity of style than I can furnish, but what I have to say at least presents the facts in, I trust, readable form. My only doubt is as to the literary value of the composition. Your and Mrs. Emery's corrections have shown me my weaknesses, but I believe that in the main the picture as it will be presented will do.[47]

Livingood urged Nolen in the same letter to write "the chapter that will be of interest to town planners and projectors of similar enterprises." Fay, Spofford & Thorndike's firm were expected to write a summary of public utility installations. Finally, Livingood concluded, Mrs. Emery's opinion coincided with Nolen's that the land had not been purchased cheaply, or at least "it is unwise to say that any of the land was bought cheap." It is clear from this exchange of letters that Livingood, protective of his authorship, expected his brochure to serve as the primary publication extolling the virtues and opportunities of Mariemont while reaching an audience of purchasers and renters.

The starting gun for any significant construction at Mariemont was in Livingood's hand, everyone knew, and his frequent instructions to his manager, George Mirick, were passed along to the next in line in the Mariemont Company's chain of command. By September 12, Livingood felt confident that there was "organization enough to erect buildings as well as complete the construction of Mariemont in general—a matter of several years certainly." He expected to start the foundations for the Howe & Manning houses on Denny Place as well as those for the Mariemont Inn designed by Zettel & Rapp. Construction of the inn was to be undertaken by a general contractor, not the Mariemont Company, because of its steel supports and elaborate plumbing. Mirick was further instructed to begin work on the hospital, a structure of particular concern to Mary Emery, according to Livingood.[48]

Livingood closed with his suggestions on garages and curbing, both details that fascinated him throughout the life of the project. Curbs might restrain the "countrified appearance of Dale Park," he wrote, and sidewalks were to be used sparingly. Garages were to be constructed of stucco and be placed as "a sort of communal garage for [the] neighborhood." He was "still firm in the conviction that in Mariemont garages shall not be placed on prominent locations simply for the publicity, which is what the average builder and filling-station operator wants, no matter how this unsightliness of the automobile business damages a neighborhood. The people will have to come to our garages wherever we see fit to put them. We are not out to make money on them."

September brought visits from Nolen's office staff, with Hale Walker arriving for two days, as did Philip Foster.[49] Landscaping concerns were discussed with the resident landscape architect, J. F. Whitney, who recommended that rapidly growing nursery stock be planted around the group and individual houses and not confined just to public areas. Foster was alarmed by the unsatisfactory grading of certain streets, lanes, and lots. This observation apparently met with Livingood's disapproval, for Mirick chastised Foster's report, especially the third paragraph that was "very distasteful to Mr. Livingood. He does not agree with you at all." Foster wisely recommended staining the concourse superstructure a light brown and not painting "the woodwork white as has been suggested . . . [as] very conspicuous and staring which added to the fact that it is in line with the smoke from the yards below and difficult to paint after once covered with vines makes it impractical." Foster concurred in the need to hide the garages where possible in grouped units and away from the fronts of houses, embracing a cardinal principle of town planning. This advice was followed by Livingood for garages in the Dale Park section, except a few that were entered from the street through the façades of the Ripley & LeBoutillier town houses.

Mariemont's operators celebrated the first occupancy of any living unit when the Carl Lutkehaus family moved into one of the Dana houses on October 1, 1924, just as Livingood returned from an eastern trip and once again shepherded the Mariemont Company brochure toward printing. Nolen was given copies of some of the text along with a sample of the cover illustration by Avinoff, with a reminder that the artist had drawn the scene from Livingood's description. The text was written to appeal to the businessman, he wrote. This was an unusual focus, as the village encouraged wage earners and their families as renters. An impressive slogan approved by Livingood for the brochure and subsequently for the village was Nolen's epithet: A National Exemplar.[50]

The federal-period club house of the Literary Club of Cincinnati, just down Fourth Street from the home of Mr. and Mrs. Charles Phelps Taft (now the Taft Museum) and facing Lytle Park, hosted a dinner and talk by Livingood on November 1. His presentation did not generate the same excitement as had the announcement in April 1922, when Nolen and Livingood had dazzled a

A row of townhouses, begun in 1924 by the Boston firm of Ripley & LeBoutillier, abutted the two apartment buildings they designed for the old town square. Garages opening onto the street were provided for a few units, a rare instance where garages were not hidden on Mariemont Company properties.

Commercial Club meeting with plans and slides featuring the then-secret Mariemont venture. Livingood's lecture, with only a few edits, drew on the lead portion of the manuscript for the Mariemont Company brochure, not off the press until 1925. Livingood recalled to Nolen their appearance together before the Commercial Club, asking "How do you think it looks in print? I read it at the Literary Club standing on the very spot you stood and I thought of you often and wished you were present." Two days later the *Cincinnati Times-Star* indulged Livingood and devoted a full page to his talk, including eight illustrations of the church under construction, the first residents of Mariemont at their front door, and on-site scenes.[51]

This article and others in the press intoned Mary Emery's name with every mention of Mariemont, a not unusual credit considering the financial underpinnings she provided. At this time, correspondence between the director of the art museum and the various art dealers pursuing Mrs. Emery noted her focus on the project (at least, that was their reading of her concern). Director Gest wrote to a dealer that "her absorption in the real estate investment at Mariemont must be very positive at this time."[52] But aside from Mrs. Emery's financial commitment to the project and endorsement of Livingood's management of it, she was its chatelaine and not its major domo. More and more since she had turned the spade to inaugurate Mariemont, she was a seldom-seen shadow.

By November, 42 houses were completed, and 300 living units were under construction. At year's end, 250 families lived in the new town, and 300 children packed Dale Park School. Mariemont was no longer a dream. Mirick continued to grouse at Nolen, complaining about his "treatment of the Industrial Road . . . the sidewalk between the cars and the loading platform [at Westover, the industrial section]," and a rail station at Westover. "I also can see no advantage whatever in [it]." His closing postscript wished that Nolen "would not forget us altogether. Things are moving fast here and we ought to see you once a month." Quick response came from Nolen, who forecasted that the rail line would expand its service eventually, as "it is only a question of time when these lines will be electrified and cater to the suburban district about Cincinnati."[53] His prophecy was unfulfilled.

Nolen was anything but elusive about visits to his planned community, for he or his associates made six excursions to Mariemont in 1924, the last by Nolen on December 29–30. Throughout their relationship, Mirick's treatment of Nolen was imperious and abrupt. He also misunderstood Nolen's significant role in Mariemont's evolution, inserting his bureaucratic manner without cause between the partnership of Nolen and Livingood. An organizational chart approved by Mirick (and probably with the blessing of Livingood) in late 1924 assigned Nolen to an equal position with the consulting engineers, the architects, and Mirick, who was placed conveniently at the center of the chart with the many departments and functions of the Mariemont Company flowing through him.[54]

Between October, when Livingood ecstatically reported to Nolen his approval of progress and planning for Mariemont, and November, the Mariemont Company belatedly weighed its operating costs. And on November 29, 1924, a bombshell was tossed at Nolen by Livingood.

As soon as we got back this Fall, Mr. Hogan and I at once got together to see if we could not reduce the terrific over-head which threatened to injure the MARIEMONT project seriously.

We have most reluctantly decided that your retaining fee of $300 per month must be saved and a proper time seems to be to close our contract with you in this respect with the close of the year.

This is like cutting off our own head, but it will not be so bad as that if you will agree to consult with us from time to time for a fee and thus remain closely attached to the project. We want your name to appear as hitherto as Town Planners of MARIEMONT and for this reason I wish you would at once prepare as such your chapter for the Brochure which is now almost ready for the press. As it is to be a final statement on many points, and the town planning has been completed, we wish your Statement to be as full but concise as possible just as we are asking F. S. & T. to make theirs as Constructing Engineers.[55]

Nolen was aghast when he received the news in North Carolina. Expecting the professional relationship to continue, an arrangement that successfully launched Mariemont since he had begun work on the project in 1920, Nolen would not accept his termination. He recalled for Livingood that "the town planner's account is now so small, financially speaking, in the Mariemont budget, that it does not figure as an important item in an undertaking as large as that at Mariemont. Even if only a very little of the town planner's advice were followed, it would easily offset its cost, unless the advice was not worthwhile." He then sidestepped the termination by outlining for Livingood an essay with a peculiar title, "The Place of Town Planning in Town Planning." He hoped to write it for town planner and patron alike, with answers to questions he posed. Perhaps this was intended to negate Livingood's message, for his outline included, "What is town planning anyhow? Is a general town plan enough? Where does the town planner come in during the construction period? Or, doesn't he? What tests should be applied to engineering and architecture and landscape architecture, and costs and social welfare, to find out if they fill in their part in the broad scheme? Is town planning a technical art, or is it just something that anyone can do? Has town planning to do mainly with design, or mainly with avoiding waste? Or both?"

Nolen was willing to accept "an intermittent service, but feel very strongly that only a continuous service can be of any real value. If we are to be consulted only when difficulties arise, it would seem the part of wisdom for you to make some provision for forestalling those same difficulties. The Chinese idea of the doctor is in many ways a better one than ours." Nolen earnestly believed that his work as planner must persist during the construction period, as what "counts for us is personal and professional pride in good permanent work and in creditable final results." He denied that he was terminated, considered his association with Mariemont still intact, and told Livingood that "if at any time the Mariemont Company does not want our services, you must say so in direct words."[56]

It was a reasoned response and also a denial of a concluded contract. Even the questions he thought he could answer in a future article gently chided Livingood. No doubt his wise counsel swayed the president of the Mariemont Company, for Livingood's fateful letter was corrected after Christmas.

> In amendation of my letter to you of November 29 it is now understood between your Mr. Nolen and myself to-day that the Mariemont Company continues to retain your firm as Town Planners on the basis of $100 [$500 is typed in the letter at this point, but crossed out and the new figure inked over it] per month, payment to be made quarterly with such periodical visits as may prove necessary, for which your Mr. Nolen will receive a per diem honorarium of $50 per day and expenses and others a lesser per diem and expenses. For work to be done at your office such as drafting, blue prints, etc., you are to charge as heretofore.
>
> I believe it was the mutual understanding that this is not a contract but merely an agreement to show that your firm is to be continued as part of the project of Mariemont so long as it is mutually satisfactory.[57]

A year of accomplishment, 1924 ended with dozens of families settling in America's newest community. Mariemont's youngsters waited in freshly fallen snow for the arrival of Santa Claus, who joined them at the illuminated Christmas tree on the tiny green in front of the Mariemont Memorial Church on a cloudy and cold December 24. After carols were sung, the rector of Christ Church, Frank Nelson, spoke to the children about Christmas, and the Packard limousine of Mary Emery brought the "Lady Bountiful" to the celebration. The first Christmas in the new town ended with a turkey dinner "in a restaurant" for everyone.[58] The next year would be the last one for Nolen on the Mariemont team.

6 · YEAR OF PROGRESS, YEAR OF TERMINATION

There was no hiatus for the builders of Mariemont during the winter of 1924–25. Although construction laborers frequently were laid off in cold weather, a large contingent worked on, plasterers and painters finishing interiors, glaziers and roofers closing in houses and apartments. Mariemont's borders now included 420 acres and embraced a section restricted to industrial use, called Westover, on the village's western limits. In January, it was clear to Livingood, Nolen, and Hogan that more capital was needed to support the pace of construction. Late in the month the officers of the Mariemont Company, obviously led by Livingood, who had the ear of Mrs. Emery, voted to increase the number of shares. After the vote, Mary Emery's investment rose to $4 million in the 39,995 shares held in her name.[1] There is no evidence that this amount, staggering for its day, prompted any reluctance on Mary's part. As so much of the village's cost by 1924–25 was consumed in its infrastructure, with no income realized for the Mariemont Company from sale of lots, construction costs for living units and grand-scale public buildings pressured the financial underpinnings of the new town. The financial cloud might darken if Mrs. Emery's support ended or if factors beyond her control limited the project's development.

Nolen outlined his continuing services for Livingood on New Year's Day, 1925, reflecting on his visit a month earlier. He expected to conduct "Bimonthly Conferences" on site, discuss "General Problems" dealing with "Architectural expression" and deed restrictions, and plan for "areas to be developed in the immediate future, . . . Types of construction for special places, . . . Lot enclosures, . . . Planting for streets and public areas, and the Planting of lots."[2] Nolen's report concluded with a recommendation that his office should prepare complete plans for Westover, then only some weed-covered fields across Whiskey Creek from Mariemont's residential section.

As he outlined his continuing involvement with Mariemont, Nolen intended to tout his Ohio project in an exhibition in New York City, the Architectural and Allied Arts Exposition to be held at the Grand Central Palace, April 20 through May 24, 1925. Nolen busied himself in January collecting photographs and plans while choosing illustrations for the exposition's accompanying catalogue.[3] He noted that "airplane pictures are not common yet and the popular appeal always makes it an interesting exhibit provided the scale is not too small."[4] Under the auspices of the American Institute of Architects, the American Society of Landscape Architects, and the International Conference on Town and City Planning, among others, the exposition offered good public exposure for the Mariemont project to leading professionals.

In mid-January, Nolen reported to Livingood his impressions of his visit on December 29–30, 1924, outlining on five pages a detailed account of his positive and negative reactions. At Mariemont, Nolen had conferred with Livingood, Hogan, Mirick, Cellarius, Whitney, and Schindel in the field and elsewhere.

> The most vivid impression of my visit came from a general observation of the large amount of construction work that has gone on during the autumn, facilitated as it was by favorable weather conditions. I had an opportunity to see progress in house building, including groups by Dana, Mackenzie, Ripley, Kruckemeyer and Strong, Ziegler, Gilchrist, McGoodwin and Short. There are many points of excellence in the work of each, architecturally considered. Just how far the work of each will contribute to a good total impression it is not possible to say at present, because nothing is finished, and the final result will be greatly influenced by the work that still remains to be done, not only upon the buildings but on the lots and streets; also the planting. One impression that I did receive was the feeling of overbuilding on the land. There seemed to be a greater density than one would naturally expect in an outlying section like Mariemont.[5]

Nolen's criticism was correct, given the open land elsewhere in the village. Also, Nolen was well aware that Livingood, not he, assigned the architects to specific locations. Nolen reminded Livingood of this, but he was not so critical of other parts of Mariemont, tactfully addressing progress with the streets and concourse and "the good promise that another twelve months holds forth." Nolen also inspected the Memorial Church, Dale Park School, the transformer station, garages in various locations, farm buildings, and the heating plant. He admired each of these buildings, or groups of buildings, as "an achievement in itself" and said he "enjoyed especially [the] progress with the Memorial Church, the school building and the farm group."

Landscaping and planting concerned him particularly, he wrote to Livingood. Especially valuable were his meetings with Joseph Whitney, the project's resident landscape architect. His worries about the color of pavement for Albert Place and adherence to named streets and their trees ("i.e, oaks for Oak St.?") were serious ones for him. For Livingood they were not high priorities. Throughout Nolen's town planning career, his roots were in landscape architecture, the field that had launched his life's work. Thus, he felt strongly that man-made Mariemont must marry comfortably and aesthetically with its natural environment. Nolen rightly perceived in the buildings and streets that a community of neighborhoods was rapidly developing, although the trees were saplings and the village had a fresh appearance everywhere.

At January's end, Livingood responded to Nolen's rather critical report of his Mariemont visit. In his response he elaborated his philosophy regarding group housing, the dominant type in the Dale Park section, and reflected on growing economic pressures.

> I realize that the North-west Section looks a little over-built but this appearance will improve with the planting of trees and the sodding, not to mention the painting of trim, store fronts, sash bars, etc., by which we will tie the whole thing a little closer together. The truth of the matter is that we were obliged to cover more of the lots than we would wish because of the excessive high cost of building. There *is* an economy in group house construction and to this we resorted in order that we might furnish some cheap homes at least for the wage earner. It should be remembered, however, that we are not building to improve a housing shortage but to illustrate different types of housing such as is being done because of economical pressure in various parts of the world. If I were sure that the present high scale of wages would continue indefinitely I would spend more money on the exteriors as is being done especially in Holland.

Referring to only one of your points, I intend to confer more closely with Mr. Whitney about landscape architecture to be done the coming season and have already disposed of Dale Park itself. We have concluded for the present to get along with a very few paths and steps. The rest will come as the need develops. Frankly I don't want to sink too much money into permanent developments at this time when housing is the real need. Nevertheless we shall face the culvert ends this Spring because this will be of permanent value but provide no bridges or things of that sort until we have more population.

Our choice of street names was so good that I am not going to be persuaded by any Cincinnati officials to change just because there happen to be similar streets in Cincinnati itself. We may never become part of Cincinnati. At any rate the neighborhood will always be known as Mariemont.[6]

Livingood's obsession with sidewalks, driveways, and lawns filled three more paragraphs of the letter. "Here is a chance to show what we can do in the way of a well made macadamized road surface and frankly I think a cement walk but not glaring white, would be appropriate," he wrote, with Albert Place (then called Albert Close) in mind. His "very definite ideas" about grass and lawn spaces were reiterated, "about which I have talked to you several times." He liked Nolen's proposals for the exhibition in New York City but professed distrust of some architects and the press. Livingood did not want to invest much in the exhibition, for he thought there would be no effect on the Mariemont project, adding that "architects generally and newspapers have been so neglectful of the project that I do not feel that I owe them much. All the same I do want to help forward the idea of City Planning as an Art and to give due credit to both City Planner and the various Architects for the large part they played in carrying out our ideas."

The costs of construction caused increasing concern in 1925. Livingood's letters to Nolen seldom avoided the topic. By late February, $265,024 had been tallied as expenses for the Dana buildings, the first housing units undertaken by the Mariemont Company. Exclusive of land costs, this was a staggering amount for construction, overhead, and architect's fees.[7] The three costliest portions of construction, carpentry ($61,216), brick masonry ($36,885), and plumbing ($28,735), accounted for about 47 percent of the total expenses. Richard Dana's fee as architect was $15,901, or 6 percent of project cost, a percentage comparing favorably with national statistics in the 1920s. Overhead charges were assigned at $23,852, or 9 percent of the total, covering unnamed expenses but perhaps including the Mariemont Company's supervisory staff as well as Nolen's fees. This cost accounting for the Dana complex is the only detailed report known to exist for any one of Mariemont's housing units.

Making another of her rare recorded visits to her National Exemplar since groundbreaking in 1923, Mary Emery arrived on February 6 to tour various points around the village, according to the diligent Warren Parks, resident engineer and diary chronicler of events. She visited again on April 12, 1925, driven by her chauffeur, Charles Singer, and accompanied by her nurse, Helen Baird. Unfortunately, her impressions after these visits were not recorded by Parks in his diary, nor did the minutes of the Mariemont Company meetings mention this visit or others. Mary Emery visited Mariemont's construction site infrequently, which is indicative of her detachment from operations and construction progress.

The first visit to Mariemont in 1925 by either Nolen or Foster occurred on March 19–20, prompted by repeated requests that their trips occur more frequently. Foster's report, after his trip, sprinkled his concerns with sensible observations. He reported that his first hours were spent outlining the display being arranged, complete with photographs and titles, for the exposition to be held in New York. After this discussion, two trips were made to the "works," as Livingood often described Mariemont at this stage of its development. Foster branded the Dale Park section as "rather closely built up. This, however, is partly due to its being in contrast with the present open country, a contrast that will disappear with the building up of the remainder of the scheme. The other impression is that of distinct, separate, unrelated groups of houses." Foster expected that the plantings and street trees would eventually create pleasant vistas, however. He added that the "project as a whole has considerable charm which will increase as other units are added and age has had its opportunity to soften the newness and harshness of the lines."[8] Foster included in his report recommendations to plant "field crops," such as alfalfa or hay, to reduce weed growth throughout the village and to finish several streets to improve circulation for vehicles. He ended with a plea to complete the athletic field because of its usefulness in drawing people to its outdoor activities and entertainment.

Aside from the Mariemont Church, the most conspicuous building in Mary Emery's new town was the Mariemont Inn. Livingood sited it on Nolen's plan at the intersection of Wooster Pike and Madisonville Road, the major corner on the town square, and construction began on April 20, 1925. A Cincinnati firm, Zettel & Rapp, drew plans for a V-shaped structure stretching a block in each direction, a grandiose scheme never fully realized. Only one part of the architects' plan, about one-half of the original design, was built. Tudor Revival in style and intended to complement the theater block designed by Steinkamp for across the street, but not built, the Inn anchored the town center. John Zettel (1881–1950) and George W. Rapp (1852–1918) had worked together as early as 1903, joining forces in their own firm by 1913. Rapp's son, Walter, worked with Zettel after George Rapp's death and during the period when the inn was planned. This centerpiece of Tudor vernacular, illustrated by its oak timber and stucco walls, steeply pitched slate roofs, narrow casement windows, and massive chimneys, provided shops, rooms for transients, a tea room, and rental offices for the Mariemont Company. As the inn's construction seemed interminable (it opened for business only in 1929), public notice of the building and its advertising effect were negligible until rental and leasing activities began on its ground floor.

Both Livingood and Mirick wrote testy letters to Nolen in late April, the latter complaining about Nolen's possible involvement in an article recently published, for "neither Mrs. Emery nor Mr. Livingood liked it at all." Livingood's letter griped about the location of and charges for installing the New York exhibition, but he was particularly distressed that the Mariemont project was not displayed prominently.[9] Mirick's upbraiding of Nolen for the article did not mention that Foster's report was never shared with Livingood, an oversight that seems to be intentional. Poor Nolen already had received Livingood's complaint that "Foster following his visit in March made no report whatsoever to me at least, and should not put in per diem honorarium as you do." Nolen's relationship with Mirick always was distant, if not antipathetic, as in his response to Mirick: "I know nothing whatever about the *New York Times* article except what I heard from Jack. I never saw it, and know nothing whatever of its origin except that I had nothing to do with it, nor did anyone connected with my office have anything to do with it. Under these circumstances I have no re-

In 1926, the Mariemont Company actively pursued renters and purchasers of lots. Because of its prominent location on the town square, the Mariemont Inn became the primary sales and rental office (as the sign over the door indicates) for Mariemont properties.

sponsibility, and deem it wise to ignore even the existence of the article. Certainly I cannot be responsible for what appears in the newspapers about Mariemont. Do you not think I am right?"[10] Nolen's postscript urged Mirick to show Foster's report on his March 19–20 visit to Livingood, a remarkable request that exposed Mirick's neglect of sharing Foster's detailed account and recommendations.

Just as Nolen prepared for his first visit to Mariemont in 1925, the Mariemont Company felt the crunch for building funds and increased its capitalization to $6 million.[11] Little return on this investment was possible at this time, for lots were not selling readily and rents did not offset the enormous investment in the town's infrastructure and construction costs. Fortunately, there were no investors to satisfy, only Mary Emery, who realized that there was little likelihood of any reimbursement to her or the Mariemont Company for her generous provision. The Mariemont Company's brochure succinctly stated its founder's reasons for financing the new town.

Mariemont is not a philanthropy or in any way paternalistic. Its sponsor, Mrs. Mary M. Emery, herself a lifelong resident of Cincinnati, is simply showing in a very practical way her interest in the proper development of home life and home ownership by providing an ideal place for home building. The Mariemont Company will do part of the building, and when all the lots and building have been disposed of, it will dissolve, so far as the village of Mariemont is concerned. It is anticipated that, a good start having been made, the public, seeing the advantages, will make Mariemont one of the most thriving of Cincinnati's suburbs.[12]

Renters saw the advantages just as Nolen and Livingood intended. One renter, a parishioner of Christ Church, conveyed her pleasure to Rev. Frank Nelson, and he quoted her words to Mary Emery in a letter addressed to "Mother Two." The renter, a woman of modest means who loved the "fresh pure air" for her children, paid thirty-five dollars per month for her "cozy lovely home."[13]

Nolen's first visit to Mariemont in 1925 occurred on May 8–9, and afterward he reported promptly to Livingood his impressions and suggestions. Apparently he met only with Mirick and Whitney, Livingood being unavailable, but he noted his reaction in six positive points. These reflect his appreciation of the practical results of his town planning theory. Nolen was struck specifically by "the architectural work beginning to show up favorably in finished form" and by

the happy way in which the large distribution of the organic parts of Mariemont is working out—the street and highway scheme, the location and boundaries of Dogwood Park, Dale Park and the Stadium site, Miami Bluff Parkway, the main town center and the subordinate center in the Dale Park section, the various classes of residential property, including especially the Dale Park section of concentrated housing and the "Places," the Farm Group, the Concourse and the main north and south axis in which it terminates, and the church and the school as public features.

He commented further on the soundness of the town's layout, the underground wires and utilities, and the heating plant. Mariemont would be successful, Nolen maintained, because of its "better method of providing for the growth of cities by means of a decentralized community." Continuing, Nolen extolled "the development of local industries in Westover, within walking distance of

Mariemont, and the advantage of giving additional attention to the social organization of the community." His sixth and final point urged a visit to Mariemont by someone from his office at least once every three months.[14]

At Mariemont, the declining new construction in 1925 was capped when houses for Sheldon Close, designed by Grosvenor Atterbury (1869–1956), were begun on June 1. In that same month, Livingood updated his list of assigned architects on the Nolen map, continuing to record Allen W. Jackson and Wilson Eyre & McIlvaine. Jackson's Tudor-style houses were to be placed, the architect thought, at prominent locations south of Wooster Pike at the corners of Pleasant Street and Mariemont Avenue, with a secondary assignment at the intersection of Cachepit and Mariemont Avenues. His handsomely delineated buildings filled a page in the Mariemont Company's brochure, where it was noted that they characterize the "housing that will prevail in the higher-priced sections of Mariemont." Elegant villas "in the Italian style" were Eyre & McIlvaine's intended contribution to the architectural scheme. The villas were intended for Hopkins Place (a cul-de-sac later called Emery Lane). These latter two firms never fulfilled their assignments, however.

Atterbury's ten residences for Sheldon Close, assigned to him on May 8, 1925, nestle into a cul-de-sac south of the town center and symmetrically balance McGoodwin's Albert Place buildings to the west. Atterbury's buildings richly blend steep roofs of slate, half-timbering, stone, and stucco. At the center point of the street, an arched gate and parking area suggests a cottage farmyard in the Cotswolds. Another piece of Nolen's orderly plan for the town center and its streets, radiating out into the surrounding residential neighborhoods, was in place. Atterbury's houses became the third residential section to be built south of Wooster Pike (after Albert Place and Denny Place), suggesting to future homeowners the preferred architectural style for homes they might build themselves. Two of the Atterbury buildings were double residences, while the remainder were single units, all echoing but not replicating his work at Forest Hills Gardens, another planned community dependent on philanthropy and begun in 1909.

Born in Detroit and educated at Yale and the architecture school of Columbia University, Grosvenor Atterbury worked in the New York office of McKim, Mead & White and in Paris for the Atelier Blondel. His important res-

·SHELDON·CLOSE·MADISONVILLE·ROAD

GROSVENOR·ATTERBURY·ARCHITE
STOWE·PHELPS·&·JOHN·TOMPKINS·Ass

GE·OF·MARIEMONT·CINCINNATI·OHIO·

Probably the best-known architect engaged at Mariemont was Grosvenor Atterbury of New York City, whose houses for Sheldon Close, begun in 1925, were the last residences constructed by the Mariemont Company. Atterbury's drawing was meticulously interpreted on the cul-de-sac that bore the name of Mary and Thomas J. Emery's elder son.

Boston architect Allen W. Jackson prepared elevation drawings, probably in 1924, for single and two-family houses suggested for Pleasant Street and Mariemont Avenues, the "higher-priced sections of Mariemont," according to the Mariemont Company brochure. Jackson was at odds with Charles Livingood from time to time, and his "cottages" never were built.

idential and country estate commissions from wealthy New Yorkers led to Forest Hills Gardens and the American Wing of the Metropolitan Museum of Art. Atterbury's interest in improving the workingman's environment through the Forest Hills experiment recommended him to Nolen, and he appeared in 1922 on Nolen's list of suggested architects.

The need for capital for Mariemont's burgeoning construction increased dramatically in 1925. In January, the Mariemont Company's funding was $4 million; by May 5, it was $6 million; by September 1, it had reached $7 million.[15] A small part of that underwriting paid for the brochure ordained by Livingood and finally available in the summer of that year. This was the only publication of any substance on its new town issued by the Mariemont Company. A leading printer and publisher in Cincinnati, Allen Collier, produced the brochure and wrote his observations to an architect friend in Boston, calling it "a very pretentious book." Collier's assessment of Mary Emery's purpose in founding

Mariemont was only partly true: "She is building this model town not for the purpose of making money out of it, although it is claimed that the enterprise will be profitable after a while, but more largely as a monument to her husband and herself. While he was living he was more interested in accumulating a large fortune than in doing anything for the city. I shall try and send you one of these books when it is completed."[16]

Collier's opinion did not matter, for others welcomed the publishing of the Mariemont Company's brochure. Art museum director Joseph Gest received his copy from Mary Emery herself and wrote her, "In glancing over it I see that it will answer questions that have been in my mind as I have watched the building month by month." By this time, Nolen was deeply involved in the planning of new towns in Florida, such as Belleair and Venice, and his commitments to those communities drew him southward many times during his work for Livingood. Returning from one trip to Florida, he praised the new brochure only faintly to Mirick.[17]

Villas in the "Italian style" were rendered in a drawing by Wilson Eyre & McIlvaine, Philadelphia architects, and published in the Mariemont Company brochure in 1925. Although the street was developed (and later called Emery Lane), the houses never were built.

The two houses on either side of the entrance to Sheldon Close (one shown nearing completion in 1925) illustrate Grosvenor Atterbury's interpretation of the Tudor style.

In October 1925, Nolen began to lose touch with Mariemont, partly because of the decreasing need for his expertise and partly because of Livingood's obvious disengagement from Nolen. Nolen nevertheless expressed his continuing interest in this project, which had involved him since 1920. Early in October, Nolen complained to Mirick that he received short notice for his visits and then praised town planning and what it had done for Mariemont.

> I would rather see Mariemont just now than any other project. Each progress report adds to my zest, because I realize, not only how much has happened, but the particular significance from a town planning and town building point of view of the work that is now going on. More and more, town planning discussion is emphasizing the third dimension in town planning—the actual up-building on the general ground plan. That is almost actually true, from the administrative point of view, in the social and community organization which is now proceeding so successfully at Mariemont.[18]

Nolen wrote just one day later to his client, effusively describing Mariemont as a project that "grows and flowers like a plant" and "how gratified on the whole I believe you will be with the results of the summer."[19]

Nolen made his last official visit to Mariemont as its town planner on October 20, 1925. He did not encounter Livingood but sent his impressions to him after returning to Cambridge. His comments were not specific, telling Livingood that

> I had a good opportunity to discuss matters fully with Mr. Mirick and Mr. Whitney, and to go over the ground several times. Quite by accident I ran into Mr. Schindel in the lobby of the Gibson Hotel one evening, and we had a good talk. He mentioned that Paul Cret had been at Mariemont. If he has made any report or recommendations, as supervising architect, relating to town planning, I should be very much pleased to see a copy—assuming, of course, that it is something that you want me to see. I am particularly keen about the town center and the way in which that is to be worked out from a town planning point of view.[20]

Nolen's lack of specificity no doubt caused Livingood to wonder whether Nolen's services as town planner were still needed. As the plan was fully developed, the infrastructure completed, and construction well under way, the expense must have outweighed the advantages of retaining Nolen.

Joined to Nolen's visit to Mariemont was his appearance on October 22 as speaker before the Ohio State Conference on City Planning, a luncheon and meeting sponsored by the Chamber of Commerce, Dayton. Unaware that his official involvement with Mariemont was soon to end, Nolen had reached his career peak by this date. He was president of the National Conference on City Planning, commissions were numerous, and the Depression of the 1930s had not yet affected the nation and his work. Nolen's lecture in Dayton permitted him to push his favorite topics, regional planning and the end of the "growth of cities by formless additions making them unwieldy, haphazard agglomerations." He applauded Mariemont, calling it "the most comprehensive development of its kind in this country" and adding, "When completed, Mariemont will illustrate how people of moderate means can live well near great cities."[21]

Nolen succinctly and plainly advocated the blessings of town planning in his Dayton lecture. Each of his seven points, or methods designed to achieve good results, was applicable to Mariemont, and the new town's proximity to the lecture site offered Mariemont as a logical case study. Nolen recommended first that "an official planning board" be established. The Mariemont Company functioned in this capacity as the agency in charge of planning and executing the village but under Livingood's personal control. There should be "adequate provision for the legal side of city planning" and "a broad yet sound financial policy," Nolen then stated. When property was acquired before Nolen's employment, Mary Emery was the legal owner. It is certain that her legal interests were reviewed carefully by several of Cincinnati's leading attorneys, men like Robert A. Taft and John Hollister, who determined that she had clear title to the property she purchased. After the Mariemont Company was formed, land purchases and expenditures were under its control. While it may be debated that a "sound financial policy" existed with Livingood at the helm, there was access to Emery millions.

Nolen's Dayton lecture urged further the "constant fundamental education of public opinion, year in and year out, in the press, the public schools and in other ways," and "timely publicity on all important single city planning projects" was desirable. Livingood knew the value of publicity, especially at the local level, in encouraging renters and purchasers of lots. But Nolen contributed much more in publicizing Mariemont in the national forum through his lectures throughout the United States, primarily as part of his official leadership of the professional organization representing town planners but also because of the large number of cities and towns that bore his design mark. He never flagged in his endorsement of favorable public opinion that would support town planning's virtues.

Finally, Nolen proposed that "printing of city plan reports, the discussion of planning proposals, local exhibitions, the use of motion pictures, etc." could link with "a persistent local citizen's committee" to secure support of city planning. As a private town, essentially, under the Mariemont Company's control, Mariemont had no citizens' committee to engage in discussions or approve any facet of the development. And until Mariemont established its own governance with incorporation in 1941, this portion of Nolen's advocacy was not applicable.[22]

December 1925 was not a pleasant month for Nolen. His longtime associate and a mainstay of his office, Philip W. Foster, left Nolen's employment in November or early December. This separation was disheartening, he wrote to Livingood. Foster had been involved with the Mariemont project from its beginning, when, in Nolen's absence, he had received in 1920 the "mysterious visitor," Livingood, in their Cambridge office. In the same letter Nolen acknowledged hearing of Joseph Whitney's resignation as resident landscape architect, stating that he knew "nothing further about it" but offering his services for landscape design.[23] The next communication from Livingood brought Nolen his termination notice.

Livingood asked Nolen to turn in any "unfinished business" and abruptly ended Nolen's official connection with Mariemont. "The fact is," Livingood wrote, "that the work generally is rapidly tapering off, and while we don't want you to 'resign' we appreciate that as your office is excessively busy and that we shall do nothing but construction, mostly large buildings, during the coming year or two, we hardly feel the necessity of retaining you on the salary list after the close of this year. You can see for yourself that very little was required of you or your office during the past months." He assured Nolen that "we are very grateful for having started us so well on the project, for MARIEMONT is an actuality, with nearly 200 families, stores, a school and much that will be occupied by next summer."[24]

Nolen reacted to his firing less vigorously than he had in November 1924, when Livingood had first proposed but then retracted a severance of Nolen's services. No doubt Nolen recognized that his Mariemont commissioners were less concerned about the program he had recommended at the year's beginning. Nolen's repeated plea that town planners should be consulted throughout the maturing phase of any new town was ignored. Landscape and planting plans, problems of lot enclosures, deed restrictions, and other needs suggested by Nolen were not critical in Livingood's eyes. However useful Nolen's talents might have been during the years of continuing construction, Mariemont ended its five-year affiliation with America's greatest town planner at the end of 1925.[25]

7 · THE CURTAIN DROPS

With John Nolen's dismissal at the end of 1925, town planning for Mariemont, at least in the hands of a professional, was finished. He did not endorse his removal, of course, but he graciously accepted his termination and maintained a cordial relationship with Livingood and the working group. Nolen shared his true feelings, however, in a letter written to John Schindel, an officer of the Mariemont Company, telling him "that Mr. Livingood is of the opinion that the town planning for Mariemont is at an end. You also know, I think, my own view, not as a personal matter, but as a professional opinion."[1]

The curtain dropped at the beginning of 1926, not only on Nolen but on those architects whose projects were canceled and never went beyond preliminary discussions or drawings. Architects selected by Livingood, beginning on December 28, 1922, remained on lists prepared on May 8 and June 30, 1924. Livingood's selections were based in part on Nolen's draft submitted in 1922. Their names are sprinkled through the Nolen-Livingood correspondence, noting specific commissions intended for some of them. The canceled architects were more than notations on a list, for it is clear from correspondence between Livingood and Nolen that their commissions were not mere pipe dreams. Reasons for the cancellations probably include the Mariemont Company's apprehension about cash flow, as sales of building lots were not brisk by this date, although rentals were progressing satisfactorily. And Livingood, not particularly adept at long-range planning, was worried, no doubt, over Mary Emery's deteriorating health and the consequences of estate settlements. Deferral of new construction must have seemed a wise course for the Mariemont Company after the Dale Park section and the McGoodwin and Atterbury groups had been completed.

The canceled Mariemont architects included Allen W. Jackson of Boston; Garber & Woodward, Herbert Spielman, and Joseph G. Steinkamp & Brother of Cincinnati; Henry O. Milliken of New York; and Arthur E. Brockie and Wilson Eyre & McIlvaine of Philadelphia. Garber & Woodward's office had been involved for several years with plans for the recreation center, an essential component of Mariemont's plan. Still unknown are the reasons for the building's eventual assignment to George B. deGersdorff, a New York architect, friend, and Harvard classmate of Livingood.[2] Two architectural firms, F. W. Bourne of Boston and Mellor, Meigs & Howe of Philadelphia, were recorded on Livingood's list in 1922 but never received any specific commissions. Paul P. Cret of Philadelphia was retained as consultant and advisor on the town center and public buildings, but his sole published listing with the Mariemont project occurs as "consultant" with Steinkamp's never-completed "Theatre Block" or "Rows." It is unfortunate that Steinkamp's imposing four-story range of shops, offices, apartments, and theater with an arcaded walk was not executed. Its monumental and elegant bulk would have balanced the Mariemont Inn and forecasted what might be done, but was not, with the buildings eventually built around the town center.

Nolen's dismissal, beginning in January 1926, did not preclude requests for his office to provide copies of plat plans to assist the selling of Mariemont lots. He maintained a continuing interest in the project he had nurtured, but his other commissions in the United States gave him a new focus. Mariemont's resident engineer, Warren W. Parks, correctly ascertained that Nolen was not wasting away. Parks knew about Nolen's "large developments in Florida of which I hear from time to time. Many of the fellows who were here are now engaged in that part of the country."[3]

Mariemont's appearance changed dramatically when the Mariemont Inn took its place on a prominent corner of the town center. Livingood reported to Nolen "that we have begun, indeed have almost under roof, the first building of the big town center, 'Ye Inn,' in the lobby of which we expect to have all the offices of the Mariemont Company by June 1st." His letter concluded with a report of the community's progress. "Deer [*sic*] Park is pretty well shaped up, with more than 325 homes practically completed and in spite of the very rough winter (42 snowstorms since October 2nd, to this date) we have had people moving in almost every day and there are now 250; all stores are occupied, the barber is in one of the flats and our shoemaker in a Gilchrist house. The school has over 300 pupils in it. On Sundays it takes care of all religious services, which are many because, even yet, our church is not done."[4]

The town's building association, first mentioned by Livingood in this same letter, was created by the Mariemont Company to facilitate the sale of lots and to provide building loans for those needing them. It functioned as rental agent, also, for the apartments and townhouses in the Dale Park section, an operation managed by William Hall in the company's offices in the Mariemont Inn. In 1926, with most of the Dale Park section finished, the company's concern shifted to selling of lots and improving cash flow. Livingood's carefully worded explanation in the Mariemont Company's brochure signaled his intentions for the village's future development.

> To show its faith in Mariemont as a place of residence, The Mariemont Company is itself planning to create other residential districts around such spots as Denny Place, Albert Place, etc., that is, specially-designed groups of single houses with large grounds about them, to establish standards of excellence up to which individual home builders must measure, and to which all may aspire. In this way, the buyer of a lot will know in advance the character of his neighborhood. For the Company believes it is just as important that a man's cherished, though modest, home should not be overshadowed by a pretentious, inappropriate structure next door as that the builder of a fine house should not have his values depreciated by a building out of harmony. As in every American village there are always neighborhoods, superior locations, more elevated sites, manifestly more valuable for homes than others, so Mariemont will be seen to have special beauty spots which will command higher prices for the land and be occupied by more costly houses. These will be eagerly sought after by skilled artisans, foremen, heads of departments, and others able to build for themselves.[5]

Prospective homeowners who purchased lots were obliged to meet the terms and restrictions imposed by the owner, the Mariemont Company. Lots could be purchased with payment in full or by land contract. Lots sold for $45 to $60 per front foot, ranging in total price from $1,800 to $3,600. Purchasers were expected to have a down payment of 10 percent at least, with the balance in installments at 6 percent interest. Construction plans and exterior house design required approval from the Mariemont Company prior to sale of a lot. House prices were predicted to range from $3,000 to $7,000 but were higher in actual sales. Rents were scaled from $25 to $120, with most apartments renting at $35 to $60 per month.

Lots "may be assigned to anyone acceptable, like yourself, to the company," a special promotion brochure stated, and future sales by owners required this same approval.[6] Both rentals and land purchases were prohibited at that time to non-Caucasians in the wording in deeds and land contracts. Persons of African and Asian heritage were specifically excluded in these documents. Such prohibitions were common in Cincinnati and other cities in the 1920s, where segregated schools, housing, and entertainment centers prevailed. It is ironic that these prohibitions by the Mariemont Company were instituted, for their tenor was contrary to Thomas J. Emery's compassionate interest and long record, as well as Mary Emery's, in support of African-American causes, whether segregated (as with orphanages) or when demanding equal admittance for black as well as white students to the Ohio Mechanics Institute.

The first issue of the *Mariemont Messenger,* the newspaper published expressly for the new town, was in Nolen's hands in March 1926, along with a letter from Livingood. Nolen wrote back appreciatively to Mirick, "Mariemont is still by all odds the best thing of its sort on the United States map, and I am glad you are at the helm." But to Livingood he wrote more congratulatory words "on the progress and success of recent developments in Mariemont." He liked especially Mrs. Emery's "Greetings," which appeared in the first issue of the *Mariemont Messenger,* and Leavitt's article, "The Romance of Mariemont." Mary's brief statement on the newspaper's front page embraced her love of children through the concept for healthy suburban living she was providing. In its simplistic charm, it remains her only recorded address to the inhabitants of Mariemont: "Good morning. Is the sun a little brighter there in Mariemont? Is the air a little fresher? Is your home a little sweeter? Is your housework somewhat easier? And the children? Do you feel safer about them? Are their faces a bit ruddier, are their legs a little sturdier? Do they laugh and play a lot louder in Mariemont? Then I am content."[7]

Nolen's lecture circuit gave him ample opportunity to preach his town planning principles. With his employment at Mariemont and with other new towns, not replanned cities, the impetus of lecturing urged his promotion of appropriate urban development. As president of the National Conference on City Planning, his viewpoint, certainly shared by his colleagues, was center stage in the formal remarks he repeated across the country. His plan for Mariemont figured prominently in most addresses he gave after 1923, such as the one given in Saint Petersburg, Florida, in the spring of 1926, when he pleaded for "action more deliberate, to plan and build new towns and cities by intention, and to do it with knowledge and skill and understanding. These new towns should express new standards and new ideals, and be an attempt to meet in new ways the modern conditions of life and the peculiar opportunities that these conditions and resources offer."[8]

Mariemont, suggested as a model of opportunity for "limited dividend companies" by Nolen, was linked with Letchworth and Hampstead Garden Suburb in his talk in Saint Petersburg. His experience with Mariemont and its reliance on a single patron for its financing urged him to speak out to enlist public opinion that might replace such unusual financing for future communities. That, he lectured, was necessary to build a "movement for the planning and building of new towns," yet both Nolen and Livingood found little response nationally to their joint efforts to establish Mariemont as a national exemplar of town planning.

After Nolen's termination at the end of 1925, there were only minor attempts to modify or change elements in Mariemont's plan. There was one correction needed, Livingood thought, at the intersection of Wooster Pike and West Street, where the roadway changes from 80 feet to 150 feet in width, broken by a median strip. Cincinnati's City Planning Commission requested that the corners of the intersection "be rounded off—preferably by means of a flat reverse curve."[9] Livingood appealed to Nolen about this, and Nolen's deliberate, cautious nature and professional experience combined in a gracious rebuttal. "The best arrangement for important street intersections is a subject for study and discussion, and there is room for difference of opinion. The arrangement proposed at the corner of West Street, Emery Row North and South and Wooster Pike does not look very good to us here. However, it may prove to be the best arrangement, all things considered."[10]

Livingood entered the discussion from his vacation retreat in Canada, complimenting Nolen on his many commitments before adding his reading of the problem and telling him, "You are certainly a busy man, you and your associates, what with laying out the comprehensive city plan for Columbus, Georgia, getting out two illustrated books on Town and City Planning, a complete development for Sarasota, Florida (for all of which brochures I thank you heartily; and did I not see a press notice of a book by you on Gardening?) so I hate to burden you but noting the discussion that has come up about shaving off corners of your plan at Wooster and West St., I will give you my layman's reaction."[11]

Livingood, like Nolen, expected that a change in road width might encourage drivers to reduce their speed through the village, but he was annoyed by motorists running over the curb. Still, he saw no need for reducing the right angle at the intersection. The most important issue was not the curb problem, however, as Livingood was "most anxious to comply with a request of the City Planning Commission, especially as it is the only one they make which is therefore a great compliment, for without their unqualified approval we can't record the plat. This we are most anxious to do at the earliest possible moment as we are beginning to sell lots."

The issue would not die, and Nolen remained firm that he had no information on traffic conditions, nor did he attempt a special study of the layout. He offered two observations, often made today by town planners, on traffic flow and road design in residential neighborhoods. In these, he foresaw part of the future problem caused by automobile traffic passing through a community.

The arrangement of the two roads is not an unusual one either in this country or abroad. It is the kind of treatment that is often provided to fit local conditions, and to furnish an interesting and logical variety. Each particular case, however, must be decided on its merits.

The second point of importance is, how far it is desirable to make intersections easy so that traffic can move rapidly, and how far it is desirable to make intersections reasonably convenient and orderly, but of such a character that traffic must slow up somewhat at such intersections in the interests of safety. This latter point comes up constantly in establishing the radius for the rounding out of corners. Such corners can be too short or they can be rounded out too much. There is no rule that can be mechanically applied. It is always a question of good judgment and knowledge used to meet the local conditions; and of course these local conditions themselves change from time to time.

This may seem a somewhat indefinite answer. It is the best that I can do with the information that we have. It would please us very much to consider the matter further for you if we can be of any service. In that case we would like to know just what the traffic requirements are, and also the present traffic conditions and a forecast of what in local judgment is likely to happen in the future.[12]

Livingood continued during July to badger Nolen about his perception of the accident-prone corners at the problem intersection. He wrote that he was "awaiting your reaction" and brought up another, equally unwarranted, query that illustrated Livingood's inability to understand fully the role of the town planner. "Now, here is another problem which I trust you can answer before you sail for Vienna," he asked. "I have always wondered why you made Plainville Pike stop at Wooster Pike. Why should it not drive right thru to Field-house Way? I know that we always wanted Denny Place to be the quietest spot in Mariemont but there is no thru traffic in it possible, yet the tenants are already complaining that they must walk all around a long city block to reach Plainville Pike where one takes the buses." Livingood thought it was a simple matter to construct a street connecting Denny Place with Plainville Pike. He closed agreeably, "You are the doctor, and will be held responsible for the very best city planning so I do not wish to over-persuade you, but this is a practical question and you will have to grant that we have asked for very few changes which is the best encomium I can give to Dr. John Nolen, City Planner."[13]

Nolen's contract with the Mariemont project was ended, yet Livingood sought the town planner's advice from time to time in 1926. There was no mention of consulting fees for Nolen's counsel, and this probably accounts for his tactful avoidance of further professional involvement. Yet Mariemont was dear to his heart, and he longed to see his role as town planner continued. Nolen wrote Livingood that his "interest in the town is so great that I feel it is a real hardship to have six months or more go by without an opportunity to observe results and to hear the story from those who are carrying out the project. An occasional visit would also be of value as a background to the expression of opinion upon questions which have already arisen and other questions which will no doubt arise in the future."[14]

Nolen continued to skirt the issue of recommending any change in the intersection on Wooster Pike, but his observations on traffic conditions apply today as readily as prophesied in 1926. "The mere fact of another accident," he regretted, "is not conclusive argument for a change. Accidents occur under the very best street arrangements and experience has shown in many places that new street arrangements and regulations intended to improve traffic conditions and reduce accidents have often worked the other way. I am not of the opinion that that is the case in this instance, although we have a feeling here that one of the objections to the plan proposed is that so far as our knowledge goes, it is likely to lead to faster driving across this intersection and indirectly may therefore make the crossing more dangerous."

Nolen objected to an extension of Plainville Road, then called Plainville Pike, as far as Denny Place, noting that the question had been discussed "in the beginning and we were all of the opinion then that on the whole it had better be stopped at Wooster Pike." Further, he thought that an extension for the few residents of Denny Place was not justified, nor were additional crossings on Wooster Pike desirable. The intimacy and privacy of this charming area must be preserved, he advised correctly. Nolen's closing sentences in his July 23 letter promoted the necessity for continued town planning, gently chiding Livingood. "Furthermore, the general plan of the town whether it is a new town or an old one, requires reconsideration of details when actual execution takes place or when new conditions arise. It is partly because of these facts that town planning services should be retained during the period of development, if a project is to have the benefit of the town planning point of view."

Throughout their years of correspondence, Nolen's letters were more reasoned and less tinged with personal preferences than were Livingood's, but as the commissioner of the entire project, the latter enjoyed his role as final arbiter. Perhaps because his leadership of the Mariemont project was never questioned, Livingood expressed his feelings freely, particularly his satisfaction with accomplishments as well as his dislikes, in writing to Nolen. Certainly, the exchange of letters between the two men forms an almost complete record of patron-planner involvement in the creation of a world-renowned new town.

The letters between the two in the summer of 1926, written well after Nolen's involvement as town planner, reflect the pleasure both shared in Mariemont's growth.

Livingood wrote to Nolen with the good news of success in renting houses and apartments, with

> nearly 300 families in residence now, so the streets in Dale Park section are animated, especially around the little Center. Visitors are struck by the contentment shown on the faces of the grownups, and by the healthy appearance of the children. At evening one feels as if they were in an English village already. We oriented just right. Frankly I am wondering if anything else will be as beautiful as Dale Park where you took every advantage of nature. Yet wait until you see the charm of Denny Place. It grows on one every day. Atterbury's Sheldon Close is approaching completion; he has been out again and takes intense interest in all details.[15]

Mariemont had an amazing occupational mix from the start. Its first renters in 1926 included shopkeepers, tradesmen, and doctors. Advertisements in the local newspaper, the *Mariemont Messenger,* usually listed the owner or shopkeeper's occupation as well as his or her address in Mariemont. Doctors Samuel Herman and John Hermanies lived near each other on Chestnut Street, not far from the barber shop run by Frank Schweitzer at 6708 Chestnut Street. A nationally recognized photographer, Nancy Ford Cones, lived with her husband and daughter at 6655 Chestnut, close to pharmacist Roy Willis, who rented in the Ripley & LeBoutillier apartments on the square.[16] Most renters remain anonymous, however, as rental records, when found, lack job associations. The number of wage earners employed in Cincinnati businesses and factories and residing in Mariemont in 1926 cannot be determined. But their anonymity does not mean that they were absent.

Most of Mariemont's residents were middle class in 1926. This socioeconomic character was intended from the beginning, even at Livingood's initial contact with Nolen's office, where he proposed a village "for all classes of people."[17] However, through the planning phase in 1920–25 and sporadically thereafter, news accounts, lectures, and publications often referred to Mariemont as a community primarily for workers, meaning by this term those who worked in factories or at other jobs with limited skills or abilities. This characterization

In 1926, the first year after completion of Mariemont's major building program, the town square at Oak and Chestnut Streets bustled with activity. The shops on the ground floor of the Ripley & LeBoutillier apartment buildings provided many of the services needed by the community. Nearly three hundred families lived in the new town by that year.

falsely promoted the new town and somewhat discouraged its appeal to families of higher financial status. Bleecker Marquette, executive secretary of the Better Housing League in Cincinnati, felt it necessary in 1927 to correct this image: "There still continues to prevail on the part of many citizens the feeling that Mariemont should be a workingman's home development and that it has failed in its purpose. We have tried repeatedly to make it clear that Mariemont is not intended to be a workingman's home development, but aims to provide an outstanding example of the importance of scientific planning to good housing."[18] During the 1940s and afterward, the village gradually evidenced an upper-middle-class population, especially in the area of single homes south of Wooster Pike, as families sought the benefits of a planned community.

In 1926, Livingood's sales operation became active. Office space on the main floor of the Mariemont Inn was appropriated for a headquarters and building association to arrange loans to prospective purchasers of lots. Livingood's eldest daughter, Josephine, was employed to plan and equip the tea room in the inn, an attraction Livingood hoped would lure customers with its terrace that overlooked sunken gardens. "This building," Livingood wrote, "puts into the shade anything I have seen in Garden Cities thus far. It simply is full of possibilities thanks to its location and shape of lot."

But Livingood was cautious about Mariemont's future and its operating expenses. In his letter to Nolen, he cited some restraints to the village's progress:

> I am not going to start the Town Center Building, even though the plans were ready. We must have more population. Building costs are still too high. The Hospital also could be opened this Fall but I want to take my time over the equipment and personnel. It, too, can wait but the Farm is in full blast, we get splendid crops, the Nursery has been most helpful and we have a dandy little herd of Guernsey cattle, right from the Island. The Concourse is rapidly shaping up and will be a great feature. Mr. Mirick will soon have his irrigation installed so we can keep our public places green. Indeed everything is so perfect that the slightest inconsistency or neglect sticks up like a sore thumb.[19]

Livingood's pride in Mariemont's coming-of-age was expressed clearly. His intention to create an English village seemed to have been realized. Since Mariemont was a private enterprise, owned and operated by the Mariemont Company, with restrictions imposed on all residents alike, property owners as well as renters, there was little chance that any visual or functional erosion would set in. Lawns and landscaping, parks and streets, were all maintained by the company, and any idiosyncratic treatment of the exterior of buildings was discouraged, if not prohibited.

It is curious, however, that Livingood did not permit the inn and the hospital to operate immediately after their completion or intend to build the Town Center Building until the population grew and construction costs declined. Neither of these conditions occurred, at least to Livingood's satisfaction, and the monumental Town Center Building designed by Steinkamp with Paul Cret's consultation was denied forever. A special article on Mariemont in *Architecture* circulated the most extensive and professionally prepared information, in illustrations and words, yet published on Mary Emery's planned community. Its author is unknown, although architect Edmund Gilchrist is credited with suggesting the article to the magazine's editors. Only one glaring error (listing the village's founder as "Mrs. Mary G. Emery") appears in its thirty-one pages of text and black-and-white images of buildings and their plans.[20]

Nolen responded to Livingood's glowing appraisal, sending his remarks to his patron just before sailing for Europe and stating that he "never wavered in [the] belief that it would come out well and that we should all ultimately be proud of it." He correctly assessed the real determinant of the project and revealed his fears. "The final test is the human one," he wrote, "and your reference to contentment on the face of the people and the appearance of the children is very much to the point. And I am also glad to have your comment on the planting and the careful reservation and preservation of the natural features. So often these are destroyed, and there were times when I feared that the liberal policy with reference to these natural features would not be retained."[21] Nolen did not elaborate his reference to the "liberal policy" that might affect the environment of Mariemont, yet his statement reflects his keen awareness of the landscape's significance as the setting for a planned community, an awareness of natural beauty and resources. Certainly in Mariemont, Nolen had found a rich terrain of woods, farmland, scenic bluff, and winding river to incorporate into his superbly conceived plan.

An appraisal of Mariemont's status in November 1926, ominously indicating a slowdown in sales of lots and home construction, was reported to Nolen by the Mariemont Company's general manager, George Mirick: "We are closing down our building program to some extent. The lots are selling slowly but I believe as soon as people wake up to what they are getting for what they pay that they will move much faster."[22] Although all of the houses were rented and the school brimmed with 360 pupils, Mirick stated encouragingly, the Mariemont Inn and hospital were completed but unoccupied by their intended users. There were other problems with new residents. The allotment gardens were not successful because of inadequate care, and there were too few garages to meet the demand. The gardens were soon converted to playgrounds and automobile garages. Mirick was most impressed, he told Nolen, that the traction line along Murray Avenue, on the northern border of the village, would soon provide frequent service between Mariemont and downtown Cincinnati. This provision for public transportation, later supplanted by buses, greatly aided the sale and rental of housing.

Sales of home lots lagged below expectations. But the most significant news in Mirick's same letter to Nolen was the long-awaited arrival of sixty tons of roof stones, first discovered by architect Louis Jallade at the Calcot tithe barn in the summer of 1926. Acquiring the stones permitted the completion of the Mariemont church. The village's unique architectural elements, the fourteenth-century stone tiles forming the undulating roof of the town's centerpiece, were installed by the dedication date of the new church the following year.

In the first months of 1927, a drastic reduction occurred in the Mariemont Company's work force when one-half of the work crew was laid off. Once there had been one thousand workmen engaged, but only a skeleton corps was left by February 1927. No electricians were retained on the job, only one truck driver remained, and but six laborers still worked at the rock quarry.[23] Although the economic hardships of the Depression were not yet being felt, a reluctance to invest more of Mary Emery's money in the project surfaced at this stage. The Mariemont Company had found fewer buyers for their lots than they had envisioned. No doubt feeling the financial pinch, although Mrs. Emery's great wealth certainly could have sustained continued expansion of the project, Livingood pulled back from further construction.

Livingood occasionally expressed to Nolen his views on a long-past event, recalling his disdain of conferences and architectural exhibitions. In the only known letter he wrote to his town planner in 1927, he griped about receiving few requests for the Mariemont Company's brochure. The city engineer of Hamburg, Germany, had asked for a copy, Livingood stated, but

> frankly this is the *first result* from that conference [the town planning conference in New York City that Nolen attended in 1925], although we sent many hundred copies of the then brochure, with an insert stating that a completed copy of the brochure with illustrations would be sent to all who make application, etc. It is as I thought would be the case; for there is very little value to conventions, excepting plans on walls at such conventions. About all that people get from them is a knowledge of the type and character of men, and at this point I will say that I selected you because of the good impression you made at various conventions where I watched you closely. I selected you because of your sanity and strong character. So, if anybody asks you in the future what I think of conventions quote the above with my compliments.[24]

The interlocking planes and angles of the Mariemont Memorial Church, constructed between 1923 and 1927 to plans of Louis E. Jallade, are attractive features of the Norman-style church capped by its medieval roof.

In the spring of 1927, Mary Emery became ill and submitted to two operations in Cincinnati. She then convalesced at her summer home in Rhode Island. Nolen heard of Mrs. Emery's illness and offered his sympathy to Livingood in a letter that again extolled Mariemont and its place in his heart.

> Mr. Mirick and Jack [Nolen's son] gave the most glowing accounts of Mariemont. The building of a new town takes time, and requires not only skill and business acumen and devotion to ideals, but also patience, and then more patience. One must be willing to wait. Critics are usually persons of impatient temperament. Again I offer my most hearty congratulations. Beauty in towns is too rare a plant in this country. May Mariemont be an influential exemplar!
>
> Indeed we all hold Mrs. Emery in high estimation, and it grieves us to hear of her illness. May she have a speedy recovery. Her words—and yours—about "New Towns for Old" [Nolen's recently published book] give me great pleasure. In many ways Mariemont is the best to date, and deserves its significant place at the beginning and end of my little story.[25]

Mary Emery failed to improve during her stay in Newport, and she returned to Cincinnati in late August. In early October she contracted a cold that soon developed into pneumonia, and she died at her home, Edgecliffe, on October 11, 1927. Newspaper headlines cited her as "Cincinnati's Most Revered Philanthropist," and the *New York Times* in its obituary on October 12 called her "one of America's richest women, founder of the model city of Mariemont." Work was canceled at Mariemont on the day of her funeral, October 14, and two days later a memorial service was held at the Mariemont church. Pastor Paul Hoppe recounted her many benefactions, noting that Mariemont "was her especial pet project, which she followed in detail up to the very last."[26] For Mariemont, her death ended the fulfillment of the 1921 plan fashioned by Nolen and masterminded by Livingood.[27] For charities she supported across the nation and in Europe, her death ended a spectacular record of generous sharing of wealth.

8 · EMERY, NOLEN, AND LIVINGOOD

After Mary Emery's death, Mariemont retreated from its energetic beginnings and its frenzied construction. There was a sense of prosperity and fulfillment in the village, however, as new residents moved into their rented apartments and houses. Landscape and nursery crews planted shade trees along the streets, the elementary school was filled with children, and a few shops offered their services. For the next few years, until Nolen's death in 1937, Livingood and his town planner carried on a desultory correspondence. Their letters focused on Mariemont, primarily, providing observations on its earliest years. Correspondence between the two men often expressed their satisfaction that Mariemont was a working community, a lively and functioning town.

Throughout Mariemont's development, Livingood's hauteur was expressed in his dealings with the architects and builders, probably because he felt that they could challenge his taste, vision, or instructions. No doubt frustrated by lagging sales of lots for home builders, Livingood berated the architectural profession in a letter to Nolen: "Frankly our greatest trouble with builders is their plans, I mean the exteriors." Some potential homeowners, he said, objected "to paying 6% to an architect and would rather deal with a builder who having just finished such a house can *guarantee* them the cost, whereas architects today have not time and do not know anything about the cost of a *house*. On this point every one of my architects fell down." Construction costs worried Livingood throughout the course of Mariemont's building, although his entire career in Cincinnati was based on the use of others' financial support, the Emery family's millions. "It is strange to me that the Profession as a whole has not taken up the matter of costs," he wrote, "for after all artisans' wages are practically

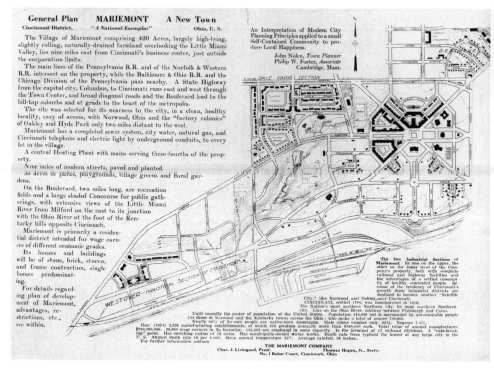

The plan published in 1925 to promote Mariemont showed a town slightly larger than the one illustrated by John Nolen in 1921. Houses and churches were proposed on the 1925 plan, but lot lines for future building were not shown. An important addition to the plan was the Westover industrial section, which adjoined the southwest edge of Mariemont. This revised plan was used in the Mariemont Company brochure and was given as a flyer to prospective buyers and renters.

uniform in this country; building supplies are in the hands of rings so that cost is almost a full day's work for a day's pay. Here in Cincinnati our Model Homes Company and the Better Housing League have frankly thrown up their hands and say it is impossible to build houses for the people. Even $6,000 is not enough for 4 or 5 rooms. Luckily we built group housing heavily and there is some economy in that, though not very much because of the exorbitant cost of plumbing and the expense of interior finish."[1]

By 1928, only 50 houses had been built by individuals in Mariemont. Most of these owners needed loans through the Mariemont Company's building association. Part of the reason for the slow building of private, individual homes might have been Livingood's complaint that Mariemont was "too far out of town, and moreover the architectural restrictions we do impose drive people to neighborhoods where there is no regard for quality of building nor taste." Livingood haughtily disdained the rapidly developing suburbs of Cincinnati and "would rather see Mariemont stand idle than to have it develop as these modern subdivisions are being thrown together. Luckily we have a large enough rent roll to carry our project and that is where I was wise if I say so myself. If I had built houses to sell I would be in the soup."

Most of the rental apartments were occupied, but Sheldon Close, Albert Place, and Denny Place were not. Livingood thought these special groups of

All of the buildings constructed by the Mariemont Company by 1928 are shown in this aerial view. The clusters of houses south of Wooster Pike (at *right center:* Denny Place, Albert Place, and Sheldon Close) are the only new buildings in the undeveloped and wooded areas.

houses were "rather isolated and cater to a class of people who would rather build their own homes. Nevertheless I am not discouraged, because I have built for 20 years ahead. I believe that with continuing prosperity and enlarging of ideas about the value of a beautiful home people *will* live some day in these and similar houses: in other words, be unwilling merely to exist as they are now doing in tenements and in the crowded districts downtown." These comments indicate that Mariemont's developed sections, the closes south of Wooster Pike, as well as undeveloped lots available to purchasers, lagged in rentals and sales. Livingood had expected, no doubt, much more activity outside the Dale Park district.

Housing starts were finished for the Mariemont Company by 1928. Only the public structures were under construction. Foundations were in place for the boathouse by January 1928. This fanciful stone-roofed recreational chalet nestled at the eastern end of a shallow lagoon in Dogwood Park had been designed by Charles F. Cellarius, a Cincinnati architect, on the site where Nolen had assigned it in 1921 as the "Bath House." The hospital and church neared completion, and work on the recreation building designed by George deGersdorff was scheduled to begin in the spring of 1929. Livingood thought that the hospital "will soon be another added reason for living in Mariemont for it is one of the most perfectly appointed and best located hospitals in the country. The views from those porches are simply marvelous, and you know the rooms are so constructed that the beds may be drawn out on to the porch."[2]

In April 1930 Nolen extolled Mariemont as "permanently in my mind as one of the leading projects, if not *the* leading project, of the twenty-five year record which I am just concluding."[3] Earlier, he had sought other residential developments to design, but a downturn in his activity was in the wind. Livingood was not helpful with recommendations, and his discouragement in assessing opportunities for new communities was obvious.

> I am sorry to say that I know no one interested in a large residential development *anywhere,* for frankly even I, with all my enthusiasm for better housing, would not wish to draw any one into the vortex of building under present prices. The only kind of house that is being built in quantity today is the cheaply-built, pretentious, stucco imitation Spanish, which is pure clap-trap. The reason is very simple. Just as people who come into money suddenly deck

themselves out with fancy togs that in a month or two are worse than nothing, so the masses today who know nothing about the importance of good construction and good materials are caught up by the frills of housing: the pink walls, the variegated imitation tile roof, the colored bath tubs, frigidaires, dish washing machines, etc. I was most fortunate in being *willing* to rent, for if I had waited to *sell* I would certainly be in the hole. Mariemonters are a picked class, the discerning kind, and they are coming from all parts of the country, some even by airplane. . . . Out of 350 houses that we ourselves built approximately all but 25 are occupied, and a large number of people have begun to build for themselves. So, ours, is a going concern.[4]

Livingood's optimism was tarnished by the American stock market collapse in 1929, which ushered in an economic disaster replete with bank failures, factory closings, and high unemployment. Activities had slowed in Mariemont even before the crash, except for basic maintenance and the construction of the recreation building, dedicated eventually on May 17, 1930. The boathouse opened its slips for canoes and rowboats in the summer of 1930. This oak-timbered and stone building contained restrooms, a fireplace, a meeting room, and storage areas for small boats. It was destined to serve boaters in the warm months and skaters in the winter when the lagoon froze, but its use was compromised when the tiny lake was filled in after World War II.[5]

Layoffs at the village site were predicted as the Depression's grip tightened, and resident engineer Parks recorded in January a cutback of all laborers except for six men for odd jobs, with the entire force laid off for one month beginning on July 24, 1930.[6] Few lots were sold to prospective builders in the early 1930s, and practically no homes were built by individuals during the troubled years of Franklin D. Roosevelt's first term as president. Vacant rental units were common then in Mariemont, adding to the pall throughout the neighborhoods. Early in 1931, the Thomas J. Emery Memorial offered for sale the Rhode Island estate of Mary Emery. It was a poor time to expect the sale of a large house and its tract of sixty acres, with extensive gardens and expensive maintenance. Mary's summer home, the estate that had given the name to Nolen's planned community and the retreat she had loved and developed into one of America's premier garden spots, was sold by Livingood for only $43,970.87.[7]

Financial pressures of the Depression and the Emery Memorial's recognition

Designed by New York architect George deGersdorff, the recreation building was dedicated in 1930. It was the last major building constructed by the Mariemont Company. Its Italianate style, characterized by its dominant campanile, or clock tower, long arcade, and red roof tiles, added a new appearance to the architectural mix in Mariemont.

that a more streamlined administration of Mary Emery's estate and the new town of Mariemont was needed caused the Mariemont Company to consider its own dissolution. On December 8, 1931, the company's stockholders, with Livingood representing Mary Emery's holdings, passed a resolution to dissolve the company and transfer its assets to the Thomas J. Emery Memorial.[8] This transfer eliminated much duplication of effort and staff resources with the two agencies. At the end of December 1931, the Mariemont Company passed its control of Mariemont to the Emery Memorial, a nonprofit foundation. Moving quickly immediately afterward, Robert A. Taft, Mrs. Emery's attorney and a trustee of the Emery Memorial, visited Warren Parks in his office to explain the terms of the transfer and how this action would affect employees of the company. On New Year's Day, the *Mariemont Messenger* informed village residents of this startling action.[9]

With this new ownership, the village created and financed by Mary Emery became the property of the nonprofit foundation she had formed in 1925. Nolen's plan and further construction of proposed buildings were doomed by the Depression, Mrs. Emery's death, and the new corporate structure of the Emery Memorial. This foundation gradually moved away from the singular focus of Mariemont and into a wider philanthropic mission. The town hall, town center shops and arcade, automobile bridge over Whiskey Creek, fieldhouse, library, pensioners' cottages, post office, additional churches, and extension of the Mariemont Inn now were only dreams. They were never built. John Nolen's noble design for the national exemplar of town planning would not be realized in all its parts. Livingood's architectural embellishments for his plan remained incomplete.

Nolen and Livingood continued their correspondence, a few letters each way until Nolen's death. No design work was requested in the 1930s from the town planner of Mariemont, but the two men enjoyed congratulating each other or, in Livingood's case, justifying his goals for the new town. Livingood seldom touched on the economic problems besetting the nation and Mariemont's growth. His air of confidence never failed him, as indicated in a letter to Nolen in May 1932.

> I am sure that if you should see this property as Mrs. Livingood and I did yesterday, a sunny, crisp afternoon, and heard the Carillon ringing [a bell tower had been erected in 1930 in Dale Park, a gift from Isabella Hopkins in memory of her sister, Mary Emery], you would agree that ours is a going concern and a success certainly from the material standpoint. Our planting, while a little tardy in getting full growth, adds much of course to the layout. But I really think we can claim that our buildings are as attractive as those in most model towns. For instance, I have just seen so-called "garden cities" in France and Spain and a short while ago saw again Welwyn and Cadbury's. Their recreation buildings cannot compare for a minute with ours completed a few years ago.[10]

But beneath this positive outlook, Livingood was dismayed that there were many unrented properties in 1932. In spite of his opinion about "the material standpoint" of the village and its buildings, streets, infrastructure, parks, and landscaping, he rationalized to Nolen that he had really been building for the future.

As the newness of Mariemont disappeared and the frequency of newspaper and magazine articles diminished, Livingood felt the loss of publicity and recognition for his accomplishments, as he noted in the same letter. He regretted especially the lack of credit given to Mariemont by "all editors in summarizing the garden city movement with the illustrations before them, [who] seem to think that we made no contribution at all to the housing problem; that masses will have to live in rabbit warrens as seems to be the outlook in Germany and Austria at least. I still stand by my guns and believe that with the higher intelligence, better earning power and more equable climate in the Temperate Zone, Americans will insist upon individual homes."

Nolen's record of accomplishments and his role as president of the International Federation for Housing and Town Planning, a post he held until his death, had the potential to open many doors of developers and government agencies in Europe and the United States, those who might be keen on planning new communities. Unfortunately, the economic downturn in the world sidetracked many fine intentions, leaving mere concepts instead of construction. Nolen maintained his usual optimistic outlook, however, even as commissions shriveled. The good times of 1920–25 were well remembered when he wrote to Livingood that "the *Mariemont Messenger* and your very kind letter brings me great happiness, because Mariemont stands out as the most worthwhile project on which I ever had the privilege of being professionally engaged. The first decade has passed. It will take at least another ten years to demonstrate Mariemont's full value, and the contribution which Mrs. Emery has made under your leadership to one of the chief problems of the modern world—housing and town planning as a basis for wholesome American neighborhood life."

The Depression's crush was sorely felt by Nolen, who reported sadly to Livingood in that letter that he was

> fallen upon hard times. It is not easy to determine the way out, but of one thing
> I feel sure, and that is, that any permanent way out for this country must be associated with the type of development which Mariemont represents, and with
> the spirit which brought it into existence. For the first time in more than
> twenty-five years I find myself, not without employment, but without employment that yields any income. My time is given practically entirely now to public work. But alas, being without financial resources, I am confronted with the
> same baffling problems which beset the unemployed working man. A net an-

nual deficit larger than my average annual income for a number of years furnishes cause for reflection and some anxiety. It is a time when many must suffer.[11]

Nolen's belt-tightening was repeated across the nation, and Mariemont's small staff felt the crimp, too. Parks's letters to Nolen, unlike Livingood's, relayed the brutal facts of the downturn. In the late autumn of 1932, there was a second salary cut of 10 percent for all workers still on the payroll, Parks stated, and he wondered whether Nolen knew of any job prospects for "a man with my experience." He expected a termination but thought it was "fortunate for me that I can still be of some service here for a while, anyway."[12]

Parks continued to write to Nolen about conditions at Mariemont in its nascency, regretting that "everything is being pared to the bone at present" and "our present organization is now a mere skeleton so that it is a constant task to keep the necessary work going." Particularly difficult for the village was the decrease in rentals, thus affecting the cash flow that maintained the Emery Memorial's responsibilities. "The vacancies in the rental property are at a high water mark," Parks wrote to Nolen, "and of course the maintenance operations do not decrease. We are not discouraged, however, for Mariemont is well founded and when conditions return to normal it will surely come into its own."[13]

Nolen's planned communities held his interest even after his work with them was concluded, and he peppered Parks with inquiries about Mariemont's status in the years after his dismissal. As Parks was one of the few staff members left from the earliest days of Mariemont, his comments were especially appreciated. In November, Parks noted some rental and house purchase statistics, providing a review of 1932 prices for housing in Mariemont.

The number of families now living in Mariemont is about 290. We have a large number of vacancies at present—probably 40%. The population, in round numbers, is 1,000. The prices of houses range from $7,500 to $25,000. Rentals on houses vary from $28.50 for 3 rooms, bath and garage, to $70.00 for 6 rooms and garage. With central heat included the rent varies from $70 for 6 rooms to $150 for 9 rooms and 4 baths. The apartment rentals which include heat and janitor service but not garage, range from $12.50 for one room and bath to 5 rooms at $45. Three room apartments rent at from $25 to $32.50 and 4 rooms from $35 to $45. The garage rental is $4.00. Many of the residents commute to

Cincinnati but there are also a large number of traveling men living in the Town. The majority of the residents are of the "white collar class."[14]

Nolen returned to Mariemont for brief visits in 1934 and 1935, the last times he saw the community he had designed. In October 1934, he arranged to interrupt a trip from Saint Louis to Washington, D.C., but the stopover was unannounced and he missed seeing Livingood.[15] Nolen's visit in 1935 brought him and other distinguished conferees to Cincinnati for a joint meeting of the American City Planning Institute, American Civic Association, and National Conference on City Planning. A conference event especially appealing to Nolen was the luncheon held at the Mariemont Inn on May 21. This brought Nolen and his fellow planners to the center of his greatest work. Hoping to see Livingood once again, Nolen confided that "the work at Mariemont and association with you is one of the pleasantest features of my whole professional life."[16] The two apparently did not meet on this occasion for "one of the old-time talks" Nolen so relished, as no acknowledging letter exists from the ever-polite Nolen. They never encountered each other again.

John Nolen, town planner of Mariemont, America's preeminent urban designer, died after a short illness at his home, 10 Garden Street, Cambridge, Massachusetts, on February 18, 1937. Although his professional life was curtailed for a few years before his death because of the economic downturn, Nolen's career had been richly active during the first third of the twentieth century. It included more than four hundred public planning projects, the redesign of fifty cities in twenty different states, and his authorship of several dozen books, reports, and articles.[17] The dean of American city planning and probably its most talented theorist and practitioner was three years younger than his Mariemont employer, Charles J. Livingood, who outlived him by fifteen years. On February 26, 1952, Livingood expired at Holmes Hospital, Cincinnati.[18] His life and career since 1890 had been synonymous at first with the interests of Mary and Thomas J. Emery and, after 1906, with Mrs. Emery's alone and the estate she had inherited. A major part of his solicitous care of Mary Emery and her philanthropies involved his role with Mariemont. With his death, the remarkable triumvirate of Mary Muhlenberg Emery, John Nolen, and Charles J. Livingood lost its third and last member.

9 ✦ WAS MARIEMONT
THE NATIONAL EXEMPLAR?

In the January–February 2000 issue of *Preservation,* the magazine of the National Trust for Historic Preservation, the editor reported that "wonderful models already exist" for those seeking something better in the suburbs instead of sprawl, sterile streets, isolation, acres of lawn to mow, automobile dependence, and a host of other negatives. Mariemont is one of those wonderful models, yet only a few enlightened town planners, architects, and historians of urban culture have recognized this town's achievements and those of other planned communities developed before World War II in the United States. Among perceptive urban historians, Witold Rybczynski considered Mary Emery "an enlightened developer" and Mariemont "a fully realized garden suburb in the United States." Further, he rated Mariemont as "an extraordinarily subtle exercise in axial formalism combined with a very relaxed form of grid planning." Walter Creese, historian of the Garden City movement and its derivative expressions, credited Mariemont with "a certain intrinsic American quality . . . an amplitude of scale and a devotion to entrance gates, parks and playgrounds, and green Olmstedian strips." Gwendolyn Wright's important study of American housing succinctly assessed Mariemont's place among new suburbs in the twentieth century, yet she recognized the ambiguity in deciding whether Mariemont was a model suburb, a town for workers, a real estate development for return of investment, or a pure philanthropy.[1] It was all of these, but, in addition, Mariemont was allowed to function freely in the real estate market. Because of this, its renters and homeowners are more diverse today, economically speaking, than they were at the town's conception. Wright's recognition of Mariemont's contribution to housing underscores its "diversity of possible housing

types—rather than one neglected solution as the dominant image of quaint suburbia—that makes this period [the 1920s] important."[2] These writers are a sampling of the historians, architects, planners, and developers who have given adequate credit to nineteenth- and early-twentieth-century examples of planned communities. A wider, more appreciative audience is needed beyond disciples already committed.

Builders and developers after the war's conclusion in 1945 produced a patch-work quilt of housing developments that smothered the landscape all across America. Many of these developments were called planned communities, but they went awry and showed little understanding of exemplary models and their adaptation to present requirements.[3] Some new planned towns or suburbs seemed to rise like the phoenix from the ashes, and suddenly the planned community seems to have been freshly invented—a new idea with no precedents to be credited. Many of the new urbanists are looking back, however, to planned communities like Letchworth or Hampstead Garden Suburb in England and Forest Hills Gardens or Mariemont in the United States as models no longer forgotten.[4] The principles espoused by Nolen for Mariemont are now incorporated in the planning philosophy of some of the major practitioners of town planning, such as Andres Duany and Elizabeth Plater-Zyberk, who "*conceived* [my emphasis] five principles of neighborhood design."[5] That Duany and Plater-Zyberk venerated the "remembered idea" of communities like Mariemont is acknowledged in their writings and plans. A catalogue accompanying an exhibition of their planned projects, held at Harvard University in 1990, included illustrations of planned communities that influenced their work. Among the chosen illustrations in a very select group was John Nolen's plan of Mariemont.[6]

Were the principles of Duany and Plater-Zyberk conceived, or were they merely reinvented? Although Nolen may not have described them so precisely, certainly Mariemont employed them. Duany and Plater-Zyberk's first principle required the neighborhood to have an identifiable center and edge, and the second urged a limited breadth so that residents could walk easily from point to point in the neighborhood. Third, a mix of residential and commercial property in close proximity was advocated. Fourth, a network of interconnected streets was required, and fifth, public buildings and places must be located in the plan. A look at Mariemont's genesis and development clearly indicates that each of these principles of neighborhood design was actively engaged by Nolen in this Ohio community, beginning in 1920.

John Nolen coined Mariemont's motto: a National Exemplar. The vision shared by Mary Emery, Nolen, and Livingood successfully demonstrated the virtues of a well-planned community. Beyond its accomplishments as a practical example of suburban living for its residents, both Nolen and Livingood hoped that other planned communities would replicate Mariemont elsewhere in the United States. Like many philosophical theses, Mariemont was nobly conceived. Its practical application was proven in better living for its residents. Mariemont offered a new community blessed with many amenities generally lacking in urban centers. Thus, in Mariemont's achievements, the standard set can rightly be regarded as an exemplar. In so many ways, Mariemont exemplifies the best in linking patronage, town planning, and sensible architecture in a new community.

An assessment of Mariemont requires a review of Nolen's basis for the village's plan. This plan, he succinctly stated in the Mariemont Company's brochure, was based on three considerations. The first consideration of a town planner and the "root and basis" for his design of Mariemont derived from "a clear conception of the kind of community that [it] was to be when fully built up."[7] Nolen's plans for Mariemont conformed to his patron's instructions, of course, as delineated at the start of their five-year involvement. Livingood's conception of Mariemont derived from the models of certain English and American planned communities. He insisted that his new town provide housing and amenities that coincided with his vision for an entire town complex. This new town was not a Utopia or ideal community but "a convenient, practical, and beautiful town; practical from the point of view of use; beautiful from the point of view of appearance." Its purposes embraced "the whole of the family's social life," an achievement seldom sought in the usual suburban development today. To Livingood's eye, when Mariemont was built up, it would present itself as a conservative, well-established suburb with an English village flavor, offering a range of shops, businesses, and services. Every public and commercial part of Mariemont was conveniently located for the town's residents. To comply with his aesthetic requirements, its architecture would echo Norman, Tudor, Queen Anne, and Georgian historical styles in revival form.

A significant element in Nolen's design for Mariemont is expressed in his second consideration. In the Mariemont Company brochure, he required "a study of the site itself and the region in which it is located and to which it should be conveniently oriented." His plan revered the chosen site. Nolen respected the topography and natural components of the farmers' fields and woods that Livingood had selected for the new town. Both Nolen and Livingood recognized the advantages of living near a large city, and neither of them expected Mariemont to be an independent, self-sustaining community, as the English garden cities hoped to be. Cultural and job opportunities in nearby Cincinnati were always in mind, and Livingood thought at one time that Mariemont might eventually be annexed to Cincinnati. A "fluid society . . . socially and economically mobile" defined the intended residents of the town Livingood developed.[8]

Nolen estimated that his plan assigned approximately one-half of the available acreage to house lots, one-quarter to public property, and one-quarter to streets. This balanced proportioning of space is evidenced in his third consideration, that there must be a "regard for the principles of town planning." His work assumed "that at every point in the development of the new town some sense of the form of the whole will be preserved."[9] That is, once the overall plan or framework was established, there would be no intrusions or changes to negate the effectiveness of the whole plan. Nolen realized that Mariemont would experience change as the years passed, but he felt that any modification or insert into Mariemont's fabric should be compatible with his plan and the town's architecture, engineering, landscaping, and maintenance program. Nolen recognized that unregulated or unsympathetic change to a plan is a serious challenge. For the most part, Mariemont has met this challenge successfully.

One example of irresponsible change occurred in the 1960s and early 1970s, when the local electric and streetlight company began replacing the original cast iron lamp posts with clumsy, wooden examples of no distinction, claiming that the original posts were difficult to repair or replace. Objections from the Mariemont Preservation Foundation resulted in a plan for the village to assume control of the streetlight system. In this plan, the village purchased cast iron replicas of the original posts to replace the wooden ones. Electricity was purchased from the electric company, and the village became responsible for the maintenance of its streetlights. To pay for this, the Mariemont Preservation Foundation appealed successfully to the Thomas J. Emery Memorial, the foundation formed by Mary Emery in 1925 and one of Cincinnati's major philanthropic agencies, to match the village's investment in the restoration project. This effort launched other preservation and renewal activities under the leadership of the Mariemont Preservation Foundation.

Nolen's third consideration urged that "Mariemont finally is to be tested in terms of human satisfaction, for above all it aims to be 'an interpretation of modern city planning principles applied to a small self-contained community to produce local happiness.'" From its beginning as an idealistic concept to provide good housing in an attractive suburban setting and until the dissolution of the Mariemont Company, Mariemont had been articulated with care. The town achieved its goal of providing "a place of residence for a wide range of families of different economic degrees." As a residential development, it was not "a laboratory for sociological experiments in the problem of housing," nor was it a company town or industrial village. Nolen planned a "complete town . . . as an illustration of how well people of moderate means can live,"[10] a town expected to house 5,000 to 10,000 residents. This projected population was never reached. The U.S. Census of 1990 recorded 3,118 men, women, and children, a rather constant number maintained throughout the decades since World War II.

In Mariemont's plan, there were housing opportunities for two types of residents: renters (primarily in Dale Park's apartments and townhouses) and builder-owners (scattered throughout the village) in freestanding houses. Group housing in buildings erected by the Mariemont Company was intended for one class or type of renter, and Livingood used various terms to define this typical renter: "worker," "the humblest dweller in Mariemont," "average wage-earner," and "people of moderate means." Beginning in 1925 and except for the earliest years of the Depression, Mariemont found ready renters for its apartments and townhouses, as the letters and reports attest.

Unfortunately, some critics of Mariemont have incorrectly assessed the village's accomplishments. For example, one author wrote that Mariemont implemented "a desire for nothing more than a private housing program at low interest rates."[11] This argument is belied by Mariemont's well-published intentions and the high occupancy rate of rental apartments by people of modest means several years before the effects of the Depression were felt. Another critic complained that "Mariemont not only failed to provide new homes for the wage earner, but it apparently failed as a model for other subdivisions, too."[12] It may not have been replicated as a model community, but its housing for lower-income and middle-class families met its goal, for the wage earner had a selection of apartments with varying rents as well as small houses available for purchase through the Mariemont Company. During the Depression years, rents were reduced to accommodate families on very limited incomes. Rental units continue to offer moderately priced housing in Mariemont.

Builder-owners generally were more affluent, able to purchase a lot and build a house, either through their own financing or with a loan from the Mariemont Company. This type of resident had more freedom than the renter in determining the location, size, and style of his residence, but even these factors were regulated by the Mariemont Company and later by the Emery Memorial. To suggest the character of a neighborhood and to guide prospective homebuilders, the company created a few pockets of houses apart from the Dale Park section, such as Denny Place, Albert Place, and Sheldon Close, and these suggested acceptable architectural styles and standards of construction.

Individual house lots in Mariemont were of normal size for a middle-class community in the 1920s. Average lot size for a detached house was 50–80 feet in width and 120 feet in depth, not particularly spacious by today's expectations for homebuyers. Normal lot size for a group house was 16 by 100 feet. Only five or six lots suitable for building single-family, freestanding houses remained in 1999 among Mariemont's 750 residential lots originally drawn on Nolen's plan. The town's unexpandable boundaries and limited number of lots encourage homeowners to renovate and improve their residences. In the 1990s, many modest-size houses sprouted additions and conversions of attached garages into living space, filling the lot to the limits of the building code. Unfortunately, many of these expanded houses appear too large and overbuilt for the size of their lots.

Livingood dictated Mariemont's appearance as a recreated English village, and this aesthetic principle remains in place today. This applies to commercial as well as residential property. In 1992 a large building housing a Kroger super-market (its brickwork decorated by touches of stucco and half-timbering) next to the Mariemont Inn on Wooster Pike, and only a short stroll from the town square, was acquired by the owner of the inn. He and his architect were sensitive to the Tudor Revival style of the inn, so the new structure erected eventually on the Kroger site, now called the Strand, echoes its neighbors with its slate roof, sham half-timbering, arcade of shops, and brickwork. Even the clay chimney pots enhance the Tudor look.

Livingood expected that new houses built by individuals would emulate the models and styles erected by the Mariemont Company, as the "Englishness" of the community was predetermined. Throughout the village, the Tudor Revival style is evident in many residences constructed in the late 1920s and 1930s. Prime examples of this style are on Center Street, an enclave of two- and three-story single-family homes adjacent to a row of four-family apartment buildings. All of these buildings exhibit Tudor characteristics: brick construction, steeply pitched roofs, and stucco and half timber on exterior walls.

After the houses on Sheldon Close were finished, the Mariemont Company did not build other residences in the village, so home-builders sought their own architects. There were restrictions on architectural design and style, however, from the beginning. Charles Cellarius, one of the architects commissioned by Livingood, served as a kind of artistic czar with the Mariemont Company and the Emery Memorial, owners of the village until its incorporation in 1941. The one-floor, ranch-style house was disdained, and only a few were ever built in Mariemont. The Tudor or Georgian Revival style was preferred for a typical, two-story residence. But, as architect and town planner Robert Stern points out, "Once the town began to grow again after World War II, the idealism of its origins was ignored, so that much of Mariemont's architecture is indistinguishable from that of any other suburb of the post-war period."[13]

Single ownership of all of the Dale Park apartments and townhouses was in place for over twenty-five years after Mariemont's inauguration. Group housing designed by Gilchrist, Dana, Mackenzie, Ripley & LeBoutillier, Ziegler, and Kruckemeyer & Strong was owned originally by the Mariemont Company and then by the Thomas J. Emery Memorial after 1931. In the 1950s, all of these units were sold to a realty firm in Cincinnati, the Chelsea-Moore Company, whose owner was a great-nephew of Mary Emery. During this period of ownership by single parties, maintenance and landscaping for housing and grounds were unified, and each unit received the same care. A high standard for the appearance of the buildings, yards, and gardens was maintained, especially by the Mariemont Company and Emery Memorial. No individual interpretation of a building's exterior was permitted. Paint colors, roof shingles, and any exterior changes had to respect the original design of the architects, and eccentric or inappropriate changes that varied from the original were prohibited. Thus, the visual cohesiveness of groups of buildings or within a single structure was carefully observed.

An ordinance protecting the exteriors of historic district properties (those built primarily by the Mariemont Company) was enacted by the village in 1983. This historic district ordinance is instrumental in maintaining the integrity of the architecture and the relationships of buildings to each other and as part of Nolen's plan. Interior improvements, renovations, and upgrades for group housing units have a spotty record of success, however, in the Dale Park section. Interiors are not governed by this ordinance.

Income levels of Mariemont residents have risen dramatically since World War II. In the early years, differences in income levels were not great between renters and homeowners. A Dale Park apartment renter's income was not much lower than a homeowner's who might live on a street south of Wooster Pike. Gradually, beginning after World War II, more affluent families recognized the merits of Mariemont, and with their moves into the village a significant gap between low and high incomes developed. But in the Dale Park section of Mariemont, the most densely populated part of the village, relatively low-cost housing for renters continues. A major premise of Mariemont's mission is preserved, even under multiple owners who have purchased townhouses and apartment buildings for investment purposes.

A major accomplishment of Mariemont is the neighborhood experience. While many cities and suburbs had the sidewalks, porches, closely grouped houses, parks, and shops that contribute to the neighborhood setting, Mariemont's residents were free of the blights of many decayed or overcrowded metropolitan areas. Mary Emery intended to provide good quality housing, shops, schools, parks, and services, establishing a healthy suburban alternative to the slums and smoke of a city. The smoke that once blackened most major cities is gone, so that concern is not faced today. Other problems have surfaced in America's cities, however, such as the increased distances of shops and stores from people's homes, growing crime in some neighborhoods, and deteriorating public schools and transportation.

Mariemont's plan attempted to avoid these problems. Even with today's ready access to malls and downtown shopping (the latter still available in some cities), the provision for shops that were integrated into the street level of the Ripley & LeBoutillier apartment buildings and along the feeder streets into the main town square is an advanced concept now being reinvented in towns like Seaside and Celebration in Florida. This provision harked back to earlier requirements for city living, that shops and small stores should be integrated into residential developments. One writer reminded readers, "Putting homes atop small retail shops was once the norm for most cities, but the practice was eventually outlawed by zoning codes. What is happening now, city planners say, reflects the limitations of sprawl and the desire of people to get out of their cars."[14] This integration was key in the scheme for the Dale Park neighborhood, especially, with Livingood requiring the architects to provide shops in the ground floor of apartment buildings at the old town square. By the 1990s, none of the dozen or so retail shops that once operated in the Ripley & LeBoutillier units were still in business. Offices and designers' studios now occupy the shop premises.

Although small shops no longer exist in this part of Mariemont, a thriving array of stores and services ring the center of town in the main square. This growth was envisioned by the Mariemont Company, but only the Mariemont Inn was built on the square before the company dissolved. Today, in addition to a reopened and remodeled movie theater facing the town square, there are doctors' and dentists' offices, barber and beauty shops, several restaurants, an ice cream and pastry shop, two banks, a gift shop that provides post office services, and a realty firm. At the Strand, the new structure where the Kroger supermarket once stood, a dozen more shops and services are available, including a delicatessen, dry cleaners, coffee shop, optometrist, and photographer. In spite of the proliferation of malls, reliance on the automobile for even short journeys, and the decline of small retail merchants, it is comforting that the concept for neighborhood shopping within easy walking distance of people's homes continues to thrive in Mariemont. A Georgian-style building at one corner of the square houses Mariemont's administrative offices and the police and fire departments. Sadly, the banal design of this building does not reflect the elegance and refinement of Hubert Ripley's imaginative rendering of a town hall drawn for Livingood in the 1920s.

Within this neighborhood experience, the public schools play a significant role that was not imagined in the 1920s. The Mariemont school district now includes, besides the village of Mariemont, two other communities, Fairfax and Terrace Park, along with an unincorporated section of Hamilton County. Since the early 1990s, Mariemont's demographics have registered a growing number of younger families with school-age children, reversing a "graying" tendency in its population. The school district is highly regarded, ranking among the top ten in Ohio. New renters and homeowners frequently cite the quality and accessibility of the public schools as the reasons for moving to Mariemont, making it more desirable than ever before in its history for renters and homeowners alike.

Unlike many suburban housing developments in the United States, with their bland streetscapes and lack of neighborhood attractions, Mariemont is often cited by recent and longtime citizens for its provisions for children. Mariemont teenagers interviewed for a segment of Peter Jennings's nightly news program on ABC television (July 21, 1999) highlighted the easy access they enjoy by walking or bicycling to the swimming pool, tennis courts, ball fields, schools, ice cream shop, stores, movie theater, and their friends' homes. Within the village, it is not necessary to chauffeur children from activity to activity. Although comments by the interviewed teenagers did not recognize the town planning principles that make this livability possible (and most of them are unaware of Mariemont's history), their conversation with the television interviewer underscored Mariemont's achievement as a family-friendly community.

For all of Mariemont's successes, parts of Nolen's plan and Livingood's objectives never were fulfilled. The most obvious omissions were the public buildings drawn on the plan of 1921 but not constructed. A particularly significant omission in the layout of the village, never envisioned, is a greenbelt. Extending out from the boundaries to soften, shield, and act as buffer for the residential and industrial sections, greenbelts were required in the garden city models, but Livingood protested that the purchase of additional property to the north of Mariemont was too difficult. Although the western edge of Mariemont was blocked by the village of Fairfax and the southern side dropped down the bluffs to the Little Miami River, to the east there was little development when acreage was being purchased. In hindsight, Livingood could have easily and cheaply acquired land to the east of Mariemont's present limits. With additional land, Nolen's plan could have been sited to provide a greenbelt between Mariemont and Fairfax to the west and between Mariemont and the unincorporated township to the east, with its strip mall, fast food chains, roadside businesses, and deserted gasoline stations. This was not to be. An opportunity did exist in the 1980s to acquire about nineteen acres of undeveloped land adjacent to Mariemont's eastern edge, but a misguided village proposal and a negative reaction by the voters killed the project.

Several public buildings were charted on Nolen's 1921 plan, and Livingood enlisted architects, notably Hubert Ripley, to prepare imaginative renderings early in the planning stage. With the exception of the Mariemont Inn, no building proposed for the town square ever materialized, not the post office, bank, city hall, or Steinkamp's shops and apartments. As for churches in the community, Mary Emery insisted that the first religious edifice in Mariemont be nondenominational, but there were no restrictions by her or the Mariemont Company on subsequent churches of any denomination. Only the Mariemont Memorial (now Community) Church was built according to Nolen's plan, although four other churches were assigned positions.

It was Livingood's intention to integrate the athletic stadium and swimming pool with the recreation center, positioning them to the rear and side of the building. A simple athletic field for the first high school was constructed in the 1930s behind the center, and the swimming pool that Livingood delighted in discussing eventually was placed at the Madisonville site. The recreation center's rear exterior wall and terrace remain unfinished and unattractive. The sale of the recreation center to the Mariemont Community Church, converting it to a parish hall and removing it from its intended audience, thwarted the usefulness of the last major building erected by the Mariemont Company.

Nolen's original plan had reserved a site for the high school on Wooster Pike between Plainville Road and the Mariemont Inn. Construction began in 1937 on land purchased by the newly formed public school district. Harking back to Hubert Ripley's imaginative drawing of the proposed town hall, rendered in 1922, the high school's Georgian Revival style seems to derive its cupola, restrained symmetry, pedimented porch, four classical columns, and rich brickwork from Ripley's unrealized structure. Reflecting the village's expanded school-age population, the Mariemont Elementary School now is the building's occupant. The neighborhood school within reasonable walking distance of every residence in Mariemont, always touted by the Mariemont Company with Dale Park School, remains a present-day asset of the community. This is frequently and correctly praised as one of Mariemont's most attractive selling points for homeowners and renters.

Building purposes were altered for several other structures in the plan. A "museum" (actually an open pavilion with a few exhibition cases) to commemorate the prehistoric Indians was designed by Nolen and his associate, Philip Foster, but not built. In 2000, Nolen's design was reproduced by the Mariemont Preservation Foundation at its intended, original location. The central heating plant and the boathouse, both highly touted in publicity by the Mariemont Company, functioned for some years and then ceased to operate. When termites infested the walls of the tunnels that provided steam heat to homes and businesses, the system was discontinued, as residents sought to operate their own furnaces. The boathouse, its surrounding woods, and the lagoon for small boats are remembered affectionately by older residents, but boating ended when the lagoon was filled in to eliminate silting and mosquitoes. The full-service hospital, which opened years after its completion and was operated by the Sisters of Mercy, was converted to a nursing facility in the 1990s, fulfilling Livingood's dream for a "convalescent" home but ending its original use.

The historic Ferris house, maintained by the Mariemont Company to display architect's drawings and plans for house lots and streets, survived as a museum only briefly into the 1930s. Currently, an educational consulting firm owns the building. Nolen's graceful arched bridge across Whiskey Creek was doomed by its high projected cost. It would have joined the Westover industrial section with the end of Mariemont Avenue, but it was a fortunate failure, for it would have brought truck traffic directly into the heart of the residential neighborhood south of Wooster Pike. Westover, located at Mariemont's western edge and easily accessible through the neighboring town, Fairfax, served after its acquisition in 1924 as a railhead for building supplies. The first factories were built on Westover's forty-five acres in 1928, followed by other manufacturing plants that filled the available acreage. Jobs in Westover drew workers mostly from greater Cincinnati, and in recent decades few local residents have found employment there. Westover's incorporation in Nolen's plan offered more than employment opportunities, however, as the tax base from industry generates considerable revenue for the operation of the village. The demonstration farm in the Resthaven scheme operated for a few years into the 1930s, producing milk from its dairy herd, feed for the cows, and shrubs and trees in its nursery. The cottages for Emery pensioners were never more than ghosts on a blueprint. A fieldhouse, to be placed at one end of its namesake street near the playing fields of Dogwood Park, never emerged from the drawing stage.

Probably the best-known architectural landmark in Mariemont is the Mary M. Emery Carillon Tower, a memorial gift in 1929 from Isabella F. Hopkins, Mrs. Emery's sister. The massive stone structure and its racks of bronze bells were not sited by Nolen and Livingood, nor even imagined among the village's necessary components, but the carillon's presence in a corner of Dogwood Park and its frequent concerts are an attractive background for the good life in Mariemont: children playing on the grass or on the ball fields, families lounging in chairs listening to chiming hymns, the woodsy smells of Dogwood Park, a safe and quiet haven all around. Today, the carillon tower's outline forms the primary element in Mariemont's official seal.

All of the missing or incomplete elements in the Nolen-Livingood plan failed because of one or more factors: severely curtailed financial support due to Mary Emery's death and the settlement of her estate, the Great Depression and its economic ills, and the dissolution of the Mariemont Company. The successor-owner of Mariemont, the Thomas J. Emery Memorial, under Livingood's presidency continued to maintain the village, however incomplete it was, but Livingood and his fellow trustees retreated from their advocacy of Mariemont as a national exemplar to be attempted elsewhere. The missing parts of the plan did not affect Mariemont's significance as a planned community, however. Fortunately, Nolen's skeleton of residential and feeder streets maintain their original integrity. The median strip of several blocks separating east- and westbound traffic joins a small, beautiful woods of sycamores and dogwoods immediately east of the town square. This buffer slows traffic because of the restricted number of lanes, and the town square calms the flow around it and circulates vehicles easily.

Without question, the automobile has had the greatest effect on the present condition of Mariemont. Not only does the automobile and its proliferation create increasing problems with through traffic and parking on residential streets, but town planners in the New Urbanist movement suggest that the automobile "is the root cause of personal isolation and malaise: automobility creates urban sprawl and breeds, in the cul de sacs of sidewalkless suburbia, a terrible, destructive loneliness."[15] The detrimental effect of the automobile was unimagined in the 1920s, although in 1924 Nolen wrote prophetically in a letter, "If I am not mistaken Mariemont will soon be a busy place and streets like Wooster Pike will have to take care of considerable automobile traffic, both trucks and pleasure vehicles." Nolen endorsed Roger W. Babson's predictions and quoted them in *New Towns for Old,* where Babson optimistically foresaw a "phenomenal suburban movement" due to good roads and the popularity of the automobile encouraging a flight from cities to the suburbs. His ominous prediction, "With more than ten million motor cars now in use in the United States, we have an average of one car to every ten persons,"[16] has been submerged in a superabundance of automobiles.

Americans' love affairs with their automobiles seem to have no limits. For all of its positive and practical uses, the automobile is an increasingly pernicious force in the livability and ambience of Mariemont. Nolen is said to have "appreciated the special characteristics of the automobile suburb,"[17] yet branding Mariemont as an intentionally planned "automobile suburb" is fallacious. The myth persists, however. One author writing on the urban landscape credits Mariemont as "an extraordinarily subtle exercise in axial planning, which is all the more impressive when one appreciates that this is among the first suburbs planned expressly for the automobile. Nolen provided space for on-street parking, and rear lanes giving access to garages. (The British garden suburbs did not have to contend with the automobile; private car ownership was so low.)"[18]

True, the automobile made Mariemont accessible to residents working in Cincinnati or nearby, but Nolen and Livingood were not partial to the automobile in their planning efforts. The automobile was not a priority in their planning. Some streets were too narrow to accept two curb lanes of parked cars plus moving traffic, there were too few garages, and the assumption of one car for one family reigned.

Traffic on the major highway, U.S. Route 50, which cuts through the town, had reached excessive levels by the 1980s. Trucks and passenger vehicles bring increasing congestion, noise, and exhaust fumes unknown in the first fifty years of Mariemont's existence. Throughout the day and especially during peak rush hours in early morning and late afternoon, a steady stream of vehicles transits the village. A count of twenty thousand cars, trucks, and buses per day was recorded in 1999. These numbers increase at an estimated 2 percent each year for U.S. 50 in Mariemont, according to the Ohio Department of Transportation, as suburban growth accelerates beyond Mariemont's eastern border. This growth was unforeseen in the 1920s, and Nolen and Livingood could not imagine the dramatic rise in the number of privately owned passenger automobiles and their dominance of suburban life.

Families that shared one car decades ago now frequently have one for every licensed driver in a household, including any sixteen-year-old children. Working spouses and teenagers wanting their own transportation increase demand for parking space in garages or on driveways and streets. Group housing in the Dale Park section offered few garages for residents, not even one space per housing unit, and the conversion of the allotment gardens to garages did little to alleviate the urgent need. Nolen had no authority to increase garage spaces, for Livingood determined that all renters would not enjoy the luxury of automobile ownership. That was true until the years after World War II. Apart from traffic problems, the automobile produced visual clutter in Mariemont, with densely packed, on-street parking, the result of too few garages and too many automobiles per resident. An ordinance prohibits overnight parking on the streets but is frequently exempted for residents in the Dale Park neighborhood and elsewhere in the village. The automobile's equally unattractive contribution to Mariemont is evident where homes have converted garages into extra rooms or remodeled kitchens, leaving the family's two or three automobiles on the driveways. Consequently, the fronts of many residences have the appearance of commercial parking lots.

Mariemont resembles other American towns and cities in its decreasing use of public transportation, although bus service to and from Cincinnati exists. Passenger and commuter train service through Mariemont, once admired by Livingood and Nolen, ended long ago. Even in the 1920s and 1930s, rail travel to Cincinnati was not popular, although Livingood "hoped that rapid train service will be supplied to commuters at low, monthly ticket rates. This will be a great boon to those who work down-town." Robert Stern remarked that "the railroad station was usually placed at the heart of the planned suburban villages,"[19] but Mariemont had no proper station on the tracks below the high bluffs on the town's southern edge.

Mariemont's genesis depended on three perspicacious individuals. Together they fashioned a planned community in the 1920s that had no American peer. Inspired primarily by English examples, Mariemont was conceived by Livingood as a quaint country village providing good housing for people of lesser means. It was born on farmland not far from a great midwestern city and touted as a commercial development, not a philanthropy. But philanthropic it was, for Mariemont's birth depended exclusively on the wealth of its generous founder, Mary Emery, who was committed to its well-intentioned purpose and who never realized any financial return on her support. She was keenly aware of housing needs in the Cincinnati area and excited by the prospect of developing an example that might illustrate the finest standards of planning and construction. She relied on her personal representative, Charles J. Livingood, for day-to-day supervision and management. He became the ultimate authority on all matters pertaining to Mariemont's conception, executing the dream. He wisely chose America's premier town planner, John Nolen, to design the American town that derived from the English garden city and to produce what Nolen called a "National Exemplar."

John Nolen optimistically forecast the future of planned communities shortly after he drafted the plans for Mariemont, echoing the hopes of his benefactress when he predicted that similar enterprises "will be prosecuted with like energy into an indefinite future and carried to great consummation. They not only will transform suburban countrysides into smiling garden cities and towns, but will react also with rejuvenant beneficence upon the cities themselves, purging them of their slums and changing them into institutional centers for the radiation of metropolitan activities out over the land—replanned for the new day and architecturally worthy of it all." Although Nolen's optimism has not been fully realized, Mariemont served as the "anticipatory example of this future" for Mary Emery, John Nolen, and Charles Livingood.[20] Mariemont remains so today in its presence and promise.

APPENDIX

Mariemont Site Landowners and Acreage in 1924

Although the landowners of Mariemont's original acreage were recorded by John Nolen in the scrapbook he compiled in July 1922 (John Nolen Papers, Carl A. Kroch Library, Cornell University) and illustrated in a drawing, owners' names and the land and buildings they sold to Mary Emery or to the Mariemont Company were more accurately indicated two years later in Mariemont Company Deed Layout, Section 9, T4, FR 2, Columbia Township, Plan No. M-153, File No. E6, dated December 30, 1924 (Mariemont Preservation Foundation). This deed layout does not record all land purchases made by the Mariemont Company during its tenure, such as Westover or other land acquired between late 1924 and the Mariemont Company's dissolution. The deed layout is useful, however, as the official list of owners and their acreage when Mariemont was initiated and recorded at the Hamilton County Court House. The owners (sellers) are listed with the acreage they sold. Sometimes this acreage was in various locations within the site. Total land acquisition on this deed layout records just over 299 acres.

C. F. Aicholz	0.7 acres	John C. Henderson	7.57 acres
George Aicholz	34.39 acres	Herman H. Hoffman	50.40 acres
Katherine Aicholz	3.8 acres	R. L. Houchins	6.35 acres
John H. Bricking	0.8 acres	George L. Jones	0.86 acres
Martha H. Bridge	1.25 acres	Charles Marback	0.92 acres
Howard M. Carpenter	4.06 acres	Ida Mathis	5.017 acres
Harry L. Crane	30.20 acres	Leota Nash	5.60 acres
John F. Fahrenkamp	25.72 acres	Minnie and Henry Prosch	3.21 acres
James Ferris	20.84 acres	M. and S. T. Richardson	2.05 acres
L. and E. Fitzwater	2.04 acres	Elsie W. Scheve	0.25 acres
Dr. Gau [?]	[?]	E. C. Snyder	0.069 acres
Katie A. Hammet	19.70 acres	William L. Stites	1.49 acres
Thomas M. Hartman	20 acres	Solomon Williams	6 acres
Harvard University	20 acres?	Louis Wocher	7.01 acres
Adolph Heinert	19.55 acres		

NOTES

Sources quoted in the notes use the following abbreviations:

CAM	Cincinnati Art Museum
CAMA	Cincinnati Art Museum Archives
CHS	Cincinnati Historical Society
CJL	Charles J. Livingood
Gest	Joseph Henry Gest
JN	John Nolen
MME	Mary Muhlenberg Emery
MPF	Mariemont Preservation Foundation
NCU	John Nolen Papers, Carl A. Kroch Library, Cornell University
Steele	Lela Emery Steele

1. New Town, New Concept

1. *Cincinnati Enquirer,* October 12, 1927; Spring Grove Cemetery, Cincinnati, interment records; Certificate of Death, Board of Health, Cincinnati, No. 824, October 15, 1927.

2. Marriage Register, St. John's Church, Cincinnati, Archives of the Episcopal Diocese of Southern Ohio.

3. CJL to MME, November 11, 1890, Steele.

4. Biographical Folder, Harvard University Archives (HUG 300). See also typescript biography [by CJL?], c. 1922, NCU.

5. *Cincinnati Enquirer,* November 25, 1900.

6. Hamilton County, Ohio, Probate Court, Will Record No. 98, and Affidavit of Alphonse P. Ruick, Town Clerk's Records, Middletown, R.I., February 20, 1906.

7. *Providence Sunday Journal,* March 4, 1906. The *New York World,* March 3, 1906, stated that, "according to the probate officers of Middletown, Mr. Emery was one of the wealthiest men in the United States."

8. *Cincinnati Commercial Tribune,* April 23, 1922. This reference, as well as Glass, *John Nolen,* 109, reports that Thomas J. Emery initiated the concept of Mariemont and that MME then pursued her husband's interest and commissioned CJL to implement their dual wish. Hancock, *The American City Planning Movement,* 368–69, credits both husband and wife as originators "following their progressive era study of housing in Cincinnati, America's third most congested city." This is an assumption not supported by other accounts.

9. Leavitt, "The Romance of Mariemont," 5. His story of Mariemont and its development, written in 1925–26, is a credible account and had CJL's blessing in an introductory statement he provided for Leavitt's article. Nolen, *New Towns for Old,* 121, 123, attributes the village's origin solely to MME, linking her wish to her husband's desire.

10. Scott, *American City Planning,* 6–7.

11. Silberstein, *Cincinnati Then and Now,* 121.

12. Fairbanks, *Making Better Citizens,* 34, 36. CJL was a member of the board of the Model Homes Company, acting as executor of MME and her estate.

13. Ibid., 37.

14. Mirick, "The New Town of Mariemont," 220; Sexton, *Mariemont,* 7; *Eastern Hills Journal,* August 24, 1966; Baker, "Mary Emery's Mariemont," 73–74. Mirick in 1924 stated that MME and CJL jointly had conceived the idea for Mariemont "fifteen years ago." Sexton wrote that CJL learned of the "Emery Project" in 1910. The others assign 1910 as the conception date.

15. *Eastern Hills Journal,* August 24, 1966; Baker, "Mary Emery's Mariemont," 73. Because CJL had been reared in Reading, Pa., and JN, America's most renowned town planner, had engaged in the replanning of this old city in 1910, it is likely that CJL studied JN's work and understandable that he would return to this master ten years later with a major commission.

16. *Cincinnati Times-Star,* November 26, 1940.

17. CJL, "Biography," 3, NCU.

18. Howard, *Garden Cities of To-morrow,* 76.

19. Creese, *The Search for Environment,* 302.

20. Fishman, *Urban Utopias,* 24.

21. Creese, *The Search for Environment,* 309.

22. This definition is given by F. J. Osborn in Howard, *Garden Cities of To-morrow,* 26.

23. Creese, *The Search for Environment,* 246–47.

24. CJL, Diary, June 10 and June 17, 1930, Virginius Hall Jr. Papers.

25. Ibid., August 1, 1933.

26. Ibid., [undated entry] 1933.

27. Leavitt, "The Romance of Mariemont," 5.

28. Stern, *The Anglo-American Suburb,* 34.

29. Metz, "The Prehistoric Monuments," 119. This is the first published account of the site, located in Section 9, Columbia Township, Hamilton County, Ohio, about ten miles east of downtown Cincinnati.

30. Hooton, "Indian Village Site and Cemetery," 1–10. Hooton's account summarizes primarily the activities of the Peabody Museum, Harvard University, from 1882 to 1911. His account, however, provides the early history of Dr. Metz's excavations.

31. Harvard University, *Thirty-first Report of the Peabody Museum,* 1897, 10.

32. Shine et al., *Art of the First Americans,* provides information on and illustrations of many important finds from the Madisonville Site now in the museum's collections.

33. Leavitt, "The Romance of Mariemont," 5.

34. These Cincinnati suburbs once functioned as independent districts, but annexation by Cincinnati was complete by the date of Mariemont's launch: Linwood in 1896, Hyde Park in 1903, Madisonville in 1911, and Oakley in 1913.

35. Both Indian Hill and Mariemont were incorporated as villages in 1941.

36. Survey, Thomas B. Punshon, Civil Engineer, 705 Glenn Building, Cincinnati, August 1918, NCU. The blueprint of Punshon's survey now in the Nolen Papers, Cornell University, is also dated in red pencil: "Rec'd Oct. 25, 1918." This marking seems to be CJL's handwriting. The blueprint's scale is 200 feet per 1 inch.

37. Reading *left* to *right, top* to *bottom* on the blueprint, the notations by CJL include [north of Wooster Pike in the Dale Park district] Solid Rows of Cheap Houses, Village Church, The Glade; [immediately east of Plainville Pike and north of Wooster Pike] Pool, Auditorium, and Upper Green; [at the center point of the village, in line with Grove Avenue and between Murry [*sic*] Avenue and Wooster Pike] stores with small apartments, Garage, Hotel, Town Hall, and Movie; [in present Resthaven area] Workshop for convalescents, Small farm allotment, Truck gardens, Barns, Pasture, Convalescent Home, Hospital, 40 Pensioners' Cottages, Trolley Station; [beginning with the so-called Harvard Tract and moving easterly to Plainville Pike] Village Burial Ground, Dogwood Park, Lagoon, The Beeches, Factory Recreation Field, and Factory Sites; [east of Plainville Pike to south of Indianview Avenue] Flower Gardens, Esplanade, and the Belvedere; [streets not included in original plan for Mariemont but illustrated on the survey] Indianview, Petoskey, and Pochahontas [*sic*] Avenues; [below the bluff and adjacent to the railroad and the river] Lookout over valley, Sewage Disposal Farms, and Community Farms.

38. John Nolen, Mariemont Scrapbook, July 1922, Plate 1, NCU, and Plat Records, MPF. The known owners were C. F., George, and Katherine Aicholz;

John H. and M. Bricking; Martha H. Bridge; Howard M. Carpenter; Harry L. Crane; John F. Fahrenkamp; James and Joseph Ferris; L. and E. Fitzwater; Dr. Gau; Katie Hammit; Thomas M. Hartman; Harvard University; Adolph Heinert; John C. Henderson; Herman H. Hoffman; R. L. Houchins; George L. Jones; Ida Mathis; Charles Morback; Leota Nash; Minnie and Henry Prosch; Minnie and Samuel T. Richardson; Elsie W. Scheve; E. C. Snyder; William H. Stites; Solomon Williams; and Louis Wacher (or Wocher).

39. Leavitt, "The Romance of Mariemont," 7.

40. Baker, "Mary Emery's Mariemont," 74; Sexton, *Mariemont,* 8; *Eastern Hills Journal,* August 24, 1966; *New York Times,* August 24, 1927; Nolen and Baxter, "Modern City Planning Principles," 25.

41. Leavitt, "The Romance of Mariemont," 7.

42. Parsons, Mariemont, Ohio, Project No. 241, NCU. Each of the Nolen projects, spanning the years 1913–37, was assigned a number. For each project in Parsons's account, she recorded the project's name, the dates when Nolen began and ended his service, the principal persons involved or responsible for the project, the city government or citizens' organizations involved, dates for field trips to the project site, a published history of the project, if known, and a description of the project's history.

43. Philip W. Foster, "Mr. Livingood's Visit to the Office September 1920," NCU. Scribbled on the bottom of the Foster memorandum in JN's hand: "What plans did he see? Did he take any of our publications?"

44. CJL to JN, November 18, 1920, NCU. The letter is written on letterhead of Office of Thomas Emery's Sons, 414 Walnut Street, Cincinnati, but also bears a typed home address in Cincinnati for CJL, 2766 Baker Place.

45. JN to CJL, November 22, 1920, NCU.

46. Scott, *American City Planning,* 228.

47. Hancock, *The American City Planning Movement,* 295.

48. Ibid., 425.

49. For extensive biographical information on Nolen, see Hancock, "The Background of a Pioneer Planner" and *The American City Planning Movement.* Summaries of JN's life and career are included in Mace, "John Nolen," 490–91, and Wilson, "John Nolen."

2. Nolen's Town Plan Unfolds

1. Nolen, *City Planning,* 3.

2. Hancock, "The Background of a Pioneer Planner," 307. JN's account in Nolen, *New Towns for Old,* 3, 121, and in other writings credits Letchworth with an abiding influence on his many projects, especially Mariemont.

3. Nolen, *New Towns for Old,* 112–18.

4. Ibid., 117.

5. Ibid., 146, 148.

6. Parsons, "Summaries of Selected Projects," 2. Although Hancock, *The American City Planning Movement,* 370, states that JN met MME on this first visit, there is no record in JN's papers of this encounter, and CJL does not mention it.

7. JN, "Mariemont Notes, J.N., Visit, Nov. 29, 1920," NCU. It is not known whether JN took photographs on this visit or whether CJL supplied him with various views of the purchased property before his visit. One slide in his extensive collection (Glass Slide U8, NCU) is labeled "Existing Conditions" in Mariemont and shows a near-slum neighborhood of crumbling frame buildings, outhouses, and lines of laundry hanging in the breeze. The density of buildings is too great to illustrate the pastoral Mariemont site, but the slide may depict certain neighborhoods in sections of Cincinnati or nearby towns.

8. Foster's quote of fifty dollars per day plus travel expenses presumably was in addition to the consultation retainer fee.

9. CJL to JN, December 3, 1920, NCU.

10. JN to CJL, December 4, 1920, NCU. Unfortunately, the recommended references are not known.

11. JN to CJL, January 4, 1921, NCU. JN reiterated his charges as discussed in Cincinnati: $2,400 per year for professional services, payable quarterly in January, April, July, and October, with additional charges for travel and drafting expenses.

12. JN to CJL, January 8, 1921, NCU. JN wrote he was sending CJL a copy of Gerald Stanley Lee's *Inspired Millionaires,* which contained an "illuminating statement of the opportunities of wealthy men and women to bring benefits to mankind." JN obviously was referring in this way to MME's philanthropic effort with Mariemont.

13. CJL to JN, January 19, 1921, NCU.

14. JN to CJL, February 2, 1921, NCU. The Farm Cities Corporation in the 1920s attempted to design and promote small towns that would integrate urban uses (community, industrial, and educational sections) with small farms. Farm cities were intended primarily for the southern United States, and JN proposed one farm city for Pender County, N.C. The letter concluded with suggested dates for Foster's visit to Cincinnati, and February 8 ultimately was selected.

15. CJL to JN, February 9, 1921, NCU.

16. CJL to JN, March 14, 1921, NCU.

17. CJL to JN, April 27, 1921, NCU. JN answered CJL on April 30, 1921, NCU, and reported progress in his new drawings with CJL's revisions.

18. The drawings (Nolen's Nos. 159, 160, 161) are known only through glass slides, NCU. One is dated (May 1921), and all bear the inscription "John Nolen, Town Planner, and Philip Foster, Associate."

19. JN to CJL, June 21, 1921, NCU. The names and addresses attached to JN's let-

ter listed Prof. Patrick Abercrombie, Prof. S. D. Adshead, Henry E. Aldridge, Victor Branford, Ewart G. Culpin, W. R. Davidge, Prof. Patrick Geddes, and Raymond Unwin.

20. Howe, *European Cities at Work*, 361.

21. Hughes, *New Town*, 9.

22. JN to CJL, July 1, 1921, NCU. JN added that good news had been received from Thomas Hogan—the "Dugan tract" had been acquired.

23. CJL to Philip W. Foster, July 7, 1921, NCU.

24. An original, hand-drawn plan, backed by linen and folded into small sheets, is in NCU.

25. JN to CJL, July 14, 1921, NCU.

26. CJL to JN, July 24, 1921, NCU.

27. General Plan, Mariemont, A New Town, July 1921, NCU.

28. CJL to JN, October 23, 1921, NCU.

29. JN to CJL, October 26, 1921, NCU.

30. JN to CJL, October 28, 1921, NCU.

31. JN to CJL, November 22, 1921, NCU.

32. CJL to JN, December 1, 1921, NCU. This response resulted from JN to CJL, November 25, 1921, NCU.

33. JN to CJL, December 16, 1921, NCU.

3. *This Is to Be a Model Town*

1. JN to CJL, February 15, 1922, NCU.

2. CJL, "A Plan for Improving Housing Conditions in Cincinnati, Ohio," February 15, 1922 [?], NCU. The document's final page lists fifteen British and German model towns and seven American examples, of which the following were visited by CJL, according to a note: Bournville, Harborne, Ealing, Hampstead Garden, Hampstead Heath Extension, Letchworth, Port Sunlight, Richmond Hill and Kew, Krupp Colonies, Hellerau, Marienbrunn, Forest Hills, Corey, Marcus Hook, Roland Park, and Whitinsville. His list records the acreage at each town, no doubt to compare with Mariemont.

3. CJL to JN, February 20–24, 1922 [?], NCU. The letter is handwritten on Lake Placid Club stationery. JN to CJL, February 25, 1922, NCU, responded that "I am firmly committed to the completion of Mariemont. It is now my greatest ambition, and nothing but your orders would turn me from it."

4. CJL to JN, March 10, 1922, NCU. The general manager of the *Cincinnati Enquirer*, W. F. Wiley, was informed of the Commercial Club event and given exclusive rights to the story if the secret was not printed until the next day's newspaper, according to Leavitt, "The Romance of Mariemont," 7.

5. CJL to JN, March 30, 1922, NCU.

6. CJL to JN, April 6, 1922, NCU; JN to CJL, April 12, 1922, NCU. JN wrote that the Russell Sage Foundation had disposed of all its stock in Forest Hills Garden to a syndicate formed by John M. Demarest, perhaps alerting CJL to a future plan for the Mariemont Company.

7. JN to CJL, April 15, 1922, NCU. Although JN's "Statistical Statement" provides data for 253.58 acres, 759 house lots, 8.6 miles of streets, and normal lot sizes ranging from 20 by 100 feet for group housing to 80 by 120 feet for detached houses, JN stated in his talk that Mariemont's official size was 365 acres.

8. "Mariemont, Cincinnati District, Ohio, Abstract of Remarks by John Nolen, Town and City Planner, Cambridge, Massachusetts. Dinner of Commercial Club, Cincinnati, Saturday Evening, April 22nd, 1922," NCU.

9. *Cincinnati Enquirer,* April 23, 1922. JN's plan of July 1921 is illustrated.

10. *Cincinnati Times-Star,* April 24, 1922.

11. "Questions and Answers: Charles J. Livingood and John Nolen," April 25, 1922, NCU. The questions seem to be CJL's, while most of the answers are JN's.

12. JN to CJL, April 26, 1922; CJL to JN, May 26, 1922, NCU.

13. JN to Clinton Mackenzie, April 26, 1922, NCU. Mackenzie to JN, April 27, 1922, NCU, is the New York architect's response, saying he could meet with JN and CJL in Kingsport and "shall try to give him the best we have."

14. JN to CJL, May 29, 1922, NCU.

15. Groben, "Union Park Gardens," 46.

16. Nolen, "Overlook Colony," 200.

17. "Proposal for Balance of Year 1922," April 29, 1922, NCU. JN was paid for services as before, $200 per month plus expenses for drafting, travel, etc. His proposed work for 1922 included finishing profiles; developing grading plans; consulting on sanitary, water, and drainage systems and on gas and electric layouts; and programming the temporary use of the property. He also suggested his "Consultation early with Architect."

18. *Cincinnati Enquirer,* April 30, 1922. Curiously, CJL is quoted in the article stating that Mariemont needed no rural land or greenbelt around it as in an English garden city, as Mariemont would be incorporated into Cincinnati. This explains, at least partially, why Mariemont was denied that environmental element.

19. CJL to Philip W. Foster, April 25, 1922, NCU.

20. CJL to Philip W. Foster, May 6, 1922, NCU.

21. JN to CJL, May 27, 1922, NCU.

22. JN to CJL, May 29, 1922, NCU. Ever mindful of publicizing his projects, JN reported to CJL in this letter that the *Boston Herald* had interviewed him for an article and wanted a photograph of MME and a list of her benefactions.

23. CJL to JN, May 31, 1922, NCU. A rare visual record, the so-called Mariemont

Scrapbook, July 1922, NCU, resulted presumably from Foster's visit to the Mariemont site, June 7–11, 1922. The scrapbook contains fifty-nine pages of labeled photographs illustrating roads, fields, woods, Indian mounds, existing houses, and vistas of the property as it looked before JN's plan was implemented.

24. JN to CJL, June 3, 1922, NCU. "Suggested Street Names," June 3, 1922, NCU, listed thirty-six names, of which JN starred seven already assigned: Grace, Cambridge, Mariemont, and Murray Avenues; Montgomery Road (not used in Mariemont proper, however); Wooster Pike ("Worcester Pike" on JN's list); and Plainville Pike.

25. "Building a New Town," 34.

26. CJL to JN, August 10, 1922, NCU. Ohio's nascent efforts to end pollution of its waterways persuaded CJL and Nolen to devote special concern to the sewer and water system to be installed by Fay, Spofford & Thorndike. CJL's letter enclosed a clipping on ending water pollution from the *Cincinnati Times-Star,* August 4, 1922.

27. CJL to Thomas Hogan Jr., July 21, 1922, NCU. The typed, seven-page letter was seen and noted by JN on August 9, 1922, according to his pencil notes in margins.

28. JN to CJL, July 19, 1922, NCU. JN sent several letters to former employers of Clarence B. Fancy, an applicant for resident engineer. Fancy had worked as resident engineer for the Sage Foundation's Forest Hills development, 1912–13.

29. Hubert G. Ripley to Philip W. Foster, August 10, 1922, NCU. Ripley's firm later was employed at Mariemont, Ohio.

30. CJL to Philip W. Foster, August 16, 1922, NCU.

31. CJL to JN, July 3, 1922, NCU.

32. CJL to JN, September 9, 1922, NCU. In JN to CJL, September 14, 1922, NCU, he complained that "it is really not necessary to employ Fay, Spofford & Thorndike to make the layout of the sewer and water systems," thinking that the newly appointed resident engineer, C. B. Fancy, could do this under JN's supervision. CJL was not dissuaded, however.

33. CJL to Philip W. Foster, September 11, 1922, NCU. The approved street names in CJL's letter were Beech, Oak, Maple, Chestnut, Elm, Cherry Lane, Linden Place, Park, Harvard, Hillside, Pleasant, Midden Way, Hammerstone Way, Cachepit Way, Flintpoint Way, Center, Mound Way, Hopkins Place, Miami Bluff Drive, Mariemont, Sheldon Place (later changed to Sheldon Close), Albert Place, Denny Place, Field House Way, West, East, Miami Road, Town Center, Madisonville Road, Service, Market, Cottage, Home (later changed to Homewood), Grace, and Hospital Lane. Some of the names were not used eventually or were changed slightly.

34. Nolen, *New Towns for Old,* 111.

35. CJL to JN, September 15, 1922, NCU.

36. CJL to JN, October 6, 1922, NCU.

37. CJL to JN, September 15, 1922, NCU.

38. CJL to Col. Harrison H. Dodge, October 16, 1922, NCU. Livingood intended to plant fifty young elms from the "original" stock at the front row of the nursery, adjacent to the trolley line, "so that every one going by will see the Washington Elms grow." The order was for 50 elms ("original" stock), 200 red oaks, 100 giant oaks, 200 white oaks, 50 tulip trees, and 50 black gum. Hancock, *The American City Planning Movement,* 376, states that 80,000 trees and shrubs were brought in to Mariemont, with JN's office supervising "distinctive planting for each of the neighborhoods."

39. JN to CJL, October 13, 1922, NCU.

40. Unwin, *Town Planning in Practice,* 360, 364, 367.

41. CJL to JN, October 16, 1922, NCU.

42. JN to CJL, October 17, 1922, NCU.

43. CJL to JN, October 19, 1922, NCU.

44. JN to CJL, October 20, 1922, NCU.

45. [JN], "Names of Architects Suggested for Consideration in Connection with Mariemont," [October 20, 1922], NCU. The list provides the street addresses for every architect except Coffin & Coffin and Richard H. Dana.

46. JN to CJL, October 24, 1922, NCU. JN also offered the driving services of his son, Jack Jr., to CJL while he was in Boston, stating that "our Buick is available." Later, JN's son was employed in Mariemont during construction.

47. CJL to JN, November 10, 1922, NCU.

48. "Suggested List of Nursery Stock for Mariemont, Ohio," November 24, 1922, NCU. R. W. Horne, "Memorandum of Decisions Reached at Conference of November 25, 1922," NCU, records that Fay's representatives, Horne and George L. Mirick, attended the meeting with CJL, JN, and Foster. Mirick later became the full-time general manager of the Mariemont project, reporting directly to CJL.

49. "Prospectus," The Mariemont Company, [1922], NCU.

50. "Articles of Incorporation," The Mariemont Company, December 1, 1922, MPF, and CJL to JN, December 29, 1922, NCU. Shareholders were MME (495 shares at $100 each), CJL, Thomas Hogan Jr., Bleecker Marquette, Frank Nelson, and John Schindel (each man owned one share at $100).

51. CJL to JN, December 4, 1922; JN to CJL, December 6, 1922, NCU.

52. CJL to Lois L. Howe & Manning, December 1, 1922, NCU. CJL disdained defining Mariemont as a "model town," yet he used this term freely in earlier and later correspondence, such as CJL to JN, March 30, 1922, and August 26, 1923, NCU.

53. JN to CJL, December 5, 1922, NCU. Inquiries from architects Clinton Mackenzie, Richard H. Dana Jr., and Frederick W. Garber were received by JN between October and December.

54. The colored charts were reproduced also in JN's files as glass slides U36, U35, and U37, NCU.

55. CJL to R. H. Dana Jr., December 29, 1922, NCU. The contract was that used by the American Institute of Architects, 1917, second edition, NCU.

56. JN, "New Ideals in the Planning of American Towns and Cities," Hanover, N.H., December 7, 1922, NCU. December also produced the third published article on Mariemont in Brinkman, "Mariemont—A Model Village," 893–94. Nolen's three watercolor illustrations of building groups in Mariemont were published in the article.

57. CJL to JN, December 8, 1922, NCU.

58. CJL to JN, December 29, 1922, NCU.

59. CJL to JN, December 26, 1922, NCU.

60. CJL to JN, December 23, 1922, NCU.

61. [CJL], "List of Architects Working on Mariemont Project to Date," December 28, 1922, NCU. Gilchrist's name and address are added in pencil at the bottom of the typed and dated list.

4. Work Begins

1. CJL to JN, January 5, 1923, NCU.

2. JN to CJL, January 9, 1923, NCU.

3. Clinton Mackenzie to JN, January 8, 1923, NCU. He offered to pay his own expenses "as they may not deem it desirable but I have never been able to put the best efforts in work when I did not feel myself closely in touch with the conditions."

4. JN to CJL, January 9, 1923, NCU. This is a second letter of the same date, apparently written only to focus on JN's request for an increased stipend. The enclosure, "Program of Work to be done—Office and Field," bears the same date.

5. CJL to Philip W. Foster, September 11, 1922, NCU. The drawings of the square plus one rendering of a street and its houses were reproduced in the *Cincinnati Enquirer,* January 14, 1923.

6. Thomas Hogan Jr. to Clinton Mackenzie, January 13, 1923, NCU. The same letter was sent to Dana, Gilchrist, and Ripley & LeBoutillier. Parsons, "Summaries of Selected Projects," 1, also records the meeting of January 22.

7. CJL to JN, January 29, 1923, NCU. The letter is written on letterhead of the newly formed Mariemont Company, 115 East Fourth Street, Cincinnati, the same address as Thomas Emery's Sons. Besides CJL as president, the masthead lists Vice-President John R. Schindel, Secretary Thomas Hogan Jr., and Treasurer F. J. Schlanser. A handwritten note clipped to CJL's letter, perhaps submitted by JN or his son, records the salary record of John Nolen Jr., serving as the guide requested by CJL. The son's monthly, beginning salary from three different employers had been $127 (surveying

camp), $144 (Fay, Spofford & Thorndike), and $150 (Panama Canal). He eventually received $192 per month at Fay, Spofford & Thorndike. Parsons, "Summaries of Selected Projects," 6, states that John Jr. was asked by C. B. Fancy, resident engineer, to join the engineering staff working on sewer and water plans. He began his new assignment in Mariemont in April.

8. CJL to JN, February 1, 1923, NCU.

9. JN, "Suggested List of Nursery Stock for Mariemont, Ohio," February 3, 1923, NCU, and JN to CJL, February 3, 1923, NCU.

10. Eleanor Manning to CJL, February 2, 1923, NCU.

11. Hubert G. Ripley to CJL, February 5, 1923, NCU.

12. "Mariemont: A Satellite Town," 777.

13. Nolen and Baxter, "Modern City Planning Principles," 21–27.

14. Philip W. Foster to JN, March 24, 1923, NCU. The letter's reference to "Myrick" refers to George L. Mirick, the engineer working for Fay, Spofford & Thorndike at this date.

15. JN, "Scheme for Organization," April 9, 1923, NCU.

16. Thomas Hogan Jr. to JN, April 13, 1923, NCU. Hogan also noted that Nolen's son, Jack, had arrived.

17. Parks served Mariemont from 1923 until 1943, when he resigned his post as chief engineer for the village. Beginning on April 11, 1923, and continuing through 1929, Parks kept a diary of daily activities, events, and insights centering on Mariemont and its construction. Eleven volumes of Parks's diaries are now in the Cincinnati Historical Society.

18. Parks, *The Mariemont Story*, 24. The low contract bid of $592,182 among ten submitted was awarded to Crumley, Jones and Crumley, Cincinnati, for the water system and to the John L. Walker Company, Hamilton, Ohio, for sewers and drains. Contracts were signed on April 23, 1923, the official groundbreaking of Mariemont.

19. CJL to JN, April 6, 1923, NCU. CJL wrote from Florence on postcards from the Uffizi Gallery.

20. CJL, Diary, April 23, 1923, Virginius Hall Jr. Papers. CJL's diaries exist for 1923, 1930, and 1933. The pages are filled with neatly printed comments and marginal notes in CJL's hand. CJL's entry for April 23, 1923, records an "overcast but very warm" day in Nimes as he and daughter Betty journeyed to Pont du Gard before moving on to Dijon.

21. *Cincinnati Times-Star*, April 24, 1923.

22. Ibid., April 25, 1923.

23. *Providence Journal*, May 21, 1925. The reporter, Robert T. Small, wrote from Cincinnati after a visit to Mariemont.

24. JN to CJL, April 28, 1923, NCU. JN's letter is addressed to CJL at the Banker's Trust Company, Paris. JN notes his satisfaction that Richard Dana and Hubert Ripley were with him in Mariemont when he inspected the site on April 18.

25. CJL to JN, May 5, 1923, NCU; Warren Parks, Diary, May 18, 1923, CHS; Thomas Hogan Jr. to JN, May 17, 1923, NCU.

26. "A Demonstration Town for Ohio," 3.

27. Thomas Hogan Jr. to JN, May 22, 1923, NCU. Hogan's letter also criticized JN for not mentioning CJL in another article published in the *National Real Estate Journal,* as "this offends Mrs. Emery, as she feels that Mr. Livingood's name should have been associated with yours and Mr. Foster's." JN to Thomas Hogan Jr., May 28, 1923, NCU, apologized for not mentioning CJL but explained that he thought that CJL wanted "to be kept in the background." JN also attributed most of the article to Sylvester Baxter. JN concluded by defending the rent estimate as compatible with CJL's plan "to provide if possible some very inexpensive three room apartments or flats, because we talked them over with the architects." JN implied that Hogan was ill informed and even misappropriating his role, which was true.

28. CJL to JN, May 18, 1923, NCU. CJL's observations were written on the backs of three postcards of views of Letchworth and Hitchin.

29. JN to CJL, May 23, 1923, NCU.

30. Parsons, "Summaries of Selected Projects," 1. An earlier meeting on June 5 in Cincinnati had been attended by JN's employee, Justin R. Hartzog.

31. CJL to Thomas Hogan Jr., June 1, 1923, NCU.

32. JN to CJL, June 13, 1923, NCU. Thomas Hogan Jr. to Henry V. Hubbard, June 12, 1923, NCU, also mentions the hiring of Hall and asks for the Harvard University professor's recommendation, noting that "Mrs. Emery will thank you to tell her, *in confidence,* your opinion of the man and his qualifications."

33. JN, "Memorandum for Mariemont Conference," July 16, 1923, NCU.

34. JN to CJL, July 19, 1923, NCU.

35. CJL to Philip W. Foster, July 30, 1923, NCU. The six postcards illustrate scenes in Josselin and Dinan, France, with notes by CJL referring to the roof stones ("Note charming texture of these roofs") and stone walls ("We shall have quantities of stone exactly like this"), the arcades under overhanging rooms, and roof stones he encountered in Malmesbury, England ("The remodelled 16th century Inn has some of the original roof stone—a delicious brownish black, much less severe than slate"; "All these buildings, centuries old, have stone instead of slate or that horrid, tiresome red tile roofs"). Three postcards, CJL to JN, August 3, 1923, NCU, add nothing to the information included in the cards sent to Foster a few days earlier.

36. Nolen, "Planning New Towns," 8–9. JN's address was derived from a paper, NCU, bearing a different title in typescript, "Mariemont—A Demonstration Amer-

ican Town," crossed out and with a new, handwritten title, "The Development of New Towns and Industrial Centers, with Special Reference to Regional Planning."

37. CJL to JN, August 26, 1923, NCU.

38. JN to Thomas Hogan Jr., September 6, 1923, NCU.

39. Robert R. McGoodwin to CJL, September 10, 1923, NCU.

40. "General Instructions Prepared by Chas. J. Livingood, Prest.," September 29, 1923, NCU.

41. CJL to Philip W. Foster, October 1, 1923, NCU.

42. Philip W. Foster to CJL, October 9, 1923, NCU.

43. MME to JN, October 5, 1923, NCU. Although the letter's reference to Mariemont may imply MME's estate, a spot she cherished and improved over many years, it is likely that she meant the town she founded in Ohio as she was writing to its planner.

44. JN to CJL, October 10, 1923, NCU. Parks's "Organization Chart" lists the initials of each man responsible for a portion of the project: Glenn Hall as landscape architect, Warren Parks as resident engineer, John Nolen Jr. as field engineer for sewer installation.

45. CJL to JN, October 27, 1923, NCU.

46. JN to Louis E. Jallade, October 27, 1923, NCU; Louis E. Jallade to JN, October 27, 1923, NCU. To provide a more imposing setting for the church, Jallade asked JN whether Oak Street could be lowered "a foot or so" in its grading. To oblige this seemingly minor request, JN agreed to lower the grade of Oak Street by one foot, and Jallade added six inches to the floor level of the church to increase its impressive siting.

47. CJL to Joseph Moore, Esq., November 15, 1923, NCU. Addressed to Moore at the Bell Inn, Malmesbury, England, the letter inquired about the cost of renovating the roof of the Bell Inn. CJL also suggested shipping roof stones from Bristol to Newport News, Virginia, in sturdy and well-packed crates. He hoped that the "fine close lichen" could be preserved on the stones.

48. CJL to JN, December 26, 1923, NCU.

49. CJL to JN, November 30, 1923, NCU.

50. CJL to Philip W. Foster, December 6, 1923, NCU.

51. JN to CJL, December 22, 1923, NCU.

52. CJL to JN, December 26, 1923, NCU. CJL sent JN a detailed chart, "Chas. J. Livingood's Ideas on North-west Section," December 27, 1923, NCU, suggesting types of street surfaces, curbs, and sidewalks and the reasons for these in the Dale Park neighborhood. Certain portions of Oak and Beech Streets were considered "our toughest neighborhood with cheapest possible housing" in CJL's chart.

53. JN to CJL, December 29, 1923, NCU.

54. JN to CJL, December 27, 1923, NCU.

55. Allen W. Jackson to CJL, December 28, 1923, NCU. Presumably the three photographs depicted an English grouping of residences.

5. Architects and Buildings

1. Leavitt, "The Romance of Mariemont," 13.

2. Fay, Spofford, & Thorndike, "Mariemont Building Construction," [1923?], NCU.

3. CJL to Allen W. Jackson, January 5, 1924, NCU.

4. CJL to JN, January 10, 1924, NCU.

5. CJL to Philip W. Foster, January 21, 1924, NCU.

6. CJL to Philip W. Foster, January 28, 1924, NCU.

7. CJL to JN, February 20, 1924, NCU. JN's first visit to Mariemont in 1924 occurred on February 3–6.

8. JN to CJL, March 21, 1924, NCU.

9. CJL to Philip W. Foster, March 27, 1924, NCU.

10. Thomas Hogan Jr., "Introductory Remarks at the Retirement of John J. Emery," February 1968, MPF. MME usually met with CJL and Hogan every day in an office in her residence, Edgecliffe, to discuss business matters. In midmorning of April 1, 1924, CJL and Hogan were about to leave when MME asked them to remain and join her and her nephew for luncheon. This required postponing the groundbreaking for several hours, which was done.

11. Leavitt, "The Romance of Mariemont," 15.

12. Parsons, "Summaries of Selected Projects," 1. In addition to JN's four visits in 1924, Foster visited on April 30 and May 1 with JN and on September 25–26; H. J. Walker from JN's office visited on September 4–5.

13. CJL to Philip W. Foster, April 9, 1924, NCU.

14. CJL, "C.J.L.'s Hopes for 1924," April 30, 1924, NCU.

15. CJL to JN, April 27, 1924, NCU. Mirick's appointment is noted in Parks, Diary, May 26, 1924, CHS.

16. J. H. Peterson to JN, May 8, 1924, NCU.

17. Allen W. Jackson to JN, April 18, 1924, NCU; JN to Clinton Mackenzie, May 5, 1924, NCU.

18. CJL to Gest, June 14, 1924, CAMA. Schindel discovered that a music teacher could handle art as well for the elementary school and until a board of education was formed. When Dale Park School opened and for many years thereafter, the Mariemont Company operated the Mariemont school system as a private enterprise in its single building. Enrollment was limited to residents of the village of Mariemont.

19. CJL to JN, June 14, 1924, NCU.

20. Published by the Mariemont Company, Cincinnati, in 1925, the brochure contains essays by Nolen and the engineers Fay, Spofford & Thorndike, with other extensive copy undoubtedly by CJL.

21. George L. Mirick to JN, June 17, 1924, NCU. The old Emery's Sons letterhead is overprinted with the new address of the Mariemont Company.

22. JN to J. F. Whitney, June 19, 1924, NCU.

23. CJL [and JN?], "Architects' Assignments," June 30, 1924, NCU.

24. "The Mariemont Memorial Church," *Mariemont Community Church Year Book, 1927–28,* [Mariemont, Ohio?], 1928, n.p. An article in the *Cincinnati Enquirer* of March 27, 1927 (LaRue, "Mariemont's Norman-English Church"), notes Jallade's presence in Malmesbury to obtain roof stones, at least by the article's report, but no date is mentioned for his trip. *Mariemont Community Church* [c. 1968], MPF, also records Jallade's search as occurring in 1926.

25. LaRue, "Mariemont's Norman-English Church." The article provides the most complete history of the barn. Until religious properties were confiscated by Henry VIII, the barn was maintained by the Cistercian Order housed at nearby Kingswood Abbey. About 1539, it was acquired by the Crown; by about 1560, it was given to Sir Nicholas Poyntz by the king. By 1795, it was the property of Thomas Estcourts, M.P., and illustrated in *Gentleman's Magazine,* May 1795. In 1927, the roof stones were sold to the Mariemont Company by then-owner Benjamin Hatherell. The barn's owner earlier in the century had been Sir Kenneth Preston.

26. *Mariemont Community Church Year Book, 1927–28,* n.p. Six carloads of stones had arrived in Mariemont by March 1927. The church was completed except for the roof by that date. The roof stones were laid in the summer of 1927, and formal dedication occurred in September of that year.

27. Livingood and Nolen, *A Descriptive and Pictured Story,* 21.

28. Leavitt, "The Romance of Mariemont," 19.

29. Livingood and Nolen, *A Descriptive and Pictured Story,* 37.

30. Mariemont Company, "Organization Chart," November 26, 1924, published in 1925 in ibid., 63.

31. Leavitt, "The Romance of Mariemont," 21.

32. Ibid., 21.

33. Ibid., 23.

34. Cole and Taylor, *The Lady Architects,* 96.

35. Leavitt, "The Romance of Mariemont," 25.

36. Ibid., 25.

37. Ibid., 31.

38. Parks, *The Mariemont Story,* 74.

39. JN, "Program of Work to Be Done—Office and Field," July 1, 1924, NCU.

40. CJL to JN, July 12, 1924, NCU.

41. George L. Mirick to JN, July 10, 1924, NCU.

42. CJL to JN, August 1, 1924, NCU. A postscript notes, "I am leaving for Murray Bay."

43. CJL to JN, August 11, 1924, NCU.

44. The article, "The City Set at the Crossroads," is unsigned. However, JN to H. I. Brock, August 27, 1924, NCU, at *New York Times* office identifies the letter's recipient as the author. See also Hall and Hardisty articles published that same year.

45. CJL to JN, August 26, 1924, NCU; JN to H. I. Brock, August 27, 1924, NCU.

46. JN to CJL, September 5, 1924, NCU.

47. CJL to JN, September 12, 1924, NCU.

48. CJL to George L. Mirick, September 12, 1924, NCU.

49. Parsons, "Summaries of Selected Projects," 1. Walker was in Mariemont on September 4–5, and Foster on September 25–26.

50. CJL to JN, October 10, 1924, NCU.

51. CJL to JN, November 6, 1924, NCU; *Cincinnati Times-Star,* November 3, 1924.

52. Gest to T. Gerrity, November 19, 1924, CAMA.

53. George L. Mirick to JN, November 24, 1924, NCU; JN to George L. Mirick, November 29, 1924, NCU. Mirick responded in haughty fashion in a letter to JN, December 1, 1924, NCU, stating "I have yours of the 29th and after reading it all over very carefully I am more than ever convinced that you are totally wrong."

54. The Mariemont Company, "Organization Chart," November 26, 1924, NCU. Charles Cellarius is listed as the "Resident Architect." Mirick's article, "The New Town of Mariemont," published that same year, ignores Nolen, mentioning him only in the next-to-last paragraph.

55. CJL to JN, November 29, 1924, NCU.

56. JN to CJL, December 15, 1924, NCU.

57. CJL to JN, December 30, 1924, NCU. A postscript noted CJL's commitment of $200 to support JN's town planning exhibit on the "Mariemont enterprise" in New York in April 1925.

58. *Cincinnati Times-Star,* January 23, 1925; Parks, Diary, December 24, 1924, CHS.

6. Year of Progress, Year of Termination

1. "Proceedings of Incorporators," Mariemont Company, January 20, 1925, MPF.

2. JN, "Program of Services—1925," January 1, 1925, NCU. A second list by JN, "Program for Work to be Done—Office and Field," January 1, 1925, NCU, identifies

more specifically JN's activities. These include consulting with Paul Cret and the other architects, preparing planting plans for the streets and park areas, drafting of detailed plans for certain areas (stadium, Dogwood Park, town center, etc.), and developing programs for temporary use of the land along with a financial and administrative policy for Mariemont.

3. JN, "Mariemont Exhibition," and "Supplementary," January 8, 1925, NCU.

4. JN, "Tentative Suggestions for a Comprehensive Exhibition of the New Town near Cincinnati, known as Mariemont, Ohio at the Architectural and Allied Arts Exposition, Grand Central Palace, New York," April 20–May 24, 1925, NCU.

5. JN to CJL, January 14, 1925, NCU.

6. CJL to JN, January 31, 1925, NCU.

7. "Construction Cost of Dana, as of February 26, 1925," NCU.

8. Philip W. Foster to George L. Mirick, April 7, 1925, NCU. It is not known why Foster addressed his report to Mirick and not to CJL. On April 29, CJL complained to JN that he had not heard about the visit. This may have been an attempt by Mirick to embarrass JN and Foster.

9. CJL to JN, April 29, 1925, NCU.

10. JN to George L. Mirick, May 2, 1925, NCU.

11. "Proceedings of Incorporators," Mariemont Company, May 5, 1925, MPF.

12. Livingood and Nolen, *A Descriptive and Pictured Story,* 13, 15.

13. Frank H. Nelson to MME, May 12, 1925, Steele.

14. JN to CJL, May 19, 1925, NCU. The remainder of JN's letter concerns plantings at the concourse, the location of baseball diamonds, a flag pole at the Dale Park School, and a design for planting the median strip in Wooster Pike.

15. "Proceedings of Incorporators," Mariemont Company, September 1, 1925, MPF.

16. Allen Collier to Winthrop D. Parker, July 22, 1925, CHS.

17. Gest to MME, October 6, 1925, CAMA; JN to George L. Mirick, September 17, 1925, NCU.

18. JN to George L. Mirick, October 7, 1925, NCU.

19. JN to CJL, October 8, 1925, NCU.

20. JN to CJL, October 26, 1925, NCU. Although JN stated that he spent "several days" in Mariemont, his office records only October 20, but this may be the only day when expenses were charged to the Mariemont Company. Mrs. Nolen accompanied JN on this trip, probably her first visit to the new town that had occupied so much of her husband's time in 1920–25.

21. JN, "The Viewpoint of City Planning," Ohio State Conference on City Planning, Dayton, Ohio, October 22, 1925, 2, NCU.

22. Ibid., 2–3.

23. JN to CJL, December 3, 1925, NCU. In a handwritten letter, Joseph Whitney to JN, November 18, 1925, NCU, Whitney had told Nolen of his discontent with CJL when he had discovered that CJL intended to dismiss him after all his plans were on paper: "I am not guessing at that but I *read* it." Whitney announced his intention of starting his own landscape business in Cincinnati.

24. CJL to JN, December 8, 1925, NCU. "Analysis of a Census of Mariemont, Ohio," December 1, 1925, NCU, recorded 521 total inhabitants, of whom 196 were children in 164 families. The average ages of adults were 38.2 years for men and 34.4 years for women. Of the total population, 32.7% were employed (167 individuals).

25. Parsons, "Summaries of Selected Projects," 8.

7. The Curtain Drops

1. JN to John R. Schindel, January 20, 1926, NCU.

2. Parks, *The Mariemont Story,* 114. The circumstances of the replacement of Garber & Woodward with deGersdorff are unknown. The recreation building was dedicated on May 17, 1930. In 1954, it was sold by the Thomas J. Emery Memorial to the Mariemont Community Church to serve as the parish center.

3. Warren W. Parks to JN, February 23, 1926, NCU.

4. CJL to JN, March 19, 1926, NCU. This letter enclosed JN's final payment of $665.51, "in full of account which covers everything up to January 1st, when our contract expired."

5. Livingood and Nolen, *A Descriptive and Pictured Story,* 29.

6. "Mariemont," *J. Walter Thompson News Bulletin,* 25.

7. JN to George L. Mirick, March 24, 1926, NCU; JN to CJL, March 24, 1926, NCU; MME, "Greetings," *Mariemont Messenger,* March 19, 1926.

8. JN, "New Communities Planned to Meet New Conditions," Eighteenth National Conference on City Planning, St. Petersburg, Fla., March 29, 1926, NCU.

9. George L. Mirick to JN, June 16, 1926, NCU. Enclosed was a request, L. Segoe, City Planning Commission to the Mariemont Company, June 2, 1926, NCU, for correcting the intersection. The letter also approved the layout of Mariemont and the recording of lots and deeds.

10. JN to George L. Mirick, June 22, 1926, NCU.

11. CJL to JN, June 29, 1926, NCU.

12. JN to CJL, July 8, 1926, NCU.

13. CJL to JN, July 13, 1926, NCU.

14. JN to CJL, July 23, 1926, NCU.

15. CJL to JN, July 27, 1926, NCU.

16. *Mariemont Messenger,* March 26, April 22, June 18, and November 5, 1926.

Other renters who advertised included Louis Dornseif, shoe repairer with shop and residence at Oak and Murray Streets; Mrs. E. P. Broadstreet Jr., writer for the *Cincinnati Enquirer,* 6733 Murray; George Zaengle, radio repairer, 6717 Maple Street; William S. Jones, hardware store operator, 6705 Murray; and Mrs. L. L. Scott, piano teacher, 3901 Oak Street.

17. Parsons, Mariemont, Ohio, Project No. 241, NCU.

18. Bleecker Marquette, *Mariemont Messenger,* January 21, 1927.

19. CJL to JN, July 27, 1926, NCU.

20. "Mariemont: A New Town," 247–74.

21. JN to CJL, August 12, 1926, NCU. In this letter and JN to George L. Mirick, August 12, 1926, NCU, the extension of Plainville Road across Wooster Pike to Denny Place is noted as "definitely abandoned. It seems to me that it would have been an unwise and regrettable change."

22. George L. Mirick to JN, November 9, 1926, NCU.

23. Parks, Diary, February 3, 1927, CHS.

24. CJL to JN, January 19, 1927, NCU.

25. JN to CJL, June 21, 1927, NCU.

26. *Mariemont Messenger,* October 21, 1927.

27. On June 1, 1927, George L. Mirick, Mariemont's general manager, resigned, and Thomas Hogan Jr. was appointed to this post, as reported in "Proceedings of Incorporators," Mariemont Company, October 27, 1927, MPF. In the same meeting minutes, George deGersdorff was retained as architect to draw plans for the recreation building to be constructed on Plainville Road. This building was sited on JN's plan of July 1921, as was the town's high school, situated on Wooster Pike, one block from the town square. Cincinnati architects Garber & Woodward were hired to design the high school, but no date for construction was set in the same minutes.

8. Emery, Nolen, and Livingood

1. CJL to JN, January 14, 1928, NCU.

2. "Proceedings of Incorporators," Mariemont Company, January 16, 1928, MPF. First blueprints for the boathouse were drawn November 16, 1927, and Cellarius's final plans were developed between July 6 and November 28, 1928.

3. JN to CJL, April 21, 1930, NCU.

4. CJL to JN, April 11, 1928, NCU.

5. The boathouse deteriorated over the years but was restored in 1999–2000 as a nature center and trailhead for Dogwood Park. Restoration costs were financed by foundations and private gifts to the Mariemont Preservation Foundation.

6. Parks, Diary, January 16 and July 24, 1930, CHS.

7. "Record of Proceedings of the Incorporators, Stockholders, and Trustees of the Thomas J. Emery Memorial," 107, January 9, 1931, MPF.

8. "Proceedings of the Incorporators, Stockholders, and Trustees of the Thomas J. Emery Memorial," 152, February 1, 1932, MPF.

9. *Mariemont Messenger,* January 1, 1932. The Hamilton County Deed Book, No. 1601, January 12, 1932, 483, records the sale for $1.00, December 29, 1931, by the Mariemont Company to the Thomas J. Emery Memorial of all its lands, buildings, parks, and improvements in Mariemont.

10. CJL to JN, May 3, 1932, NCU.

11. JN to CJL, May 9, 1932, NCU.

12. Warren W. Parks to JN, May 27, 1932, NCU.

13. Warren W. Parks to JN, November 1, 1932, NCU.

14. Warren W. Parks to JN, November 9, 1932, NCU.

15. JN to CJL, October 31, 1934, NCU.

16. JN to CJL, May 13, 1935, NCU. JN to CJL, September 18, 1936, NCU, is thought to be the last letter from the town planner to his client, closing an extensive correspondence stretching over sixteen years.

17. *New York Times,* February 18, 1937; *Boston Herald,* February 19, 1937.

18. *Cincinnati Enquirer,* February 26, 1952; *Cincinnati Times-Star,* February 27, 1952; *New York Times,* February 27, 1952. CJL's wife, Lily, had died on December 3, 1936, at their residence in Cincinnati, 2766 Baker Place.

9. Was Mariemont the National Exemplar?

1. Rybczynski, *City Life,* 189; Creese, *The Search for Environment,* 302; Wright, *Building the Dream,* 203.

2. Wright, *Building the Dream,* 214.

3. Duany and Plater-Zyberk, "The Second Coming," 20–21. This article exposed many problems and concerns with the suburbs and may be one of the earliest reappraisals of the importance of past models.

4. "Can New Urbanism Find Room for the Old?" *New York Times,* June 2, 1996. In this article Herbert Muschamp lists several notable new urbanists, including Andres Duany, Elizabeth Plater-Zyberk, Peter Calthorpe, Elizabeth Moule, Stefanos Polyzoides, and Dan Solomon, who respect the achievements of earlier town planners. To Muschamp's list, the author must add Robert A. M. Stern.

5. Langdon, *A Better Place to Live,* 217.

6. Krieger, *Andres Duany and Elizabeth Plater-Zyberk,* 12, Fig. 9.

7. Livingood and Nolen, *A Descriptive and Pictured Story,* 39.

8. Fairbanks, *Making Better Citizens,* 51.

9. Livingood and Nolen, *A Descriptive and Pictured Story,* 43.

10. Ibid., 43, 9, 15.

11. Scott, *American City Planning,* 233.

12. Fairbanks, *Making Better Citizens,* 55.

13. Stern, *The Anglo-American Suburb,* 81.

14. *New York Times,* January 1, 2000.

15. Ibid., September 6, 1999.

16. JN to J. F. Whitney, October 23, 1924, NCU; Nolen, *New Towns for Old,* 113.

17. Stern, *The Anglo-American Suburb,* 11.

18. Rybczynski, *City Life,* 189.

19. Livingood and Nolen, *A Descriptive and Pictured Story,* 13; Stern, *The Anglo-American Suburb,* 10.

20. Nolen, *New Towns for Old,* 119–20.

BIBLIOGRAPHY

The unpublished writings of John Nolen and of others recorded in this bibliography with no location noted are housed in the Carl A. Kroch Library, Cornell University. The location of other unpublished materials in a library or archives is noted. Bibliographical research was aided immeasurably by the efforts of Prof. John L. Hancock, to whom I am indebted and who prepared a detailed record of John Nolen's published and unpublished writings in his Ph.D. dissertation.

Aaron, Daniel. *Cincinnati, Queen City of the West, 1819–1838.* Columbus: Ohio State University Press, 1992.

Ackerman, Frederick L., and J. J. Murphy. *Housing Famine: How to End It; a Triangular Debate.* New York: E. P. Dutton, 1921.

Adams, Thomas. *The Design of Residential Areas.* Cambridge: Harvard University Press, 1934.

———. *Outline of Town and City Planning.* New York: Russell Sage Foundation, 1935.

Arnall, Betty. *An Historical Architectural Survey [Venice, Florida].* Venice, Fla.: City of Venice, 1990.

Baillie Scott, M. H. *Garden Suburbs, Town Planning, and Modern Architecture.* London: T. Unwin, 1910.

Baker, John D. "Mary Emery's Mariemont." *Cincinnati Magazine,* October 1973, 40–45, 72–75.

Barnett, Henrietta. *The Story of the Growth of Hampstead Garden Suburb, 1907–1928.* London: Hampstead Garden Suburb Trust, 1928.

Benoît-Lévy, Georges. *La Cité-Jardin.* Paris: Editions des Cites-Jardins, 1911.

Bing, Alexander M. "Can We Have Garden Cities in America?" *Survey,* May 1, 1925, 172–73, 190.

Brinkman, Walter. "Mariemont—a Model Village." *Popular Mechanics,* December 4, 1922, 893–94.

Brock, H. I. "The City Set at the Crossroads: A New Experiment in Town Planning to Fit the Motor Age." *New York Times Magazine,* August 24, 1924, 7–8.

"Building a New Town." *Building Age,* June 9, 1922, 34.

Caldwell, Wil F. "The Indians and the Early Settlers." *Mariemont Town Crier Special Edition,* July 12, 1991.

Candler, Martha. "A Town Made for Happiness." *Woman's Journal,* August 1928, 18–19, 30–31.

Christensen, Carol A. *The American Garden City and the New Towns Movement.* Ann Arbor: UMI Press, 1986.

Ciucci, G., M. Manieri-Elia, and M. Tafuri. *The American City. From Civil War to the New Deal.* Cambridge: MIT Press, 1983.

Clubbe, John. *Cincinnati Observed: Architecture and History.* Columbus: Ohio State University Press, 1992.

Cole, Doris, and Karen C. Taylor. *The Lady Architects: Lois Lilley Howe, Eleanor Manning, and Mary Alny, 1893–1937.* New York: Midmarch Arts Press, 1990.

Creese, Walter L. *The Search for Environment: The Garden City Before and After.* New Haven: Yale University Press, 1966.

"A Demonstration Town for Ohio." *Journal of the Town Planning Institute of Canada,* May 1923, 1–6.

"Dr. John Nolen." *Architectural Forum,* April 1937, 94.

Duany, Andres, and Elizabeth Plater-Zyberk. "The Second Coming of the American Small Town." *Wilson Quarterly,* Winter 1992, 19–48.

Engst, Elaine D., and H. Thomas Hickerson. *Urban America: Documenting the Planners.* Ithaca: Cornell University Libraries, 1985.

Fairbanks, Robert B. *Making Better Citizens: Housing Reform and the Community Development Strategy in Cincinnati, 1890–1960.* Urbana: University of Illinois Press, 1988.

Fay, Frederic H. "The Development of Mariemont, Ohio." Address to City Planning Division, American Society of Civil Engineers, New York, January 21, 1926.

Filler, Roger. *Welwyn Garden City.* Chichester: Phillimore & Co., 1986.

Fishman, Robert. *Urban Utopias in the Twentieth Century.* New York: Basic Books, 1977.

Ford, George B., and Ralph F. Warner, eds. *City Planning Progress in the United States, 1917.* Washington, D.C.: American Institute of Architects, 1917.

Fromson, Stuart. *The Garden City Suburb in America: A Study of the Town Planning Movement during the Industrial Revolution.* M.A. thesis, Miami University, Ohio, 1985.

"The Garden Suburb of Cincinnati." *Architectural Forum,* March 1932, 245–48.

Giglierano, G. J., and D. A. Overmyer. *The Bicentennial Guide to Greater Cincinnati: A Portrait of Two Hundred Years.* Cincinnati: Cincinnati Historical Society, 1988.

Glass, James A. *John Nolen and the Planning of New Towns: Three Case Studies.* M.A. thesis, Cornell University, 1984.

Glenn, John M., and Lilian Brandt. *Russell Sage Foundation, 1907–1946.* New York: Russell Sage Foundation, 1947.

Groben, William E. "Union Park Gardens: A Model Garden Suburb for Shipworkers of Wilmington, Delaware." *Architectural Record,* January 1919, 44–64.

Hall, Glenn. "Planning Recreation for a New Town." *Playground,* October 1923, 381–82.

Hanchett, Thomas W. *Sorting Out the New South City: Race, Class, and Urban Development in Charlotte, 1875–1975.* Chapel Hill: University of North Carolina Press, 1998.

Hancock, John L. *John Nolen and the American City Planning Movement: A History of Culture Change and Community Response, 1900–1940.* Ph.D. diss., University of Pennsylvania, 1964.

―――. "John Nolen: The Background of a Pioneer Planner." *Journal of the American Institute of Planners,* November 1960, 302–12.

Hardisty, Frank. "Mariemont, A Study in City Planning." *Co-operative Engineer,* March 1924, 22–26.

Hartzog, Justin. "John Nolen." *Planner's Journal,* March–April 1937, 3, 55.

Harvey, W. Alexander. *The Model Village and Its Cottages: Bournville.* London: Bateford, 1906.

Heinrich, Jacob A. *Mariemont: A Garden Suburb Project.* M.A. thesis, University of Cincinnati, 1931.

Hogan, Thomas. "Your Neighbor, Mariemont." *Cincinnati Street Railway News,* December 1928, 3–4, 12.

Holden, Arthur C. "Realty Developments and the Architect." *Architectural Record,* April 1931, 331–58.

Hooton, Earnest A. "Indian Village Site and Cemetery near Madisonville, Ohio." *Papers of the Peabody Museum of American Archeology and Ethnology,* Harvard University, 7:1–137.

Horne, R. W. "The Public Works of the New Model Town, Mariemont, Ohio." *American City,* March 1924, 247–50.

Howard, Ebenezer. *Garden Cities of To-morrow* [first published as *To-morrow: A Peaceful Path to Real Reform,* 1898; present title, 1902]. London: Faber & Faber, 1965.

Howe, Frederic C. *The British City.* New York: Charles Scribner, 1907.

―――. *The City: The Hope of Democracy.* New York: Charles Scribner, 1909.

―――. *European Cities at Work.* New York: Charles Scribner, 1913.

Hubbard, Edward, and M. Shippobottom. *A Guide to Port Sunlight Village.* Liverpool: Liverpool University Press, 1988.

Hubbard, Theodora K., and Henry V. Hubbard. *Our Cities To-Day and To-morrow:*

A Survey of Planning and Zoning Progress in the United States. Cambridge: Harvard University Press, 1929.

Hughes, W. R. *New Town: A Proposal in Agricultural, Educational, Civic, and Social Reconstruction.* London: J. M. Dent & Sons, 1919.

Ikin, C. W. *Hampstead Garden Suburb: Dreams and Realities.* London: New Hampstead Garden Trust, 1990.

"John Nolen." *American Magazine of Art,* March 1937, 186–88.

"John Nolen." *Architectural Record,* April 1937, 49.

"John Nolen." *Journal of the Town Planning Institute,* February 1937, 116–17.

"John Nolen." *New York Times,* February 19, 1937.

Krieger, Alexander, ed. *Andres Duany and Elizabeth Plater-Zyberk: Towns and Town-Making Principles.* New York: Rizzoli International Publications, 1991.

Langdon, Philip. *A Better Place to Live: Reshaping the American Suburb.* New York: Harper Collins, 1995.

LaRue, John W. "Mariemont's Norman-English Church Is to Have Roof of Ancient Stone." *Cincinnati Enquirer,* March 27, 1927.

Leavitt, Warren E. "The Romance of Mariemont." *Eastern Hamilton County Messenger,* April 19, 1973 [first published in *Mariemont Messenger,* March 19–November 26, 1926].

Livingood, Charles J. "The New Town, a National Exemplar." Address to the Literary Club of Cincinnati, November 1, 1924.

Livingood, Charles J., and John Nolen. *A Descriptive and Pictured Story of Mariemont—a New Town: "A National Exemplar."* Cincinnati: Mariemont Co., 1925.

Mace, Ruth. "John Nolen." *Dictionary of American Biography,* Supplement 2. New York: Charles Scribner's Sons, 1958.

MacFayden, Dugald. *Sir Ebenezer Howard and the Town Planning Movement.* Manchester, England: University Press, 1933.

"Mariemont." *The J. Walter Thompson News Bulletin Describing Mariemont, the New Town.* Cincinnati: Mariemont Press, 1926.

"Mariemont, America's Demonstration Town." *American City,* October 1922, 309–10.

"Mariemont, a Modern Fairyland." *Norfolk and Western Magazine,* November 1925, 972–74.

"Mariemont: A New Town, a Complete Residential Village near Cincinnati, Ohio, Planned by John Nolen and Philip W. Foster, Associate, Town Planners." *Architecture,* September 1926, 247–74.

"Mariemont: A Satellite Town in the Making." *Survey,* March 15, 1923, 777–79.

Marquette, Bleecker. "Are We Losing the Battle for Better Homes?" Address to National Conference of Social Work, Washington, D.C., June 21, 1923.

———. "Mariemont, an American Garden Village." *National Municipal Review,* May 1927, 296–301.

Maxwell, Sidney D. *The Suburbs of Cincinnati: Sketches Historical and Perspective.* Cincinnati: George E. Stevens & Co., 1870.

Maxwell, Walter H. "The Emery Estate, a Commercialized Philanthropy." *Saxby's Magazine,* September 1909, 51–65.

Metz, Charles L. "The Prehistoric Monuments of the Little Miami Valley." *Journal of the Cincinnati Society of Natural History,* October 1878, 119–28.

Miller, Mervyn. *Letchworth: The First Garden City.* Chichester: Phillimore & Co., 1989.

Miller, Zane L. *The Urbanization of Modern America: A Brief History.* San Diego: Harcourt Brace Jovanovich, 1987.

Miller, Zane L., and H. Gillette, eds. *American Urbanism: A Historiographical Review.* New York: Greenwood Press, 1987.

Mirick, George L. "The New Town of Mariemont." *Club Woman's Magazine* [Cincinnati], November 1924, 220–25.

Moss-Eccardt, John. *Ebenezer Howard: An Illustrated Life of Sir Ebenezer Howard, 1850–1928.* Aylesbury, England: Shire Publishers, 1973.

Mumford, Lewis. *The Culture of Cities.* New York: Harcourt, Brace & Co., 1938.

Munro, William B. *Government of European Cities.* New York: Macmillan Co., 1909.

"A New Suburb, Scientifically Planned, a Marvel in Construction, Beauty, and Appointment." *Suburban Life,* September 1926, 10–11.

Newton, Norman T. *Design on the Land: The Development of Landscape Architecture.* Cambridge: Belknap Press of Harvard University, 1971.

Nolen, John. "American Small Towns: I. Kingsport, Tennessee." *Town Planning Review,* July 1934, 16–24.

———. "The Art of Planning Cities." *American Magazine of Art,* January 1934, 31–32.

———. "The City of the Future: The Place of City Planning in our Present Civilization." Address at Syracuse University, May 3, 1933.

———. *City Planning.* New York: D. Appleton & Co., 1924.

———. "The City Planning Movement." *American Architect,* November 19, 1919, 627–29.

———. *Comprehensive Planning for Small Towns and Villages.* Boston: American Unitarian Association, 1912.

———. "General Discussion: Garden Suburbs." In *Housing Problems in America: Proceedings of the Fifth National Conference on Housing,* 308–9. New York: Douglas C. McMurtrie, 1916.

———. "Making City Plans" [retitled from "How to Make a City Plan," December 14, 1931]. Address at Massachusetts Institute of Technology, [January?] 1933.

———. "Mariemont, Cincinnati District, Ohio." Address to the Commercial Club, Cincinnati, April 22, 1922.

———. "Mariemont, Cincinnati District, Ohio: Scheme for Organization." April 29, 1922.

———. "Mariemont, Ohio." *Architectural Forum,* March 1932, 245–48.

———. "Mariemont, Ohio—a New Town Built to Produce Local Happiness." In *American Civic Annual,* 235–37. Washington, D.C.: American Civic Association, 1929.

———. "The Need of a Master Plan to Guide City Growth." In *Housing Problems in America; Proceedings of the Tenth National Conference on Housing,* 189–93. New York: National Housing Association, 1929.

———. "New Communities Planned to Meet New Conditions." Address to the Eighteenth Conference on City Planning, St. Petersburg, Florida, March 29, 1926.

———. "New Ideals in the Planning of American Towns and Cities." Address at Hanover, New Hampshire, December 7, 1922.

———. *New Ideals in the Planning of Cities, Towns, and Villages.* New York: American City Bureau, 1919.

———. *New Towns for Old: Achievements in Civic Improvement in Some American Small Towns and Neighborhoods.* Boston: Marshall Jones Co., 1927.

———. "New Towns vs. Existing Cities." *City Planning,* April 1926, 69–78.

———. "Overlook Colony, a Housing Project in Claymont, Delaware." *Architecture Forum,* May 1922, 74–75, 197–200.

———. "The Place of the Beautiful in the City Plan: Some Everyday Examples." In *Proceedings of the Fourteenth National Conference on City Planning, June 5–7, 1922,* 133–47. Springfield, Mass.: Loring-Axtell Co., 1922.

———. "The Plan for the Development of Reading." *American City,* June 1910, 250–53.

———. "A Plan for Improving Housing Conditions in Cincinnati, Ohio." [April 1922?].

———. "Plan of the Town of Mariemont." August 1923.

———. "Planning New Towns in the United States, or Town Planning Tendencies in the United States" [originally written as "Mariemont, a Demonstration American Town"]. Address to the International Cities and Town Planning Conference and Exhibition, Gothenburg, Sweden, August 3–10, 1923.

———. "Planning Progress in the United States of America, 1907–1928." Address to Town Planning Institute, June 28, 1928.

———. "Putting a City Plan into Action." *American City,* December 1911, 332–34.

———. *Replanning Small Cities: Six Typical Studies.* New York: B. W. Huebsch, 1912.

———. "Town Planning for Mariemont." March 31, 1925.

———. "Town Planning Tendencies in the United States." *International Garden Cities and Town Planning Federation, Report of Conference at Gothenburg, 1923,* 5:64–70.

———. "Twenty Years of City Planning Progress in the United States." Address to Nineteenth Conference on City Planning, Washington, D.C., May 9, 1927.

———. "The Viewpoint of City Planning." Address to Ohio State Conference on City Planning, Dayton, Ohio, October 22, 1925.

Nolen, John, and Sylvester Baxter. "Modern City Planning Principles Applied to a Small Community: Mariemont, a New Town in the Cincinnati District." *National Real Estate Journal,* March 26, 1923, 21–27.

Nolen, John, and Frederick Fay. "The Development of Mariemont, Ohio." *Proceedings of the American Society of Civil Engineers,* October 1926, 1619–35.

Nolen, John, and Glenn Hall. "Carrying out Mariemont Plans for a Self-Contained Town." *Engineering News Record,* April 3, 1924, 580–82.

Nolen, John, [and Charlotte Parsons?]. "Plans Book: An Index of the Plans Prepared by the Office of John Nolen, 1904–1934."

Parks, Warren W. "General Record of Work at Mariemont." In Diaries, vols. 1–9, Cincinnati Historical Society.

———. *The Mariemont Story: A National Exemplar of Town Planning.* Cincinnati: Creative Writers & Publishers, 1967.

———. "Mariemont, the New Town." *Professional Engineer,* June 1927, 12–16.

Parsons, Charlotte. "Summaries of Selected Projects. Prepared by Charlotte Parsons, Secretary to Mr. Nolen, 1913–1937."

Peterson, Jon A. "The City Beautiful Movement: Forgotten Origins and Lost Meanings." *Journal of Urban History,* August 1976, 415–34.

Plunz, Richard. *A History of Housing in New York City.* New York: Columbia University Press, 1990.

Purdom, C. B. *The Building of Satellite Towns.* London: J. M. Dent & Sons, 1925.

———. *The Garden City: A Study in the Development of a Modern Town.* London: J. M. Dent & Sons, 1913.

———. *The Letchworth Achievement.* London: J. M. Dent & Sons, 1963.

Rybczynski, Witold. *City Life.* New York: Simon & Schuster, 1996.

Schaffer, Daniel. *Garden Cities of America: The Radburn Experience.* Philadelphia: Temple University Press, 1982.

Schmidlapp, Jacob G. *Low Priced Housing for Wage Earners.* New York: National Housing Association Publications, 1916.

Scott, Mel. *American City Planning since 1890.* Berkeley and Los Angeles: University of California Press, 1964.

Sellers, Sue. *Sunlighters: The Story of a Village.* London: Unilever PLC, 1988.

Sennett, A. R. *Garden Cities in Theory and Practice.* London: Bemrose & Sons, 1905.

Sexton, P. M. *Mariemont: A Brief Chronicle of Its Origin and Development.* Mariemont, Ohio: Village of Mariemont, 1966.

Shine, Carolyn R., Mary L. Meyer, Elisabeth Batchelor, Beth Dillingham, and James B. Griffin. *Art of the First Americans* [exhibition catalogue]. Cincinnati: Cincinnati Art Museum, 1976.

Sies, Mary Corbin, and Christopher Silver. *Planning the Twentieth-Century American City.* Baltimore: Johns Hopkins University Press, 1996.

Silberstein, Iola H. *Cincinnati Then and Now.* Cincinnati. League of Women Voters, 1982.

Smith, Geddes. "New Towns for Old." *Survey,* August–September 1927, 547–49.

deSoissons, Maurice. *Welwyn Garden City: A Town Designed for Healthy Living.* Cambridge: Cambridge University Press, 1988.

Stein, Clarence. *Towards New Towns for America.* Cambridge: MIT Press, 1957.

Stern, Robert A. M., ed. *The Anglo-American Suburb.* London: Architectural Design, 1981.

Stevenson, Charles. "A Contrast in 'Perfect' Towns." *Nations' Business,* December 1937, 18–20, 112–16, 124–30.

Sullivan, Kevin B. "Mariemont, Ohio: Three Papers." November 12, 1992. F. Loeb Library, Harvard University.

Taft, Eleanor G. *Hither and Yon on Indian Hill.* Cincinnati: Indian Hill Garden Club, 1962.

Unwin, Raymond. *Town Planning in Practice: An Introduction to the Art of Designing Cities and Suburbs.* London: T. Fisher Unwin, 1920.

Warner, Sam Bass. *Streetcar Suburbs: The Process of Growth in Boston, 1890–1900.* Cambridge: Harvard University Press, 1978.

Wilson, Stewart J. "John Nolen: An Overview of His Career." M.A. thesis, University of Oregon, 1982.

Wolfe, Margaret R. *Kingsport, Tennessee: A Planned American City.* Lexington: University of Kentucky Press, 1987.

"Women and Town-Planning." *Woman's Journal,* August 1928, 21.

Worley, William S. *J. C. Nichols and the Shaping of Kansas City.* Columbia: University of Missouri Press, 1990.

Wright, Gwendolyn. *Building the Dream: A Social History of Housing in America.* Cambridge: MIT Press, 1983.

Young, Clarence E. *Mariemont, Cincinnati's Beautiful Residential Suburb.* Cincinnati: Hennegan Co., 1927.

PHOTOGRAPH CREDITS

The author and publisher are grateful to the following individuals and institutions for their permission to reproduce the illustrations in this book.

INDEX

Italic folios indicate illustrations.

About the Author

Millard F. Rogers, Jr., received his master's degree in art history from the University of Michigan and a doctor of humanities (honorary) degree from Xavier University. After graduate studies, he received the Gosline fellowship for study at the Victoria and Albert Museum, London, with Sir John Pope-Hennessy.

His professional museum career began as an assistant to the director and curator of American art at the Toledo Museum of Art. In 1967 he was appointed the founding director of the Elvehjem Museum of Art, University of Wisconsin-Madison, where he also served as professor of art history. In 1974 he was appointed director of the Cincinnati Art Museum, the fifth director of that institution since its founding in 1881. He retired in 1994 and was named Director Emeritus.

As a specialist in American art and culture, Mr. Rogers has written extensively on American and Spanish art, including *Randolph Rogers, American Sculptor in Rome* (1971), *Spanish Paintings in the Cincinnati Art Museum* (1978), and *Sketches and Bozzetti by American Sculptors, 1800–1950* (1987). In 1982 he received the Rosa and Samuel B. Sachs Prize for outstanding achievement in the arts.

Mr. Rogers has resided in the village of Mariemont, Ohio, since 1974. He has served as president of the Mariemont Preservation Foundation for many years, he conducted extensive research on the history of Mariemont and its predecessors, and he received Outstanding Citizen of Mariemont honors for his efforts. Mr. Rogers is now recognized as an authority on the genesis and planning of Mariemont and on the eminent American town planner, John Nolen.

Related Books in the Series

America's Original GI Town: Park Forest, Illinois
Gregory C. Randall

Apostle of Taste: Andrew Jackson Downing, 1815–1852
David Schuyler

The Promise of Paradise:
Recreational and Retirement Communities in the United States since 1950
Hubert B. Stroud

Redevelopment and Race: Planning a Finer City in Postwar Detroit
June Manning Thomas

Local Attachments:
The Making of an American Urban Neighborhood, 1850 to 1920
Alexander von Hoffman

The City Beautiful Movement
William H. Wilson

Hamilton Park: A Planned Black Community in Dallas
William H. Wilson